Daily Wisdom

Sayings of the Companions of the Prophet ﷺ

Abdur Raheem Kidwai

KUBE PUBLISHING

Daily Wisdom: Sayings of the Companions of the Prophet ﷺ

First published in England by

Kube Publishing Ltd
Markfield Conference Centre
Ratby Lane, Markfield,
Leicestershire LE67 9SY
United Kingdom
Tel: +44 (0) 1530 249230
Website: www.kubepublishing.com
Email: info@kubepublishing.com

Cataloguing-in-Publication Data
is available from the British Library

ISBN 978-1-84774-191-2 *casebound*
ISBN 978-1-84774-192-9 *ebook*

Original Concept Design: Imtiaz Manjra
Cover Design and internal typesetting: nqaddoura@hotmail.com
Printed by: Imak Offset, Turkey

CONTENTS

TRANSLITERATION TABLE

Arabic Consonants

Initial, unexpressed medial and final: ء ʾ

ء	a	د	d	ض	ḍ	ك	k
ب	b	ذ	dh	ط	ṭ	ل	l
ت	t	ر	r	ظ	ẓ	م	m
ث	th	ز	z	ع	ʿ	ن	n
ج	j	س	s	غ	gh	هـ	h
ح	ḥ	ش	sh	ف	f	و	w
خ	kh	ص	ṣ	ق	q	ي	y

With a *shaddah*, both medial and final consonants are doubled.

Vowels, diphthongs, etc.

Short:	a ـَ	ـِ i	ـُ u
Long:	ā ـَا	ـِي ī	ـُو ū
Diphthongs:		ـَوْ aw	
		ـَيْ ay	

PREFACE

Sayings of the Companions of the Prophet ﷺ, another volume in Kube Publishing's Daily Wisdom series, aims at acquainting the readers with their understanding and elucidation of Islam. Essentially, these sayings constitute the amplification of the life-giving message of the Qur'ān and Sunnah. Since these noble, pious souls had the unique privilege of enjoying over the years the Prophet Muhammad's company, and as they were keen on assimilating the life enriching message of Islam, their sayings have a great value and relevance. At one level, their sayings and practices serve as one of the primary sources, next to the Qur'an and *Sunnah*, in the codification of Islam. Among the jurists, Imām Mālik in particular placed much premium on the actions of the Madinan Companions. His premise was natural and logical: these Companions must have learnt from the Prophet ﷺ all that they did, for emulating him was their mission.

Most of their sayings therefore stand out for their nuanced elaboration, summarization and recapitulation, and even contextualization of the Prophet's words and deeds. Their comments underscore their sagacity, their insights into the faith and practice of Islam and their earnest attempts to preserve faithfully what they had received directly from the Prophet ﷺ. Their unwavering commitment led to the formulation and development of the vast *Ḥadīth* corpus, bearing out as it does their devotion to Islam and the Prophet ﷺ and their sincere goal of transmitting their invaluable knowledge to subsequent generations. For they were wedded unflinchingly to the cause of promoting Islam at the widest possible scale.

Needless to add, their sayings reverberate and reinforce the sayings of the Propher ﷺ, and at times, extend these in a logical fashion. Some of their sayings capture the circumstantial setting of certain Qur'anic verses. Take the following saying by 'Abdullāh ibn 'Abbās ؓ,* a brilliant Qur'an exegete in his own right, as illustrative:

> Regarding the words of Allah Most High ... and restrain their rage, [*Āl 'Imrān* 3: 134], Ibn 'Abbās said: "This refers to a man who verbally abuses you and you restrain your rage and do not answer back despite being able to do so."
>
> (al-Ṭabarānī)

---

* Whenever we say the illustrious names of the Companions of the Prophet ﷺ we should always say May Allah be pleased with them

Abū Hurayrah's following saying exemplifies a pithy aphorism:

> Yazīd ibn al-Asamm said: "I heard Abū Hurayrah say: "One of you sees a speck in his brother's eye but does not see the log in his own eye."
>
> (al-Bukhārī)

The following comment by the rightly guided Caliph. 'Umar ibn al-Khaṭṭāb is reflective of his piety and God-fearingness:

> 'Umar ibn al-Khaṭṭāb ﷺ said: "Were a lamb to perish because it got lost by the banks of the river Euphrates, I would be afraid that Allah may ask me (as the Caliph) about it."
>
> (Ibn Abī Shaybah)

Some of these sayings provide a vivid glimpse of life in the Prophet's day, especially those by 'Ā'ishah ﷺ:

> It is reported from 'Ā'ishah ﷺ that she said: "The believing women used to pray Fajr prayer with the Prophet (peace be upon him) wrapped up in their sheets and then after that return to their families without being recognized by

anyone."

(Muslim)

These Sayings are from scores of Companions, most notably the four rightly-guided Caliphs, 'Ā'ishah, Abū al-Dardā', Abū Hurayrah and 'Abdullāh ibn Mas'ūd. These have been gleaned from the authentic *Ḥadīth* collections by Bukhārī, Muslim, Mālik, Aḥmad and others.

I take this opportunity to thank Brother Haris Ahmad, CEO, Kube Publishing, without whose valuable help this work could not have seen the light of day.

Abdur Raheem Kidwai
Aligarh, India
Rabi' al-Awwal 1433 H
December 2022 CE

Daily Wisdom

Sayings of the Companions of the Prophet ﷺ

DAY 1

Abū'l-Dardā' said: "Worship Allah as if you see Him; and consider yourself among the dead; and beware of the supplication of the one who is wronged, and know that the little that is just sufficient is much better than abundance which distracts you [from Allah], and that pious works never wear off while sin is never forgotten."

(Wakīʿ ibn al-Jarrāḥ, *Kitāb al-Zuhd*)

DAY 2

Ḥammād ibn Zayd reported that ʿUthmān ibn ʿAffān, may Allah have mercy on him, said: "No doer does any work except that Allah wraps him in the raiment of his work."

(Aḥmad)

اليوم ١

قالَ أَبُو الدَّرْدَاءِ: اُعْبُدِ اللهَ كَأَنَّكَ تَرَاهُ، وَعُدَّ نَفْسَكَ فِي المَوْتَى، وَإِيَّاكَ وَدَعْوَةَ المَظْلُومِ، وَاعْلَمْ أَنَّ قَلِيلاً يُغْنِيكَ خَيْرٌ مِنْ كَثِيرٍ يُلْهِيكَ، وَأَنَّ البِرَّ لاَ يَبْلَى وَأَنَّ الإِثْمَ لاَ يُنْسَى.

وكيع بن الجرَّاح ، كتاب الزهد

اليوم ٢

عَنْ حَمَّادِ بْنِ زَيْدٍ عَنْ عُثْمَانَ أَنَّهُ قَالَ: مَا مِنْ عَامِلٍ يَعْمَلُ عَمَلاً إِلاَّ كَسَاهُ اللَّهُ رِدَاءَ عَمَلِهِ.

أحمد

DAY 3

ʿUmar said: "I want to see every young person worshipping, dressed in clean clothes."

(Wakīʿ ibn al-Jarrāḥ, Kitāb *al-Zuhd*)

DAY 4

It is reported that ʿAbdullāh ibn ʿAbbās said to his caller to prayer (*mu'adhdhin*) on a very rainy day: 'After you pronounce the two testifications of faith, in your call to prayer, do not say: 'Come to prayer' but say: 'Pray inside your homes.' The narrator continued: 'And when he saw that some people somehow decried his instruction, he said: 'Are you surprised over this? This was done by someone who was much better than me [i.e. Prophet Muḥammad (blessings and peace be upon him)]. The Friday congregational prayer must be strictly followed but I disliked for you going out and walking through mud and slippery ground."

(al-Bukhārī and Muslim)

اليوم
٣

قَالَ عُمَرُ: إِنِّي لَأُحِبُّ أَنْ أَرَىٰ الشَّابَّ النَّاسِكَ النَّظِيفَ الثِّيَابِ.

وكيع بن الجرَّاح، كتاب الزهد

اليوم
٤

عَنْ عَبْدِ اللهِ بْنِ عَبَّاسٍ أَنَّهُ قَالَ لِمُؤَذِّنِهِ فِي يَوْمٍ مَطِيرٍ: إِذَا قُلْتَ: أَشْهَدُ أَنْ لَا إِلَهَ إِلَّا اللهُ، أَشْهَدُ أَنَّ مُحَمَّدًا رَسُولُ اللهِ، فَلَا تَقُلْ: حَيَّ عَلَىٰ الصَّلَاةِ، قُلْ: صَلُّوا فِي بُيُوتِكُمْ، قَالَ: فَكَأَنَّ النَّاسَ اسْتَنْكَرُوا ذَاكَ، فَقَالَ: أَتَعْجَبُونَ مِنْ هذَا، قَدْ فَعَلَ هذَا مَنْ هُوَ خَيْرٌ مِنِّي، إِنَّ الْجُمُعَةَ عَزْمَةٌ، وَإِنِّي كَرِهْتُ أَنْ أُخْرِجَكُمْ فَتَمْشُوا فِي الطِّينِ، وَالدَّحْضِ.

البخاري و مسلم

DAY 5

Muṭarrif ibn ʿAbdullāh is reported to have said: "That I am given well-being for which I give thanks [to Allah] is more beloved to me than I be tested and I bear it patiently."

(Wakīʿ ibn al-Jarrāḥ, *Kitāb al-Zuhd*)

DAY 6

Abū'l-Dardā' said: "Remember Allah in times of ease and He will remember you in times of hardship."

(Aḥmad)

اليوم
٥

عَنْ مُطَرِّفِ بْنِ عَبْدِ اللهِ قَالَ: لَأَنْ أُعَافَىٰ فَأَشْكُرَ أَحَبُّ إِلَيَّ مِنْ أَنْ أُبْتَلَىٰ فَأَصْبِرَ.

وكيع بن الجرَّاح، كتاب الزهد

اليوم
٦

قَالَ أَبُو الدَّرْدَاءِ: أُذْكُرِ اللهَ فِي السَّرَّاءِ يَذْكُرْكَ فِي الضَّرَّاءِ.

أحمد

DAY 7

Abū'l-Dardā' wrote the following in a letter he addressed to Maslamah ibn Makhlid: "To proceed: When a servant performs an act of obedience to Allah, Allah loves him, and when He loves him He endears him to His creation. And when the servant performs an act of disobedience to Allah, Allah loathes him, and when He loathes him He makes him loathed by His creation."

(Aḥmad)

DAY 8

Abū'l-Dardā' said: "What I fear most when I am made to stand for reckoning is being told: 'You have acquired knowledge, so what did you apply of that which you have learnt.'"

(Aḥmad)

اليوم
٧

كَتَبَ أَبُو الدَّرْدَاءِ إِلَىٰ مَسْلَمَةَ بْنِ مَخْلَدٍ: أَمَّا بَعْدُ: فَإِنَّ العَبْدَ إِذَا عَمِلَ بِطَاعَةِ اللهِ أَحَبَّهُ اللهُ، فَإِذَا أَحَبَّهُ اللهُ حَبَّبَهُ إِلَىٰ خَلْقِهِ، وَإِذَا عَمِلَ العَبْدُ بِمَعْصِيَةِ اللهِ أَبْغَضَهُ اللهُ فَإِذَا أَبْغَضَهُ اللهُ بَغَّضَهُ إِلَىٰ خَلْقِهِ.

أحمد

اليوم
٨

قَالَ أَبُو الدَّرْدَاءِ: إِنَّ أَخْوَفَ مَا أَخَافُ إِذَا وُقِفْتُ عَلَىٰ الحِسَابِ أَنْ يُقَالَ لِي: قَدْ عَلِمتَ، فَماذَا عَمِلتَ فِيما عَلِمتَ؟

أحمد

DAY 9

Abū'l-Dardā' said: "A moment of meditation is better than standing in prayer a whole night."

(Aḥmad)

DAY 10

It is reported that Ḥudhayfah [ibn al-Yamān] said: "The first thing of your religion that you will lose is humble devotedness and the last thing of your religion that you will lose is the canonical prayer."

(Aḥmad)

اليوم
٩

قَالَ أَبُو الدَّرْدَاءِ: تَفَكُّرُ سَاعَةٍ خَيْرٌ مِنْ قِيَامِ لَيْلَةٍ.

أحمد

اليوم
١٠

عَنْ حُذَيْفَةَ قَالَ: أَوَّلُ مَا تَفْقِدُونَ مِنْ دِينِكُمْ الْخُشُوعُ، وَآخِرُ مَا تَفْقِدُونَ مِنْ دِينِكُمْ الصَّلَاةُ.

أحمد

DAY 11

It is reported that ʿAbdullāh said: "No state is more beloved to Allah regarding His servant than seeing him in prostration [before Him]."

(Ibn Abī Shaybah, *al-Muṣannaf*)

DAY 12

Sālim ibn Abī al-Jaʿd reported that Umm al-Dardā' was asked: "What was Abū al-Dardā's best work?" and she replied: "Meditation."

(Ibn Abī Shaybah, *al-Muṣannaf*)

اليوم
١١

عَنْ عَبْدِ اللهِ قَالَ: مَا حَالٌ أَحَبُّ إِلَى اللهِ يَرَىٰ الْعَبْدَ عَلَيْهَا مِنْهُ وَهُوَ سَاجِدٌ.

ابن أبي شيبة، المصنّف

اليوم
١٢

عَنْ سَالِمِ بْنِ أَبِي الْجَعْدِ عَنْ أُمِّ الدَّرْدَاءِ قَالَ: قِيلَ لَهَا: مَا كَانَ أَفْضَلَ عَمَلِ أَبِي الدَّرْدَاءِ؟ قَالَتْ: التَّفَكُّرُ.

ابن أبي شيبة، المصنّف

DAY 13

Abū Bakr al-Ṣiddīq, may Allah be well pleased with him, said: "O people! Indeed, I am a follower [of the Prophet, Allah bless him and grant him peace] and not a blameworthy innovator. So, if I do well, you should help me; and if I deviate, you should set me right."

(al-Baqillānī, *I'jāz al-Qur'ān*)

DAY 14

ʿAlī ibn Abī Ṭālib, may Allah be well pleased with him, said: "These hearts are receptacles, and the best of them are those who retain things well."

(Al-Sharīf al-Raḍī, *Nahj al-Balāqhah*)

اليوم
١٣

قَالَ أَبُو بَكْرٍ الصِّدِّيقُ: أَيُّهَا النَّاسُ، إِنَّمَا أَنَا مُتَّبِعٌ وَلَسْتُ بِمُبْتَدِعٍ، فَإِنْ أَحْسَنْتُ فَأَعِينُونِي وَإِنْ زِغْتُ فَقَوِّمُونِي.

الإمام الباقلاني، إعجاز القرآن

اليوم
١٤

قَالَ عَلِيُّ بْنُ أَبِي طَالِبٍ: إِنَّ هَذِهِ الْقُلُوبَ أَوْعِيَةٌ فَخَيْرُهَا أَوْعَاهَا.

الشَّرِيف الرَّضِيّ، نهج البلاغة

DAY 15

Salmān [al-Fārisī] said: "The people who will come with more sins on the Day of Judgement are the ones who talk more about disobedience of Allah."

(Ibn Abī Shaybah, *al-Muṣannaf*)

DAY 16

ʿAntarah said: "I asked Ibn ʿAbbās: which work is the best?" He replied: "The remembrance of Allah is the greatest [of works], and no group of people sit in a house dealing with the Book of Allah amongst themselves and studying it except that the angels overspread them with their wings, and they remain Allah's guests as long as they are doing so unless they engage in something else."

(Ibn Abī Shaybah, *al-Muṣannaf*)

اليوم
١٥

عَنْ سَلْمَانَ قَالَ: أَكْثَرُ النَّاسِ ذُنُوبًا يَوْمَ الْقِيَامَةِ أَكْثَرُهُمْ كَلَامًا فِي مَعْصِيَةِ اللهِ.

ابن أبي شيبة، المصنَّف

اليوم
١٦

عَنْ عَنْتَرَةَ قَالَ: سَأَلْتُ ابْنَ عَبَّاسٍ: أَيُّ الْعَمَلِ أَفْضَلُ؟ قَالَ: ذِكْرُ اللهِ أَكْبَرُ، وَمَا جَلَسَ قَوْمٌ فِي بَيْتٍ يَتَعَاطَوْنَ فِيهِ كِتَابَ اللهِ فِيمَا بَيْنَهُمْ وَيَتَدَارَسُونَهُ إِلَّا أَظَلَّتْهُمُ الْمَلَائِكَةُ بِأَجْنِحَتِهَا وَكَانُوا أَضْيَافَ اللهِ مَا دَامُوا فِيهِ حَتَّى يَخُوضُوا فِي حَدِيثٍ غَيْرِهِ.

ابن أبي شيبة، المصنَّف

DAY 17

Salmān [al-Fārisī]said: "Allah has created one hundred parts of mercy and placed one part of it amongst created beings, each of these parts beings greater than what is between the heaven and earth. It is through this one part that the mother shows compassion towards her child and the birds and wild beast drink water. Upon the Day of Judgement, Allah shall take back this one part of mercy from created beings and place it, along with the other ninety-nine parts, in those who are God fearing. That is the meaning of His saying: ... *While My mercy encompasses everything. I shall invariably inscribe it for those who are ever-Godfearing.* [*al-A'rāf*: 156]".

(Ibn Abī Shaybah, *al-Muṣannaf*)

اليوم
١٧

عَنْ سَلْمَانَ قَالَ: خَلَقَ اللَّهُ مِئَةَ رَحْمَةٍ فَجَعَلَ مِنْهَا رَحْمَةً بَيْنَ الْخَلَائِقِ، كُلُّ رَحْمَةٍ أَعْظَمُ مِمَّا بَيْنَ السَّمَاءِ وَالأَرْضِ فَبِهَا تَعْطِفُ الْوَالِدَةُ عَلَىٰ وَلَدِهَا، وَبِهَا يَشْرَبُ الطَّيْرُ وَالْوَحْشُ الْمَاءَ، فَإِذَا كَانَ يَوْمُ الْقِيَامَةِ قَبَضَهَا اللَّهُ مِنَ الْخَلَائِقِ فَجَعَلَهَا وَالتِّسْعَ وَالتِّسْعِينَ لِلْمُتَّقِينَ، فَذَلِكَ قَوْلُهُ: (وَرَحْمَتِي وَسِعَتْ كُلَّ شَيْءٍ فَسَأَكْتُبُهَا لِلَّذِينَ يَتَّقُونَ).

ابن أبي شيبة، المصنَّف

DAY 18

Al-Ḍaḥḥāk said: "When Abū Bakr saw a bird perched on a tree, he exclaimed: "O bird, how blessed are you! By Allah, I wish I were like you: You perch on a tree, eat fruits and fly away without being subjected to reckoning or recompense. By Allah, I wish I were not a human being and were instead a tree on a roadside which is chewed and eaten by a camel and then rejected as dung."

(Ibn Abī Shaybah, *al-Muṣannaf*)

DAY 19

Abū 'Uthmān reported that 'Umar [ibn al-Khaṭṭāb] appointed a man as a state official and the latter said: "I have such-and-such number of children but I have never kissed any of them." Upon this 'Umar remarked: "Certainly Allah, glorified and exalted is He, does show mercy only to those of His servants who are most dutiful.""

(al-Bukhārī, *al-Adab Al-Mufrad*)

اليوم ١٨

عَنِ الضَّحَّاكِ قَالَ: رَأَىٰ أَبُو بَكْرٍ الصِّدِّيقُ طَيْرًا وَاقِعًا عَلَىٰ شَجَرَةٍ، فَقَالَ: طُوبَىٰ لَكَ يَا طَيْرُ وَاللهِ لَوَدِدْتُ أَنِّي كُنْتُ مِثْلَكَ، تَقَعُ عَلَىٰ الشَّجَرَةِ وَتَأْكُلُ مِنَ الثَّمَرِ، ثُمَّ تَطِيرُ وَلَيْسَ عَلَيْكَ حِسَابٌ وَلاَ عَذَابٌ، وَاللهِ لَوَدِدْتُ أَنِّي كُنْتُ شَجَرَةً إِلَىٰ جَانِبِ الطَّرِيقِ مَرَّ عَلَيَّ جَمَلٌ فَأَخَذَنِي فَأَدْخَلَنِي فَاهُ فَلاَكَنِي، ثُمَّ ازْدَرَدَنِي، ثُمَّ أَخْرَجَنِي بَعْرًا وَلَمْ أَكُنْ بَشَرًا.

ابن أبي شيبة، المصنَّف

اليوم ١٩

عَنْ أَبِي عُثْمَانَ أَنَّ عُمَرَ اسْتَعْمَلَ رَجُلاً، فَقَالَ الْعَامِلُ: إِنَّ لِي كَذَا وَكَذَا مِنَ الْوَلَدِ، مَا قَبَّلْتُ وَاحِدًا مِنْهُمْ، فَزَعَمَ عُمَرُ أَوْ قَالَ عُمَرُ: إِنَّ اللهَ عَزَّ وَجَلَّ لاَ يَرْحَمُ مِنْ عِبَادِهِ إِلاَّ أَبَرَّهُمْ.

البخاري، الأدب المفرد

DAY 20

'Abdullāh ibn Mas'ūd, may Allah be well pleased with him, said: "Moderation in [following] the Sunnah is better than exerting oneself in following what is blameworthy innovated (in the *Dīn*)."

(al-Dārimī)

DAY 21

A Jewish man said to 'Umar ibn al-Khaṭṭāb: "O Leader of the Believers! Had this verse: *This day have I wholly perfected for you your religion; and completed upon you My blessing; and chosen for you Islam as your religion* [*al-Mā'idah*: 3] been revealed to us, we would have celebrated that day as a festive day." To which 'Umar replied: "Indeed. I know well the day on which this verse was revealed: it was revealed on the Day of 'Arafah which coincided with a Friday."

(al-Bukhārī and Muslim)

اليوم
٢٠

قَالَ عَبْدُ اللهِ بْنُ مَسْعُوْدٍ: الاِقْتِصَادُ فِي السُنَّةِ خَيْرٌ مِّنَ الْاِجْتِهَادِ فِي الْبِدْعَـةِ.

الدّارمي

اليوم
٢١

قَالَ رَجُلٌ مِنَ اليَهُودِ لِعُمَرَ: يا أَمِيرَ المُؤْمِنِينَ لو أنَّ علينا نَزَلَتْ هذِهِ الآيَةُ: ﴿ٱلْيَوْمَ أَكْمَلْتُ لَكُمْ دِينَكُمْ وَأَتْمَمْتُ عَلَيْكُمْ نِعْمَتِي وَرَضِيتُ لَكُمُ ٱلْإِسْلَـٰمَ دِينًا﴾ [المائدة ٥:٣]، لاتَّخَذْنا ذلكَ اليومَ عِيدًا، فقالَ عُمَرُ: إنِّي لَأَعْلَمُ أيَّ يومٍ نَزَلَتْ هذِهِ الآيَةُ، نَزَلَتْ يومَ عَرَفَةَ في يومِ جُمُعَةٍ.

البخاري و مسلم

DAY 22

Abū Bakr [al-Ṣiddīq] said: "Beware of lying for it certainly contraries faith."

(Ibn Abī Shaybah, *al-Muṣannaf*)

DAY 23

Ibn ʿAbbās said: "I sought sacred knowledge and found that it was more abundant amongst the Anṣār. And so I used to call on one of them and, upon asking about him, I may be told that he was sleeping. On hearing this, I would make my outer garment as a pillow and lie down until he came out to pray the *Ẓuhr* [prayer]. And on seeing me, he would say: 'How long have you been here, O cousin of Allah's Messenger, may Allah bless him and grant him peace?' 'For a long time,' I would answer. And he would say: 'What an evil thing you have done! Why did you not inform me [that you were here]?' And I would reply: 'I wanted you to come out to see me after you have had fulfilled your need first.'"

(al-Dārimī)

اليوم ٢٢

قَالَ أَبُو بَكْرٍ (الصِّدِيق) : إِيَّاكُمْ وَالْكَذِب فَإِنَّهُ مُجَانِبُ الإِيمَانَ.

ابن أبي شيبة ، المصنّف

اليوم ٢٣

قَالَ ابْنُ عَبَّاسٍ: طَلَبْتُ الْعِلْمَ فَلَمْ أَجِدْهُ أَكْثَرَ مِنْهُ فِي الْأَنْصَارِ، فَكُنْتُ آتِي الرَّجُلَ فَأَسْأَلُ عَنْهُ فَيُقَالُ لِي: نَائِمٌ فَأَتَوَسَّدُ رِدَائِي ثُمَّ أَضْطَجِعُ حَتَّىٰ يَخْرُجَ إِلَي الظُّهْرِ، فَيَقُولُ: مَتَىٰ كُنْتَ هَا هُنَا يَا ابْنَ عَمِّ رَسُولِ اللهِ صَلَّىٰ اللهُ عَلَيْهِ وَسَلَّمَ؟ فَأَقُولُ: مُنْذُ زَمَنٍ طَوِيلٍ، فَيَقُولُ: بِئْسَ مَا صَنَعْتَ ! لَا أَعْلَمْتَنِي؟ فَأَقُولُ: أَرَدْتُ أَنْ تَخْرُجَ إِلَيَّ وَقَدْ قَضَيْتَ حَاجَتَكَ.

الدّارمي

DAY 24

ʿAlī ibn Abī Ṭālib said: "Patience with regard to faith is the same as the head with regard to the body."

(Wakīʿ ibn al-Jarrāḥ, *Kitāb al-Zuhd*)

DAY 25

Masrūq related that ʿAbdullāh ibn Masʿūd said: "By Allah besides Whom there is no god! There is not a single *Sūrah* of the Book of Allah except that I know where it was revealed; and there is not a single verse in the Book of Allah except that I know the reason why it was revealed. And if I knew of anyone who is more knowledgeable than me about the Book of Allah, to whom one can travel on the back of camels, I would travel to him."

(Al-Bukhārī)

اليوم
٢٤

قَالَ عَلِيٌّ: الصَّبْرُ مِنَ الْإِيمَانِ بِمَنْزِلَةِ الرَّأْسِ مِنَ الْجَسَدِ.

وكيع بن الجرَّاح، كتاب الزهد

اليوم
٢٥

عَنْ مَسْرُوقٍ قَالَ: قَالَ عَبْدُ اللهِ: وَاللهِ الَّذِي لَا إِلَهَ غَيْرُهُ! مَا أُنْزِلَتْ سُورَةٌ مِنْ كِتَابِ اللهِ إِلَّا أَنَا أَعْلَمُ أَيْنَ أُنْزِلَتْ، وَلَا أُنْزِلَتْ آيَةٌ مِنْ كِتَابِ اللهِ إِلَّا أَنَا أَعْلَمُ فِيمَ أُنْزِلَتْ. وَلَوْ أَعْلَمُ أَحَدًا أَعْلَمَ مِنِّي بِكِتَابِ اللهِ تُبَلِّغُهُ الْإِبِلُ لَرَكِبْتُ إِلَيْهِ.

البخاري

DAY
26

It is reported that 'Abdullāh ibn Mas'ūd said: "We have reached a time when we no longer judge [between people] and we are no longer there; and then Allah has decreed on us that we have reached what you can see. So if anyone of you is brought a case to judge after today, then let him judge according to what is in the Book of Allah. And if it is a matter that is not in the Book of Allah, let him judge with that which His Prophet, may Allah bless him and grant him peace, has judged. And if it is a matter that has not been mentioned in the Book of Allah or His Prophet, may Allah bless him and grant him peace, then let him judge by that which the righteous have judged. And if it is a matter that has not been mentioned in the Book of Allah and His Prophet, may Allah bless him and grant him peace, and the righteous scholars did not issue a judgement about it, then he should make an effort to give his own opinion.

اليوم
٢٦

عَنْ عَبْدِ اللَّهِ بْنِ مَسْعُودٍ قَالَ: إِنَّهُ قَدْ أَتَىٰ عَلَيْنَا زَمَانٌ وَلَسْنَا نَقْضِي وَلَسْنَا هُنَالِكَ، ثُمَّ إِنَّ اللَّهَ عَزَّ وَجَلَّ قَدَّرَ عَلَيْنَا أَنْ بَلَغْنَا مَا تَرَوْنَ، فَمَنْ عَرَضَ لَهُ مِنْكُمْ قَضَاءٌ بَعْدَ الْيَوْمِ، فَلْيَقْضِ بِمَا فِي كِتَابِ اللَّهِ، فَإِنْ جَاءَ أَمْرٌ لَيْسَ فِي كِتَابِ اللَّهِ، فَلْيَقْضِ بِمَا قَضَىٰ بِهِ نَبِيُّهُ صَلَّىٰ اللَّهُ عَلَيْهِ وَسَلَّمَ، فَإِنْ جَاءَ أَمْرٌ لَيْسَ فِي كِتَابِ اللَّهِ، وَلَا قَضَىٰ بِهِ نَبِيُّهُ صَلَّىٰ اللَّهُ عَلَيْهِ وَسَلَّمَ، فَلْيَقْضِ بِمَا قَضَىٰ بِهِ الصَّالِحُونَ، فَإِنْ جَاءَ أَمْرٌ لَيْسَ فِي كِتَابِ اللَّهِ، وَلَا قَضَىٰ بِهِ نَبِيُّهُ صَلَّىٰ اللَّهُ عَلَيْهِ وَسَلَّمَ، وَلَا قَضَىٰ بِهِ الصَّالِحُونَ، فَلْيَجْتَهِدْ رَأْيَهُ وَلَا يَقُولُ: إِنِّي

And let him not say: I am afraid! I am afraid! For the lawful is crystal clear and the unlawful is crystal clear and between the two are ambiguous matters; so leave that which you find suspect to that which you do not find suspect."

(al-Dārimī)

DAY 27

ʿAbdullāh ibn Masʿūd said: "This Qur'ān is Allah's invitation, take from it as much as you can. For indeed, I know of nothing more deprived of goodness than a house in which there is nothing in it of the Book of Allah. And verily, the heart in which there is nothing of the Book of Allah is as desolate as a house which is uninhabited."

(al-Dārimī)

أَخَافُ وَإِنِّي أَخَافُ، فَإِنَّ الْحَلَالَ بَيِّنٌ وَالْحَرَامَ بَيِّنٌ وَبَيْنَ ذَلِكَ أُمُورٌ مُشْتَبِهَاتٌ، فَدَعْ مَا يَرِيبُكَ إِلَى مَا لَا يَرِيبُكَ.

النَّسَائِي

اليوم ٢٧

عَنْ عَبْدِ اللهِ قَالَ: إِنَّ هَذَا الْقُرْآنَ مَأْدُبَةُ اللهِ فَخُذُوا مِنْهُ مَا اسْتَطَعْتُمْ فَإِنِّي لَا أَعْلَمُ شَيْئًا أَصْفَرَ مِنْ خَيْرٍ مِنْ بَيْتٍ لَيْسَ فِيهِ مِنْ كِتَابِ اللهِ شَيْءٌ وَإِنَّ الْقَلْبَ الَّذِي لَيْسَ فِيهِ مِنْ كِتَابِ اللهِ شَيْءٌ خَرِبٌ كَخَرَابِ الْبَيْتِ الَّذِي لَا سَاكِنَ لَهُ.

الدَّارِمِي

DAY 28

Ḥafṣ ibn ʿInān al-Ḥanafī related that Abū Hurayrah, may Allah be well pleased with him, used to say: "Through reciting the Qur'ān in it, a house becomes expansive for its inhabitants, the angels would be present therein and the devils depart from it while its goodness increases. By contrast, by not reciting the Qur'ān in it, a house becomes too small for its inhabitants, the angels depart from it, the devils would be present therein and its goodness decreases."

(al-Dārimī)

DAY 29

ʿUmar ibn al-Khaṭṭāb, may Allah be well pleased wirh him, said: "Learn the laws of inheritance, proper Arabic usage and the Prophetic practices in the same way as you learn the Qur'ān."

(al-Dārimī)

اليوم ٢٨

عَنْ حَفْصِ بْنِ عِنَانٍ الْحَنَفِيُّ أَنَّ أَبَا هُرَيْرَةَ كَانَ يَقُولُ: إِنَّ الْبَيْتَ لَيَتَّسِعُ عَلَى أَهْلِهِ وَتَحْضُرُهُ الْمَلَائِكَةُ وَتَهْجُرُهُ الشَّيَاطِينُ وَيَكْثُرُ خَيْرُهُ أَنْ يُقْرَأَ فِيهِ الْقُرْآنُ وَإِنَّ الْبَيْتَ لَيَضِيقُ عَلَى أَهْلِهِ وَتَهْجُرُهُ الْمَلَائِكَةُ وَتَحْضُرُهُ الشَّيَاطِينُ وَيَقِلُّ خَيْرُهُ أَنْ لَا يُقْرَأَ فِيهِ الْقُرْآنُ.

الدّارمي

اليوم ٢٩

قَالَ عُمَرُ بْنُ الْخَطَّابِ: تَعَلَّمُوا الْفَرَائِضَ وَاللَّحْنَ وَالسُّنَنَ كَمَا تَعَلَّمُونَ الْقُرْآنَ.

الدّارمي

DAY 30

ʿAbdullāh ibn Masʿūd, may Allah be well pleased with him, said: "Learn the Qur'ān and the laws of inheritance, for a time is near when a man may be in need of a knowledge he used to know or he may remain amongst people who have no knowledge."

(al-Dārimī)

DAY 31

ʿAlī ibn Abī Ṭālib, may Allah be well pleased wirh him, said: "The hoarders of wealth are in peril while they are still alive while the men of knowledge last as long as Time persists."

(Al-Sharīf al-Raḍī, *Nahj al-Balāghah*)

اليوم
٣٠

قَالَ عَبْدُ اللَّهِ بْن مَسْعُود تَعَلَّمُوا الْقُرْآنَ وَالْفَرَائِضَ فَإِنَّهُ يُوشِكُ أَنْ يَفْتَقِرَ الرَّجُلُ إِلَى عِلْمٍ كَانَ يَعْلَمُهُ أَوْ يَبْقَى فِي قَوْمٍ لَا يَعْلَمُونَ.

الدّارمي

اليوم
٣١

قال عَلِيّ بْن أَبِي طَالِبٍ: هَلَكَ خُزَّانُ الْأَمْوَالِ وَهُمْ أَحْيَاءُ، وَالْعُلَمَاءُ بَاقُونَ مَا بَقِيَ الدَّهْرُ.

الشّريف الراضي، نهج البلاغة

DAY 32

ʿAbdullāh Ibn Masʿūd, may Allah be pleased with him, said: "Keep up the recitation of these scrolls [of the Qur'ān] – or he might have said: the Qur'ān - for it slips away from the breasts of men more easily than the cattle from their leash."

(Aḥmad)

DAY 33

Ibn ʿAbbās said: "Whoever reads *Sūrah Yā-Sīn* when he reaches morning shall be given ease on that day until he reaches evening; and whoever reads it at the beginning of the night shall be given ease on that night until he reaches morning."

(al-Dārimī)

اليوم ٣٢

عَنْ عَبْدِ اللهِ بن مَسعُود قَالَ: تَعَاهَدُوا هَذِهِ الْمَصَاحِفَ - وَرُبَّمَا قَالَ الْقُرْآنَ - فَلَهُوَ أَشَدُّ تَفَصِّيًا مِنْ صُدُورِ الرِّجَالِ مِنْ النَّعَمِ مِنْ عُقُلِهِ.

أحمد

اليوم ٣٣

قَالَ ابْنُ عَبَّاسٍ: مَنْ قَرَأَ يس حِينَ يُصْبِحُ أُعْطِيَ يُسْرَ يَوْمِهِ حَتَّى يُمْسِيَ وَمَنْ قَرَأَهَا فِي صَدْرِ لَيْلِهِ أُعْطِيَ يُسْرَ لَيْلَتِهِ حَتَّى يُصْبِحَ.

الدَّارمي

DAY 34

Khālid ibn Ma'dān said: "Recite the Saver – which is A.L.M. *Tanzīl* [*Sūrah al-Sajdah*] – for it has reached me that a man used to recite it so much that he did not recite anything else and he was a man of many sins, and so it overspread its wings on him and said: 'O Lord! Forgive him for he used to recite me a great deal.' And so the Lord accepted Its intercession on his behalf, and He said: 'for each sin he has committed, inscribe a good deed for him and raise him one degree.'"

(al-Dārimī)

DAY 35

'Uthmān ibn 'Affān said: "Whoever recites the last verses of *Sūrah Āl 'Imrān* at night, it will be inscribed for him [the reward of] standing up in prayer in the dead of night."."

(al-Dārimī)

اليوم
٣٤

عَنْ خَالِدِ بْنِ مَعْدَانَ قَالَ: اقْرَؤُوا الْمُنجِّيَةَ، وَهِيَ (الم تَنْزِيلُ)، فَإِنَّهُ بَلَغَنِي أَنَّ رَجُلًا كَانَ يَقْرَؤُهَا مَا يَقْرَأُ شَيْئًا غَيْرَهَا وَكَانَ كَثِيرَ الْخَطَايَا فَنَشَرَتْ جَنَاحَهَا عَلَيْهِ وَقَالَتْ: رَبِّ اغْفِرْ لَهُ فَإِنَّهُ كَانَ يُكْثِرُ قِرَاءَتِي فَشَفَّعَهَا الرَّبُّ فِيهِ وَقَالَ اكْتُبُوا لَهُ بِكُلِّ خَطِيئَةٍ حَسَنَةً وَارْفَعُوا لَهُ دَرَجَةً.

الدّارمي

اليوم
٣٥

عَنْ عُثْمَانَ بْنِ عَفَّانَ قَالَ: مَنْ قَرَأَ آخِرَ آلِ عِمْرَانَ فِي لَيْلَةٍ كُتِبَ لَهُ قِيَامُ لَيْلَةٍ.

الدّارمي

DAY 36

ʿAbdullāh ibn Masʿūd said: "Whoever recites *Sūrah Āl ʿImrān* is prosperous while [*Sūrah*] *al-Nisā'* beautifies [whoever recites it]."

(al-Dārimī)

DAY 37

ʿAlī ibn Abī Ṭālib said: "The simile of the one who is given faith but has not been given the Qur'ān is like a date: it tastes good but it has no smell; and the simile of the one who is given the Qur'ān but has not been given faith is like a fragrant basil tree: it smell good while its taste is bitter; and the simile of the one who is given both the Qur'ān and faith is like a citron: it smells good and tastes good; while the simile of the one who is not given neither faith nor the Qur'ān is like the citrullus colocynthis: it smells foul and tastes foul."

(al-Dārimī)

اليوم
٣٦

قَالَ عَبْدُ اللهِ بْنُ مَسْعُودٍ : مَنْ قَرَأَ آلَ عِمْرَانَ فَهُوَ غَنِيٌّ وَالنِّسَاءُ مُحَبِّرَةٌ.

الدَّارمي

اليوم
٣٧

عَنْ عَلِيٍّ قَالَ: مَثَلُ الَّذِي أُوتِيَ الْإِيمَانَ وَلَمْ يُؤْتَ الْقُرْآنَ مَثَلُ التَّمْرَةِ طَعْمُهَا طَيِّبٌ وَلَا رِيحَ لَهَا وَمَثَلُ الَّذِي أُوتِيَ الْقُرْآنَ وَلَمْ يُؤْتَ الْإِيمَانَ مَثَلُ الرَّيْحَانَةِ الْآتِيَةِ رِيحُهَا طَيِّبٌ وَطَعْمُهَا مُرٌّ وَمَثَلُ الَّذِي أُوتِيَ الْقُرْآنَ وَالْإِيمَانَ مَثَلُ الْأُتْرُجَّةِ رِيحُهَا طَيِّبٌ وَطَعْمُهَا طَيِّبٌ وَمَثَلُ الَّذِي لَمْ يُؤْتَ الْإِيمَانَ وَلَا الْقُرْآنَ مَثَلُ الْحَنْظَلَةِ رِيحُهَا خَبِيثٌ وَطَعْمُهَا خَبِيثٌ.

الدَّارمي

DAY 38

'Umar ibn al-Khaṭṭāb said: "This Qur'ān is Allah's speech, so I do not know why you have distorted its meaning to agree with your whims."

(al-Dārimī)

DAY 39

It is related that Mu'ādh ibn Jabal said: "The Qur'ān will wear out in the breasts of some people just as a garment wears out and then fades away. They will recite it but find therein neither joy nor delight. They are wolves in sheep's clothing; their works are done in pure covetedness [of Allah's reward] while devoid of any fear [of Allah]. If they are remiss, they say: 'We shall get there'; and if they sin, they say: 'We shall be forgiven. After all, we do not associate anything with Allah!'"

(al-Dārimī)

اليوم ٣٨

قَالَ عُمَرُ بْنُ الْخَطَّابِ: إِنَّ هَذَا الْقُرْآنَ كَلَامُ اللَّهِ فَلَا أَعْرِفَنَّكُمْ فِيمَا عَطَفْتُمُوهُ عَلَى أَهْوَائِكُمْ.

الدّارمي

اليوم ٣٩

عَنْ مُعَاذِ بْنِ جَبَلٍ قَالَ: سَيَبْلَى الْقُرْآنُ فِي صُدُورِ أَقْوَامٍ كَمَا يَبْلَى الثَّوْبُ فَيَتَهَافَتُ، يَقْرَءُونَهُ لَا يَجِدُونَ لَهُ شَهْوَةً وَلَا لَذَّةً، يَلْبَسُونَ جُلُودَ الضَّأْنِ عَلَى قُلُوبِ الذِّئَابِ، أَعْمَالُهُمْ طَمَعٌ لَا يُخَالِطُهُ خَوْفٌ، إِنْ قَصَّرُوا قَالُوا سَنَبْلُغُ وَإِنْ أَسَاءُوا قَالُوا سَيُغْفَرُ لَنَا إِنَّا لَا نُشْرِكُ بِاللَّهِ شَيْئًا.

الدّارمي

DAY 40

It is related that ʿAbdullāh [ibn Masʿūd] said: "Recite the Qur'ān in abundance before it is lifted away." Those present asked: "These copies of the Qur'ān will be lifted away but what about that which is preserved in the breasts of men?" To this he replied: "It will be taken away from them at night, and when they reach morning, they would be bereft of it, forgetting even how to say: 'there is no deity except Allah', and they would then fall in the usual talk and poetry of the pre-Islamic period. It is then that the sentence falls on them."

(al-Dārimī)

DAY 41

It is reported from Abū Qilābah that a man said to Abū al-Dardā': "Your brothers in Kufah from among the folk of remembrance convey their greeting of peace to you." And so he said: "And may the greeting of peace be upon them.

اليوم ٤٠

عَنْ عَبْدِ اللَّهِ قَالَ: أَكْثِرُوا تِلَاوَةَ الْقُرْآنِ قَبْلَ أَنْ يُرْفَعَ. قَالُوا: هَذِهِ الْمَصَاحِفُ تُرْفَعُ فَكَيْفَ بِمَا فِي صُدُورِ الرِّجَالِ؟ قَالَ: يُسْرَىٰ عَلَيْهِ لَيْلًا فَيُصْبِحُونَ مِنْهُ فُقَرَاءَ وَيَنْسَوْنَ قَوْلَ لَا إِلَهَ إِلَّا اللَّهُ وَيَقَعُونَ فِي قَوْلِ الْجَاهِلِيَّةِ وَأَشْعَارِهِمْ وَذَلِكَ حِينَ يَقَعُ عَلَيْهِمُ الْقَوْلُ.

الدَّارمي

اليوم ٤١

عَنْ أَبِي قِلَابَةَ أَنَّ رَجُلًا قَالَ لِأَبِي الدَّرْدَاءِ: إِنَّ إِخْوَانَكَ مِنْ أَهْلِ الْكُوفَةِ مِنْ أَهْلِ الذِّكْرِ يُقْرِئُونَكَ السَّلَامَ. فَقَالَ:

Tell them to give their reins to the Qur'ān for it prompts them to follow moderation and ease and makes them avoid transgression and hardship."

(al-Dārimī)

DAY
42

It is reported that Abū Mūsā [al-Ash'arī] said: "Indeed, this Qur'ān shall be a reward for you and it shall be a remembrance for you; and it shall be a light through you or it shall be an onus on you. So follow the Qur'ān and do not let the Qur'ān pursue you. For whoever follows the Qur'ān, it will land him in the meadows of Paradise; and whoever is pursued by the Qur'ān, it will push him from behind and throw him in Hell."

(al-Dārimī)

وَعَلَيْهِمُ السَّلَامُ وَمُرْهُمْ فَلْيُعْطُوا الْقُرْآنَ بِخَزَائِمِهِمْ فَإِنَّهُ يَحْمِلُهُمْ عَلَى الْقَصْدِ وَالسُّهُولَةِ وَيُجَنِّبُهُمُ الْجَوْرَ وَالْحُزُونَةَ.

الدَّارمي

اليوم ٤٢

عَنْ أَبِي مُوسَى أَنَّهُ قَالَ: إِنَّ هَذَا الْقُرْآنَ كَائِنٌ لَكُمْ أَجْرًا وَكَائِنٌ لَكُمْ ذِكْرًا وَكَائِنٌ بِكُمْ نُورًا وَكَائِنٌ عَلَيْكُمْ وِزْرًا. اتَّبِعُوا الْقُرْآنَ وَلَا يَتَّبِعْكُمُ الْقُرْآنُ فَإِنَّهُ مَنْ يَتَّبِعْ الْقُرْآنَ يَهْبِطْ بِهِ فِي رِيَاضِ الْجَنَّةِ وَمَنْ اتَّبَعَهُ الْقُرْآنُ يَزُخُّ فِي قَفَاهُ فَيَقْذِفُهُ فِي جَهَنَّمَ.

الدَّارمي

DAY 43

It is reported that ʿAbdullāh ibn Masʿūd said: "Let him receive glad tidings whoever loves the Qur'ān."

(al-Dārimī)

DAY 44

ʿAbdullāh [ibn Masʿūd] said: "Indeed, this Qur'ān is Allah's invitation to attend His bounty and so learn from it as much as you can. Verily, this Qur'ān is Allah's rope, the clear light and the beneficial healing. It is a protection for whoever holds fast to it and a safety for whoever follows it. It does not deviate such that it needs censoring nor does it get crooked such that it requires straightening. Its wonders never wear out nor does it become obsolete through oft repetition. So do recite it, for Allah rewards you ten good deeds for the recitation of each letter. Here I am not saying A. L. M. [is a letter] but I am saying [He will reward you] for A, L and M."

(al-Dārimī)

اليوم ٤٣

عَنْ عَبْدِ اللَّهِ قَالَ: مَنْ أَحَبَّ الْقُرْآنَ فَلْيُبْشِرْ.

الدَّارمي

اليوم ٤٤

عَنْ عَبْدِ اللَّهِ رَضِيَ اللَّهُ عَنْهُ قَالَ: إِنَّ هَذَا الْقُرْآنَ مَأْدُبَةُ اللَّهِ فَتَعَلَّمُوا مِنْ مَأْدُبَتِهِ مَا اسْتَطَعْتُمْ. إِنَّ هَذَا الْقُرْآنَ حَبْلُ اللَّهِ وَالنُّورُ الْمُبِينُ وَالشِّفَاءُ النَّافِعُ، عِصْمَةٌ لِمَنْ تَمَسَّكَ بِهِ وَنَجَاةٌ لِمَنْ اتَّبَعَهُ، لَا يَزِيغُ فَيُسْتَعْتَبُ وَلَا يَعْوَجُّ فَيُقَوَّمُ، وَلَا تَنْقَضِي عَجَائِبُهُ وَلَا يَخْلَقُ عَنْ كَثْرَةِ الرَّدِّ، فَاتْلُوهُ فَإِنَّ اللَّهَ يَأْجُرُكُمْ عَلَى تِلَاوَتِهِ بِكُلِّ حَرْفٍ عَشْرَ حَسَنَاتٍ أَمَا إِنِّي لَا أَقُولُ الم وَلَكِنْ بِأَلِفٍ وَلَامٍ وَمِيمٍ.

الدَّارمي

DAY
45

ʿAbdullāh ibn Masʿūd said: "Whoever seeks knowledge let him read the Qur'ān and study it with the men of knowledge for it contains the knowledge of the people of old and that of the people who will come."

(Aḥmad)

DAY
46

It is reported that Abū al-Dardā' said: " How is it that your scholars are dying out and your ignorant ones do not seek knowledge? Seek knowledge before it is lifted, for the lifting of knowledge means the passing of the men of knowledge. And how is it that you are avid for what has been guaranteed for you and squander what you have been left to seek."

(Ibn Abī Shaybah, *al-Muṣannaf*)

اليوم ٤٥

قَالَ عَبْدُ اللهِ بْن مَسْعُود: مَنْ أَرَادَ العِلْمَ فَلْيُثَوِّرِ القُرْآنَ فَإِنَّ فِيهِ عِلْمُ الأَوَّلِينَ وَالآخِرِين.

أحمد

اليوم ٤٦

عَنْ أَبِي الدَّرْدَاءِ رَضِيَ اللَّهُ عَنْهُ أَنَّهُ قَالَ: مَالِي أَرَىٰ عُلَمَائَكُمْ يَذْهَبُونَ، وَأَرَى جُهَّالَكُمْ لاَ يَتَعَلَّمُونَ، اعْلَمُوا قَبْلَ أَنْ يُرْفَعَ الْعِلْمُ، فَإِنَّ رَفْعَ الْعِلْمِ ذَهَابُ الْعُلَمَاءِ. مَالِي أَرَاكُمْ تَحْرِصُونَ عَلَىٰ مَا تُكُفِّلَ لَكُمْ بِهِ، وَتُضَيِّعُونَ مَا وُكِّلْتُمْ بِهِ.

ابن أبي شيبة، المصنَّف

DAY 47

It is reported that Ibn ʿAbbās said: "Allah has guaranteed for the one who follows the Qur'ān and acts on what it contains that he will neither go astray in this world nor be damned in the next world." Then he recited Allah's words (*then whosoever follows My guidance shall not go astray, neither shall he be unprosperous*) (*Ṭa-Ha* 20: 123)

(Ibn Abī Shaybah, *al-Muṣannaf*)

DAY 48

It is reported that ʿAlī ibn Abī Ṭālib said: "When I relate to you a Prophetic saying from the Messenger of Allah, Allah bless him and grant him peace, you should think of it that which is the most felicitous, most guiding and most fearing of Allah."

(Ibn Mājah)

اليوم
٤٧

عَـنِ ابْنِ عَبَّاسٍ: ضَمِنَ اللَّهُ لِمَنِ اتَّبَعَ الْقُرْآنَ وَعَمِلَ بِمَا فِيهِ أنْ لاَ يَضِلَّ فِي الدُّنْيَا وَلاَ يَشْقَى فِي الآخِرَةِ، ثُمَّ تَلاَ ﴿فَمَنِ ٱتَّبَعَ هُدَاىَ فَلَا يَضِلُّ وَلَا يَشْقَىٰ﴾ [طه ٢٠: ١٢٣].

ابن أبي شيبة، المصنَّف

اليوم
٤٨

عَنْ عَلِيٍّ بْنِ أَبِي طَالِبٍ قَالَ: إِذَا حَدَّثْتُكُمْ عَنْ رَسُولِ اللَّهِ صَلَّى اللَّهُ عَلَيْهِ وَسَلَّمَ بِحَدِيثٍ فَظُنُّوا بِهِ الَّذِي هُوَ أَهْنَاهُ وَأَهْدَاهُ وَأَتْقَاهُ.

ابن ماجه

DAY 49

It is related that ʿAbdullāh ibn Buraydah said: "ʿAlī [ibn Abī Ṭālib] said: "Visit one another and study *Ḥadīth* amongst yourselves, for it will be extinct if you do not do so.""

(Ibn Abī Shaybah, *al-Muṣannaf*)

DAY 50

It is related that Ibn Masʿūd said: "Verily, Allah looked at the hearts of His servants and found that the heart of Muhammad, Allah bless him and grant him peace, was the best heart of His servants' hearts and so He chose him for Himself and sent him with His Message. Then He looked at the hearts of His servants, after looking at the heart of Muhammad, and found that the hearts of his Companions were the best hearts of His servants' hearts and so He made them the helpers of His Prophet who defend His religion."

(Aḥmad)

اليوم
٤٩

عَنْ عَبْدِ الله بْنِ بُرَيْدَةَ قَالَ: قَالَ عَلِيٌّ: تَزَاوَرُوا وَتَذَاكَرُوا الْحَدِيثَ فَإِنَّكُمْ إِنْ لاَ تَفْعَلُوا يَدْرُسْ.

ابن أبي شيبة ، المصنَّف

اليوم
٥٠

عَنْ عَبْدِ اللَّهِ بْنِ مَسْعُودٍ قَالَ: إِنَّ اللَّهَ نَظَرَ فِي قُلُوبِ الْعِبَادِ فَوَجَدَ قَلْبَ مُحَمَّدٍ صَلَّى اللَّهُ عَلَيْهِ وَسَلَّمَ خَيْرَ قُلُوبِ الْعِبَادِ فَاصْطَفَاهُ لِنَفْسِهِ فَابْتَعَثَهُ بِرِسَالَتِهِ ثُمَّ نَظَرَ فِي قُلُوبِ الْعِبَادِ بَعْدَ قَلْبِ مُحَمَّدٍ فَوَجَدَ قُلُوبَ أَصْحَابِهِ خَيْرَ قُلُوبِ الْعِبَادِ فَجَعَلَهُمْ وُزَرَاءَ نَبِيِّهِ يُقَاتِلُونَ عَلَى دِينِهِ.

أحمد

DAY 51

It is related that ʿAbdullāh [Ibn Masʿūd] said: "Whoever wishes to encounter Allah, glorious and exalted is He, tomorrow as a Muslim, then let him observe these prescribed prayers diligently whenever they are called to be performed for they are of the norms of guidance and, indeed, Allah has prescribed for your Prophet the norms of guidance. And there is none of you except that he has a space for praying at home, and were you to pray in your homes, as did this person who stayed behind in his home, you would leave the practice of your Prophet. And were you to leave the practice of your Prophet, you would go astray. And it is my experience that none stays behind and misses the prayer except a hypocrite whose hypocrisy is well known. I have indeed seen men carried by a person on each side until they are placed in the rows of prayer."

(Aḥmad)

اليوم
٥١

عَنْ عَبْدِ اللَّهِ قَالَ: مَنْ سَرَّهُ أَنْ يَلْقَىٰ اللَّهَ عَزَّ وَجَلَّ غَدًا مُسْلِمًا فَلْيُحَافِظْ عَلَىٰ هَؤُلَاءِ الصَّلَوَاتِ الْمَكْتُوبَاتِ حَيْثُ يُنَادَي بِهِنَّ فَإِنَّهُنَّ مِنْ سُنَنِ الْهُدَىٰ وَإِنَّ اللَّهَ عَزَّ وَجَلَّ شَرَعَ لِنَبِيِّكُمْ سُنَنَ الْهُدَى وَمَا مِنْكُمْ إِلَّا وَلَهُ مَسْجِدٌ فِي بَيْتِهِ وَلَوْ صَلَّيْتُمْ فِي بُيُوتِكُمْ كَمَا يُصَلِّي هَذَا الْمُتَخَلِّفُ فِي بَيْتِهِ لَتَرَكْتُمْ سُنَّةَ نَبِيِّكُمْ وَلَوْ تَرَكْتُمْ سُنَّةَ نَبِيِّكُمْ لَضَلَلْتُمْ وَلَقَدْ رَأَيْتُنِي وَمَا يَتَخَلَّفُ عَنْهَا إِلَّا مُنَافِقٌ مَعْلُومٌ نِفَاقُهُ وَلَقَدْ رَأَيْتُ الرَّجُلَ يُهَادَىٰ بَيْنَ الرَّجُلَيْنِ حَتَّى يُقَامَ فِي الصَّفِّ.

أحمد

DAY
52

It is related that Ḥassān said: "Whenever a group of people introduces a blameworthy innovation in their religion, Allah takes away of their practice the like of it and never brings it back to the Day of Judgement."

(al-Dārimī)

DAY
53

A man from the Banū ʿĀmir reported that ʿAlī [ibn Abī Ṭālib] said: "Verily, I fear for you two things: long hope and following whims, for long hope makes one forget the Afterlife while following whims bars from the truth. Indeed, this world is receding and about to end and the Afterlife is coming ahead and each has its children. So be the children of the Afterlife, as today there is work and no reckoning while tomorrow there is reckoning and no work."

(Ibn Abī Shaybah, *al-Muṣannaf*)

اليوم ٥٢

عَنْ حَسَّانَ قَالَ: مَا ابْتَدَعَ قَوْمٌ بِدْعَةً فِي دِينِهِمْ إِلَّا نَزَعَ اللَّهُ مِنْ سُنَّتِهِمْ مِثْلَهَا ثُمَّ لَا يُعِيدُهَا إِلَيْهِمْ إِلَى يَوْمِ الْقِيَامَةِ.

الدّارمي

اليوم ٥٣

عَنْ رَجُلٍ مِنْ بَنِي عَامِرٍ قَالَ: قَالَ عَلِيٌّ: إِنَّمَا أَخَافُ عَلَيْكُمُ اثْنَتَيْنِ: طُولَ الأَمَلِ وَاتِّبَاعَ الْهَوَى، فَإِنَّ طُولَ الأَمَلِ يُنْسِي الآخِرَةَ، وَإِنَّ اتِّبَاعَ الْهَوَى يَصُدُّ عَنِ الْحَقِّ، وَإِنَّ الدُّنْيَا قَدْ تَرَحَّلَتْ مُدْبِرَةً، وَإِنَّ الآخِرَةَ مُقْبِلَةٌ وَلِكُلٍّ وَاحِدَةٍ مِنْهُمَا بَنُونَ فَكُونُوا مِنْ أَبْنَاءِ الآخِرَةِ، فَإِنَّ الْيَوْمَ عَمَلٌ وَلاَ حِسَابَ وَغَدًا حِسَابٌ وَلاَ عَمَلَ.

ابن أبي شيبة، المصنَّف

DAY 54

Salmān [al-Fārisī] wrote to Abū al-Dardā' the following: "There is the shade of the Throne for a man whose heart is very attached to the mosques out of love for them."

(Ibn Abī Shaybah, *al-Muṣannaf*)

DAY 55

Yaḥya ibn 'Abd al-Raḥmān ibn Ḥāṭib reported that Abū Wāqid al-Laythī said: "We have looked into which works are better and could not find anything more helpful for seeking the Afterlife than non-attachment to this world."

(Ibn Abī Shaybah, *al-Muṣannaf*)

اليوم
٥٤

كَتَبَ سَلْمَانُ إِلَىٰ أَبِي الدَّرْدَاءِ: إِنَّ فِي ظِلِّ الْعَرْشِ رَجُلاً قَلْبُهُ مُعَلَّقٌ فِي الْمَسَاجِدِ مِنْ حُبِّهَا.

ابن أبي شيبة، المصنَّف

اليوم
٥٥

عَنْ يَحْيَى بْنِ عَبْدِ الرَّحْمَنِ بْنِ حَاطِبٍ قَالَ: قَالَ أَبُو وَاقِدٍ اللَّيْثِيُّ: تَابَعْنَا الأَعْمَالَ أَيُّهَا أَفْضَلُ فَلَمْ نَجِدْ شَيْئًا أَعْوَنَ عَلَى طَلَبِ الآخِرَةِ مِنَ الزُّهْدِ فِي الدُّنْيَا.

ابن أبي شيبة، المصنَّف

DAY
56

ʿĀʾishah is reported to have said: "The Messenger of Allah (Allah bless him and grant him peace) never hit a servant or any of his wives. Neither did he strike anyone with his hand unless it be during jihad in the way of Allah. And never did he take revenge against any person who slighted him unless the sanctuaries of Allah have been violated in which case he would take revenge for Allah, glorified and exalted is He. And never was he presented with two alternatives except that he chose the easiest of the two unless it be a sin, in which case he would be the farthest person from it."

(Muslim)

اليوم
٥٦

عَنْ عَائِشَةَ قَالَتْ: مَا ضَرَبَ رَسُولُ اللَّهِ صَلَّى اللَّهُ عَلَيْهِ وَسَلَّمَ خَادِمًا لَهُ قَطُّ وَلَا امْرَأَةً لَهُ قَطُّ وَلَا ضَرَبَ بِيَدِهِ إِلَّا أَنْ يُجَاهِدَ فِي سَبِيلِ اللَّهِ وَمَا نِيلَ مِنْهُ شَيْءٌ فَانْتَقَمَهُ مِنْ صَاحِبِهِ إِلَّا أَنْ تُنْتَهَكَ مَحَارِمُ اللَّهِ عَزَّ وَجَلَّ فَيَنْتَقِمُ لِلَّهِ عَزَّ وَجَلَّ وَمَا عُرِضَ عَلَيْهِ أَمْرَانِ أَحَدُهُمَا أَيْسَرُ مِنْ الْآخَرِ إِلَّا أَخَذَ بِأَيْسَرِهِمَا إِلَّا أَنْ يَكُونَ مَأْثَمًا فَإِنْ كَانَ مَأْثَمًا كَانَ أَبْعَدَ النَّاسِ مِنْهُ.

مسلم

DAY 57

It is reported that Salmān [al-Fārisī] said: "When a servant is used to remembering Allah in times of ease and praising Him in times of prosperity and then harm befalls him and he beseeches Allah, the angels would say: 'This is a familiar voice from a weak individual,' and so they intercede for him. But when a servant does not remember Allah in times of ease nor praises him in times of prosperity and then harm befalls him and he beseeches Allah, the angels would say: 'This is an unfamiliar voice,' and so they would not intercede for him.'

(Ibn Abī Shaybah, *al-Muṣannaf*)

DAY 58

Nāfiʿ ibn ʿAbdullāh (the client of ʿUmar) reported that ʿUmar ibn al-Khaṭṭāb wrote the following to his governors: "The most important of your matters in my sight is the prayer:

عَنْ سَلْمَانَ قَالَ: إِذَا كَانَ الْعَبْدُ يَذْكُرُ اللَّهَ فِي السَّرَّاءِ وَيَحْمَدُهُ

فِي الرَّخَاءِ فَأَصَابَهُ ضُرٌّ فَدَعَا اللَّهَ، قَالَتِ الْمَلَائِكَةُ: صَوْتٌ

مَعْرُوفٌ مِنِ امْرِئٍ ضَعِيفٍ فَيَشْفَعُونَ لَهُ. وَإِنْ كَانَ الْعَبْدُ لَمْ

يَذْكُرِ اللَّهَ فِي السَّرَّاءِ وَلَا يَحْمَدُهُ فِي الرَّخَاءِ فَأَصَابَهُ ضُرٌّ فَدَعَا

اللَّهَ قَالَتِ الْمَلَائِكَةُ: صَوْتٌ مُنْكَرٌ فَلَمْ يَشْفَعُوا لَهُ.

ابن أبي شيبة، المصنَّف

عَنْ نَافِعٍ مَوْلَى عَبْدِ اللَّهِ بْنِ عُمَرَ أَنَّ عُمَرَ بْنَ الْخَطَّابِ

كَتَبَ إِلَى عُمَّالِهِ: إِنَّ أَهَمَّ أَمْرِكُمْ عِنْدِي الصَّلَاةُ،

whoever preserves it and diligently performs it has preserved his religion, and whoever squanders it will be more prone to squandering other things."

(Mālik, *al-Muwaṭṭa'*)

DAY 59

It is reported that al-Ḥasan said: "One day Salmān al-Fārisī entered in on Abū Bakr while he was alone and said to him: 'O deputy of the Messenger of Allah! Counsel me.' And so he said: 'Verily, Allah, glorified and exalted is He, is opening this world for you, so do not take from it except that which makes you do by; and whoever performs the prayer of *Ṣubḥ* is in Allah's liability, so do not break Allah's liability lest He throws you on your face in the Fire.'"

(Aḥmad)

فَمَنْ حَفِظَهَا وَحَافَظَ عَلَيْهَا حَفِظَ دِينَهُ وَمَنْ ضَيَّعَهَا فَهُوَ لِمَا سِوَاهَا أَضْيَعَ.

مالك، الموطأ

اليوم
٥٩

عَنِ الْحَسَنِ قَالَ: دَخَلَ سَلْمَانُ عَلَى أَبِي بَكْرٍ وَهُوَ يَكِيدُ بِنَفْسِهِ فَقَالَ: يَا خَلِيفَةَ رَسُولِ اللَّهِ، أَوْصِنِي، فَقَالَ لَهُ أَبُو بَكْرٍ: إِنَّ اللَّهَ عَزَّ وَجَلَّ فَاتِحٌ عَلَيْكُمُ الدُّنْيَا فَلَا تَأْخُذُوا مِنْهَا إِلَّا بَلَاغَكُمْ، وَإِنَّ مَنْ صَلَّى صَلَاةَ الصُّبْحِ فَهُوَ فِي ذِمَّةِ اللَّهِ عَزَّ وَجَلَّ فَلَا تَخْفِرَنَّ اللَّهَ عَزَّ وَجَلَّ فِي ذِمَّتِهِ فَيُكِبَّكَ فِي النَّارِ عَلَى وَجْهِكَ.

أحمد

DAY 60

ʿAbdullāh ibn ʿUmar said: "There will come a time when people gather in the mosque while none of them is a believer."

(Wakīʿ ibn al-Jarrāḥ, Kitāb *al-Zuhd*)

DAY 61

ʿAbdullāh ibn Masʿūd said: "Whoever is not prompted by his prayer to embrace what is good and to desist from what is evil will only increase in remoteness [from Allah]."

(Aḥmad)

اليوم ٦٠

عَنْ عَبْدِ اللَّهِ بْنِ عُمَرَ قَالَ: يَأْتِي عَلَى النَّاسِ زَمَانٌ يَجْتَمِعُونَ فِي الْمَسْجِدِ لَيْسَ فِيهِمْ مُؤْمِنٌ.

وكيع بن الجرَّاح، كتاب الزهد

اليوم ٦١

قَالَ عَبْدُ الله بْن مَسْعود: مَنْ لَمْ تَأْمُرْهُ الصَّلَاةُ بِالمَعْرُوفِ وَتَنْهَاهُ عَنِ المُنْكَرِ لَمْ يَزْدَدْ بِهَا إلاَّ بُعْدًا.

أحمد

DAY 62

It is reported from Mu'āwiyah ibn Qurrah that Mu'ādh ibn Jabal, may Allah have mercy on him, said to his son: "O my son! When you pray, pray as if you are going to pass on: do not think you are ever going to come back to it. And know, O my son, that the believer dies between two good deeds: a good deed he has sent forward and a good deed he has deferred for later."

(Aḥmad)

DAY 63

Al-Aswad ibn Yazīd reported that 'Abdullāh ibn Mas'ūd said: "The things that expiate sins are: performing the minor ritual ablution in cold mornings, walking to the congregational prayers and waiting for the next prayer after each prayer."

(Ibn Abī Shaybah, *al-Muṣannaf*)

اليوم ٦٢

عَنْ مُعَاوِيَةَ بْنِ قُرَّةَ قَالَ: قَالَ مُعَاذٌ لِابْنِهِ: يَا بُنَيَّ إِذَا صَلَّيْتَ صَلَاةً فَصَلِّ صَلَاةَ مُوَدِّعٍ لَا تَظُنُّ أَنَّكَ تَعُودُ إِلَيْهَا أَبَدًا، وَاعْلَمْ يَا بُنَيَّ أَنَّ الْمُؤْمِنَ يَمُوتُ بَيْنَ حَسَنَتَيْنِ: حَسَنَةً قَدَّمَهَا وَحَسَنَةً أَخَّرَهَا.

أحمد

اليوم ٦٣

عَنِ الأَسْوَدِ بْنِ يَزِيدَ قَالَ: قَالَ عَبْدُ اللهِ: الْكَفَّارَاتُ إِسْبَاغُ الْوُضُوءِ بِالسَّبَرَاتِ وَنَقْلُ الأَقْدَامِ إِلَى الْجُمُعَاتِ وَانْتِظَارُ الصَّلَاةِ بَعْدَ الصَّلَاةِ.

ابن أبي شيبة، المصنَّف

DAY
64

ʿUmar [ibn al-Khaṭṭāb] said: "The mosques are Allah's houses on earth and it is a right upon the One Who is visited to honour His visitor."

(Ibn Abī Shaybah, *al-Muṣannaf*)

DAY
65

ʿAlī ibn Abī Ṭālib, may Allah be well pleased with him, said: "Knowledge rules while wealth is ruled upon."

(Al-Sharīf al-Raḍī, *Nahj al-Balaghāh*)

اليوم ٦٤

عَنْ عُمَرَ قَالَ: الْمَسَاجِدُ بُيُوتُ اللَّهِ فِي الأَرْضِ وَحَقٌّ عَلَىٰ الْمَزُورِ أَنْ يُكْرِمَ زَائِرَهُ.

ابن أبي شيبة ، المصنَّف

اليوم ٦٥

قَالَ عَلِيُّ بْنُ أَبِي طَالِبٍ: الْعِلْمُ حَاكِمٌ، وَالْمَالُ مَحْكُومٌ عَلَيْهِ.

الشَّريف الرَضِّي ، نهج البلاغة

DAY
66

Qays ibn Ḥāzim reported the following: "Abū Bakr entered in on a woman from Aḥmas called Zaynab and saw that she did not speak. He enquired: "Why does she not speak?" They said: "She performed the pilgrimage in a state of silence." So he said: "Speak! For this is not allowed: this is of the works of pre-Islamic paganism." Upon hearing this, she spoke and said: "Who are you?" He said: "I am a man of the Immigrants." "Which immigrants?" she exclaimed. He said: "From Quraysh." "From which tribe of Quraysh are you?" she asked again. "You ask too many questions," he said and then added: "I am Abū Bakr." She said: "How long are we going to remain on this good thing that Allah has brought after pre-Islamic paganism?" He said: "You shall remain on it as long as your leaders establish what is right amongst you." She said: "And what are the leaders?" He said: "Did not your people have heads and noblemen who commanded them and they obeyed them?" She said: "Yes, indeed!" He said: "They are those people."

(al-Bukhārī)

اليوم
٦٦

عَنْ قَيْسِ بْنِ أَبِي حَازِمٍ قَالَ: دَخَلَ أَبُو بَكْرٍ عَلَى امْرَأَةٍ مِنْ أَحْمَسَ يُقَالُ لَهَا زَيْنَبُ فَرَآهَا لَا تَكَلَّمُ فَقَالَ: مَا لَهَا لَا تَكَلَّمُ. قَالُوا: حَجَّتْ مُصْمِتَةً، قَالَ: لَهَا تَكَلَّمِي فَإِنَّ هَذَا لَا يَحِلُ، هَذَا مِنْ عَمَلِ الْجَاهِلِيَّةِ. فَتَكَلَّمَتْ فَقَالَتْ: مَنْ أَنْتَ؟ قَالَ: امْرُؤٌ مِنْ الْمُهَاجِرِينَ. قَالَتْ: أَيُّ الْمُهَاجِرِينَ؟ قَالَ: مِنْ قُرَيْشٍ. قَالَتْ: مِنْ أَيِّ قُرَيْشٍ أَنْتَ؟ قَالَ: إِنَّكِ لَسَؤُولٌ. أَنَا أَبُو بَكْرٍ. قَالَتْ: مَا بَقَاؤُنَا عَلَى هَذَا الْأَمْرِ الصَّالِحِ الَّذِي جَاءَ اللَّهُ بِهِ بَعْدَ الْجَاهِلِيَّةِ؟ قَالَ: بَقَاؤُكُمْ عَلَيْهِ مَا اسْتَقَامَتْ بِكُمْ أَئِمَّتُكُمْ. قَالَتْ: وَمَا الْأَئِمَّةُ؟ قَالَ: أَمَا كَانَ لِقَوْمِكِ رُؤُوسٌ وَأَشْرَافٌ يَأْمُرُونَهُمْ فَيُطِيعُونَهُمْ. قَالَتْ: بَلَى! قَالَ: فَهُمْ أُولَئِكِ عَلَى النَّاسِ.

البخاري

DAY 67

Abū Dharr is reported to have said: "No charity on this earth is given until the whisperings of seventy satans are brushed aside, each one of them forbidding him [i.e. the person giving charity] from doing it."

(Ibn Abī Shaybah, *al-Muṣannaf*)

DAY 68

It is reported from Abū al-Aḥwaṣ that 'Abdullāh said: "The prayer of whosoever does not pay the poor-due (*Zakāt*) is not accepted."

(Ibn Abī Shaybah, *al-Muṣannaf*)

اليوم
٦٧

عَنْ أَبِي ذَرٍّ قَالَ: مَا عَلَىٰ الأَرْضِ مِنْ صَدَقَةٍ تَخْرُجُ حَتَّى يُفَكَّ عَنْهَا لِحَىٰ سَبْعِينَ شَيْطَانًا كُلُّهُمْ يَنْهَاهُ عَنْهَا.

ابن أبي شيبة ، المصنَّف

اليوم
٦٨

عَنْ أَبِي الأَحْوَصِ قَالَ: قَالَ عَبْدُ اللَّهِ: مَنْ لَمْ يُؤَدِّ الزَّكَاةَ فَلَا صَلَاةَ لَهُ.

ابن أبي شيبة ، المصنَّف

DAY 69

ʿAlī ibn Abī Ṭālib is reported to have said: "The one who withholds the poor-due is cursed."

(Ibn Abī Shaybah, *al-Muṣannaf*)

DAY 70

Abū ʿAṭiyyah reported the following: "I and Masrūq entered in on the Mother of the Believers, ʿĀ'ishah, and said: "O Mother of the Believers! There are two men among the Companions of Muhammad, Allah bless him and grant him peace, and one of them hastens both the breaking of the fast and the prayer while the other delays both the breaking of the fast and the prayer." She asked: "Who is the one who hastens both the breaking of the fast and the prayer?" We said: "ʿAbdullāh," i.e. Ibn Masʿūd. She said: "Thus did the Messenger of Allah, Allah bless him and grant him peace." Abū Kurayb added: "And the other Companion is Abū Mūsā [al-Ashʿarī]."

(Muslim)

اليوم ٦٩

عَنْ عَلِيٍّ قَالَ: لُعِنَ مَانِعُ الصَّدَقَةِ.

ابن أبي شيبة، المصنَّف

اليوم ٧٠

عَنْ أَبِي عَطِيَّةَ قَالَ: دَخَلْتُ أَنَا وَمَسْرُوقٌ عَلَى عَائِشَةَ فَقُلْنَا: يَا أُمَّ الْمُؤْمِنِينَ رَجُلَانِ مِنْ أَصْحَابِ مُحَمَّدٍ صَلَّى اللهُ عَلَيْهِ وَسَلَّمَ أَحَدُهُمَا يُعَجِّلُ الْإِفْطَارَ وَيُعَجِّلُ الصَّلَاةَ، وَالْآخَرُ يُؤَخِّرُ الْإِفْطَارَ وَيُؤَخِّرُ الصَّلَاةَ. قَالَتْ: أَيُّهُمَا الَّذِي يُعَجِّلُ الْإِفْطَارَ وَيُعَجِّلُ الصَّلَاةَ؟، قَالَ: قُلْنَا: عَبْدُ اللهِ، يَعْنِي ابْنَ مَسْعُود. قَالَتْ: كَذَلِكَ كَانَ يَصْنَعُ رَسُولُ اللهِ صَلَّى اللهُ عَلَيْهِ وَسَلَّمَ. زَادَ أَبُو كُرَيْبٍ: وَالْآخَرُ أَبُو مُوسَى.

مسلم

DAY 71

ʿAbdullāh ibn Salamah said: "A man said to Muʿādh [ibn Jabal]: 'Teach me!' He said: 'And will you obey me if I do?' The man said: 'Indeed, I am very keen to obey you!' So he said: 'Fast on some days and do not fast on others; pray part of the night but also sleep part of it; earn a living but do not commit any sin in the process; do not die except as a Muslim; and beware of the supplication of the one who is wronged.'"

(Aḥmad)

DAY 72

Abū al-Dardā' said: "Those whose tongues are moist with the remembrance of Allah will enter Paradise laughing."

(Aḥmad)

اليوم ٧١

عَنْ عَبْدِ اللَّهِ بْنِ سَلَمَةَ قَالَ: قَالَ رَجُلٌ لِمُعَاذٍ: عَلِّمْنِي. قَالَ: وَهَلْ أَنْتَ مُطِيعِي؟ قَالَ: إِنِّي عَلَىٰ طَاعَتِكَ لَحَرِيصٌ. قَالَ: صُمْ وَأَفْطِرْ، وَصَلِّ وَنَمْ، وَاكْتَسِبْ وَلَا تَأْثَمْ، وَلَا تَمُوتَنَّ إِلَّا وَأَنْتَ مُسْلِمٌ، وَإِيَّاكَ وَدَعْوَةَ الْمَظْلُومِ.

أحمد

اليوم ٧٢

عَنْ أَبِي الدَّرْدَاءِ قَالَ: إِنَّ الَّذِينَ أَلْسِنَتُهُمْ رَطْبَةٌ بِذِكْرِ اللَّهِ يَدْخُلُونَ الْجَنَّةَ وَهُمْ يَضْحَكُونَ.

أحمد

DAY 73

Abū Hurayrah said: "The one who sheds tears out of fear of Allah, glorified and exalted is He, will not enter the Fire unless milk, once milked, can go back to the udder [from which it was milked]!"

(Aḥmad)

DAY 74

Muʿādh ibn Jabal, may Allah have mercy on him, said: "Whoever knows that Allah, glorified and exalted is He, is real, that the Final Hour is coming and that Allah will resurrect those in the graves shall enter Paradise."

(Aḥmad)

اليوم ٧٣

عَنْ أَبِي هُرَيْرَةَ قَالَ: لَنْ يَلِجَ النَّارَ مَنْ بَكَى مِنْ خَشْيَةِ اللَّهِ عَزَّ وَجَلَّ حَتَّى يَعُودَ اللَّبَنُ فِي الضَّرْعِ.

أحمد

اليوم ٧٤

قَالَ مُعَاذُ بْنُ جَبَلٍ: مَنْ عَلِمَ أَنَّ اللَّهَ عَزَّ وَجَلَّ حَقٌّ، وَأَنَّ السَّاعَةَ آتِيَةٌ لَا رَيْبَ فِيهَا، وَأَنَّ اللَّهَ يَبْعَثُ مَنْ فِي الْقُبُورِ دَخَلَ الْجَنَّةَ.

أحمد

DAY
75

Shaqīq reported that ʿAbdullāh was asked about something and so he said: "Verily, I hate indeed to make something lawful for you when Allah has made it unlawful just as I hate to make something unlawful for you when Allah has made it lawful."

(al-Dārimī)

DAY
76

ʿAṭā' reported from ʿĀmir that Ibn Masʿūd and Ḥudhayfah [ibn al-Yamān] were sitting when a man came and asked them about something, and so Ibn Masʿūd said to Hudhayfah: "Why do you think they are asking me about this; it is something they know but refrain from doing." Then Ibn Masʿūd turned to the man and said: "You did not ask us about anything

اليوم
٧٥

عَنْ شَقِيقٍ قَالَ: سُئِلَ عَبْدُ اللهِ عَنْ شَيْءٍ فَقَالَ: إِنِّي لَأَكْرَهُ أَنْ أُحِلَّ لَكَ شَيْئًا حَرَّمَهُ اللهُ عَلَيْكَ أَوْ أُحَرِّمَ مَا أَحَلَّهُ اللهُ لَكَ.

الدَّارمي

اليوم
٧٦

عَنْ عَطَاءٍ عَنْ عَامِرٍ عَنْ ابْنِ مَسْعُودٍ وَحُذَيْفَةَ أَنَّهُمَا كَانَا جَالِسَيْنِ فَجَاءَ رَجُلٌ فَسَأَلَهُمَا عَنْ شَيْءٍ فَقَالَ ابْنُ مَسْعُودٍ لِحُذَيْفَةَ: لِأَيِّ شَيْءٍ تَرَىٰ يَسْأَلُونِي عَنْ هَذَا. قَالَ يَعْلَمُونَهُ ثُمَّ يَتْرُكُونَهُ. فَأَقْبَلَ إِلَيْهِ ابْنُ مَسْعُودٍ فَقَالَ: مَا سَأَلْتُمُونَا عَنْ شَيْءٍ

in the book of Allah, which we know, or the Practice of the Prophet, Allah bless him and grant him peace, except that we have told you about it. As for what you have innovated, there is nothing we can do about it."

(al-Dārimī)

DAY 77

Abū Qilābah reported that ʿAbdullāh ibn Masʿūd said: "Acquire knowledge before it is taken away, and it is taken away when the men of knowledge pass on. And beware of excessive exaggeration, engagement in hair-splitting details and blameworthy innovations, and adhere to that which was initially prescribed."

(al-Dārimī)

مِنْ كِتَابِ اللَّهِ تَعَالَىٰ نَعْلَمُهُ أَخْبَرْنَاكُمْ بِهِ أَوْ سُنَّةٍ مِنْ نَبِيِّ اللَّهِ صَلَّى اللَّهُ عَلَيْهِ وَسَلَّمَ أَخْبَرْنَاكُمْ بِهِ وَلَا طَاقَةَ لَنَا بِمَا أَحْدَثْتُمْ.

الدَّارمي

اليوم ٧٧

عَنْ أَبِي قِلَابَةَ قَالَ: قَالَ عَبْدُ اللَّهِ بْنُ مَسْعُودٍ: تَعَلَّمُوا الْعِلْمَ قَبْلَ أَنْ يُقْبَضَ وَقَبْضُهُ أَنْ يَذْهَبَ أَهْلُهُ، أَلَا وَإِيَّاكُمْ وَالتَّنَطُّعَ وَالتَّعَمُّقَ وَالْبِدَعَ وَعَلَيْكُمْ بِالْعَتِيقِ.

الدَّارمي

DAY
78

Ibn Shihāb reported that Abū Idrīs al-Khawlānī informed him that Yazīd ibn ʿUmayrah, who was a student of Muʿādh ibn Jabal, informed him saying: "Whenever Muʿādh ibn Jabal had a session of teaching he would say: 'Allah is a just Ruler; and those who have doubt are certainly doomed to destruction'. One day he said: 'There shall come to you trials whereby wealth will be abundant and the Qur'ān shall be easily available such that it will be learnt by the believer and the hypocrite, the man and the woman, the young and the old, and the freeman and the slave. So much so that a person may be tempted to say: 'Why are people not following me when I am well versed in the Qur'ān? They are not going to follow me until I innovate for them something else.' So beware of what is blameworthy innovated for whatever is blameworthy innovated is a misguidance.'"

(Abū Dāwūd)

اليوم
٧٨

عَنِ ابْنِ شِهَابٍ أَنَّ أَبَا إِدْرِيسَ الْخَوْلَانِيَّ عَائِذَ اللهِ أَخْبَرَهُ أَنَّ يَزِيدَ بْنَ عُمَيْرَةَ وَكَانَ مِنْ أَصْحَابِ مُعَاذِ بْنِ جَبَلٍ أَخْبَرَهُ، قَالَ: كَانَ لَا يَجْلِسُ مَجْلِسًا لِلذِّكْرِ حِينَ يَجْلِسُ إِلَّا قَالَ: اللهُ حَكَمٌ قِسْطٌ هَلَكَ الْمُرْتَابُونَ. فَقَالَ مُعَاذُ بْنُ جَبَلٍ يَوْمًا: إِنَّ مِنْ وَرَائِكُمْ فِتَنًا يَكْثُرُ فِيهَا الْمَالُ وَيُفْتَحُ فِيهَا الْقُرْآنُ حَتَّى يَأْخُذَهُ الْمُؤْمِنُ وَالْمُنَافِقُ وَالرَّجُلُ وَالْمَرْأَةُ وَالصَّغِيرُ وَالْكَبِيرُ وَالْعَبْدُ وَالْحُرُّ، فَيُوشِكُ قَائِلٌ أَنْ يَقُولَ: مَا لِلنَّاسِ لَا يَتَّبِعُونِي وَقَدْ قَرَأْتُ الْقُرْآنَ مَا هُمْ بِمُتَّبِعِيَّ حَتَّى أَبْتَدِعَ لَهُمْ غَيْرَهُ، فَإِيَّاكُمْ وَمَا ابْتُدِعَ فَإِنَّ مَا ابْتُدِعَ ضَلَالَةٌ.

أبو داود

DAY 79

Masrūq reported that he was walking with Ubayy ibn Kaʿb when a young lad approached and asked him: "O Uncle! What do you say about such-and-such?" Ubayy asked him: "O nephew! Has this already taken place?" When the lad said that it did not, Ubayy said: "Please spare me [such questions] until they do take place."

(Al-Dārimī)

DAY 80

ʿUbaydullāh ibn Abī Yazīd reported the following: "Whenever Ibn ʿAbbās was asked about something and its answer was in the Qur'ān, he would answer according to it; if it was not in the Qur'ān and was found in the Practice of the Messenger of Allah, Allah bless him and grant him peace, he would answer

اليوم
٧٩

عَنْ مَسْرُوقٍ قَالَ: كُنْتُ أَمْشِي مَعَ أُبَيِّ بْنِ كَعْبٍ فَقَالَ فتًى: مَا تَقُولُ يَا عَمَّاهُ فِي كَذَا وَكَذَا. قَالَ: يَا ابْنَ أَخِي أَكَانَ هَذَا؟ قَالَ: لَا. قَالَ: فَأَعْفِنَا حَتَّى يَكُونَ.

الدَّارمي

اليوم
٨٠

عَنْ عُبَيْدِ اللهِ بْنِ أَبِي يَزِيدَ قَالَ: كَانَ ابْنُ عَبَّاسٍ إِذَا سُئِلَ عَنِ الْأَمْرِ فَكَانَ فِي الْقُرْآنِ أَخْبَرَ بِهِ وَإِنْ لَمْ يَكُنْ فِي الْقُرْآنِ وَكَانَ عَنْ رَسُولِ اللهِ صَلَّى اللهُ عَلَيْهِ وَسَلَّمَ

according to it; if it was not in the Prophetic Practice and was found in the answers given by Abū Bakr and ʻUmar, he would answer according to that; if it is not found there either, he would provide his own opinion."

(Al-Dārimī)

DAY 81

Abū Ṣāliḥ reported that he heard Abū Hurayrah say: "Recite the Qur'ān for what a good intercessor it is on the Day of Judgement; it will say on the Day of Judgement: 'O Lord! Adorn him [the person who used to recite it often] with the adornment of honour,' and so he would be adorned. 'O Lord! Clothe him with the garment of honour,' and so he would be clothed. 'O Lord! Put on him the crown of honour. O Lord! Be pleased with him, for there is nothing [that is better acquired] after Your good pleasure than it'."

(Al-Dārimī)

أَخْبَرَ بِهِ فَإِنْ لَمْ يَكُنْ فَعَنْ أَبِي بَكْرٍ وَعُمَرَ فَإِنْ لَمْ يَكُنْ قَالَ فِيهِ بِرَأْيِهِ.

الدّارمي

اليوم ٨١

عَنْ أَبِي صَالِحٍ قَالَ سَمِعْتُ أَبَا هُرَيْرَةَ يَقُولُ: اقْرَؤُوا الْقُرْآنَ فَإِنَّهُ نِعْمَ الشَّفِيعُ يَوْمَ الْقِيَامَةِ إِنَّهُ يَقُولُ يَوْمَ الْقِيَامَةِ يَا رَبِّ حَلِّهِ حِلْيَةَ الْكَرَامَةِ فَيُحَلَّى حِلْيَةَ الْكَرَامَةِ يَا رَبِّ، اكْسُهُ كِسْوَةَ الْكَرَامَةِ فَيُكْسَى كِسْوَةَ الْكَرَامَةِ، يَا رَبِّ أَلْبِسْهُ تَاجَ الْكَرَامَةِ، يَا رَبِّ ارْضَ عَنْهُ فَلَيْسَ بَعْدَ رِضَاكَ شَيْءٌ.

الدّارمي

DAY
82

ʿAbdullāh ibn Masʿūd said: "The Qur'ān is an intercessor and its intercession shall be accepted just as its pleading [for those who recite it] is also accepted. Whoever makes it his leading guide, it will lead him to Paradise; and whoever leaves it behind him, it will take him to the Fire."

(Aḥmad)

DAY
83

ʿAbdullāh ibn Masʿūd said: "As long as you are in prayer you are knocking at the door of the King; and whoever knocks at the door of the King, it shall be opened for him."

(Ibn Abī Shaybah, *al-Muṣannaf*)

اليوم
٨٢

قَالَ عَبْدُ اللَّهِ: الْقُرْآنُ شَافِعٌ مُشَفَّعٌ، وَمَاحِلٌ مُصَدَّقٌ، فَمَنْ جَعَلَهُ إِمَامَهُ قَادَهُ إِلَى الْجَنَّةِ، وَمَنْ جَعَلَهُ خَلْفَهُ سَاقَهُ إِلَى النَّارِ.

أحمد

اليوم
٨٣

قَالَ عَبْدُ الله بن مَسْعُودٍ: مَا دُمْتَ فِي صَلَاةٍ فَأَنْتَ تَقْرَعُ بَابَ الْمَلِكِ، وَمَنْ يَقْرَعْ بَابَ الْمَلِكِ يُفْتَحْ لَهُ.

ابن أبي شيبة، المُصنّف

DAY 84

Ibn ʿAbbās said: "Every beast, including the fish in the sea, asks for forgiveness for the person who teaches people goodness."

(Zuhayr ibn Ḥarb, *al-ʿIlm*)

DAY 85

Jarīr ibn ʿAbdullāh reported the following: Salmān [al-Fārisī] said to me: "O Jarīr! Humble yourself to Allah for whoever humbles himself to Allah in this world, Allah will raise him on the Day of Judgement."

(Wakīʿ ibn al-Jarrāh, *Kitāb al-Zuhd*)

اليوم ٨٤

عَنْ ابْنِ عَبَّاسٍ قال: إنَّ الذي يُعلِّمُ النَّاسَ الخَيْرَ يَسْتَغْفِرُ لَهُ كُلُّ دَابَّةٍ حَتَّى الحُوتَ فِي البَحْرِ.

زهير بن حرب، العلم

اليوم ٨٥

عن جَرِيرِ بْنِ عَبْدِ اللهِ قَالَ: قَالَ لِي سَلْمَانُ: يَا جَرِيرُ تَوَاضَعْ للهِ، فَإِنَّهُ مَنْ تَوَاضَعَ للهِ فِي الدُّنْيَا رَفَعَهُ اللهُ يَوْمَ الْقِيَامَةِ.

وكيع بن الجرَّاح، كتاب الزهد

DAY
86

ʿĀʾishah, may Allah have mercy on her, said: "You are quite mistaken: the best act of worship is humility."

(Aḥmad)

DAY
87

Abū ʿUthmān said: "I was informed that Abū Hurayrah had said: 'Allah rewards the believer for every good deed a million rewards,' so I went to him and said: 'O Abū Hurayrah! I was informed that you said: 'Allah rewards the believer for every good deed a million rewards.' He said: 'Yes, I did, and even two million rewards, and the Qur'ān mentions something like this: {... and if it be a good deed He will increase it manifold} [*al-Nisāʾ*: 40], and so who knows how manifold it will be? And {and give from Himself a mighty wage} [*al-Nisāʾ*: 40], i.e. Paradise'."

(Ibn Abī Shaybah, *al-Muṣannaf*)

اليوم ٨٦

عَنْ عَائِشَةَ رَحِمَهَا اللَّهُ قَالَتْ: إِنَّكُمْ لتَغْفَلُونَ: أَفْضَلُ الْعِبَادَةِ التَّوَاضُعَ.

أحمد

اليوم ٨٧

عَنْ أَبِي عُثْمَانَ قَالَ: بَلَغَنِي عَنْ أَبِي هُرَيْرَةَ قَالَ: إِنَّ اللَّهَ يُجْزِي الْمُؤْمِنَ بِالْحَسَنَةِ أَلْفَ أَلْفِ حَسَنَةٍ، فَأَتَيْتُه فَقُلْتُ: يَا أَبَا هُرَيْرَةَ إِنَّهُ بَلَغَنِي أَنَّك تَقُولُ: إِنَّ اللَّهَ يُجْزِي الْمُؤْمِنَ بِالْحَسَنَةِ أَلْفَ أَلْفِ حَسَنَةٍ. قَالَ: نَعَمْ وَأَلْفَيْ أَلْفِ حَسَنَةٍ، وَفِي الْقُرْآنِ مِنْ ذَلِكَ: (إِنَّ ٱللَّهَ لَا يَظْلِمُ مِثْقَالَ ذَرَّةٍ وَإِن تَكُ حَسَنَةً يُضَٰعِفْهَا) فَمَنْ يَدْرِى تَسْمِيَةَ تِلْكَ الأَضْعَافِ (وَيُؤْتِ مِن لَّدُنْهُ أَجْرًا عَظِيمًا). قَالَ الجَنَّةُ.

ابن أبي شيبة، المصنَّف

DAY 88

It is reported from Qays that he said: "Once Abū Bakr [al-Ṣiddīq], may Allah be well pleased with him, stood up, and after praising and lauding Allah, he said: 'You read this verse (O believers, look after your own souls. He who is astray cannot hurt you, if you are rightly guided) [but fail to understand its true meaning], for we have heard the Messenger of Allah, Allah bless him and grant him peace, say: 'Allah is almost about to inflict His punishment on people when they see evil and do not protest against it'.'"

(Aḥmad)

DAY 89

It is reported that Ḥudayfah [ibn al-Yamān] said: "O memorisers of the Qur'ān! You have excelled [over others] a great deal, but if you turn right and left, you would go astray a great deal."

(Al-Bukhārī)

اليوم
٨٨

عَنْ قَيْسٍ، قَالَ قَامَ أَبُو بَكْرٍ فَحَمِدَ اللَّهَ وَأَثْنَى عَلَيْهِ ثُمَّ قَالَ: يَا أَيُّهَا النَّاسُ إِنَّكُمْ تَقْرَءُونَ هَذِهِ الْآيَةَ: ﴿يَـٰٓأَيُّهَا ٱلَّذِينَ ءَامَنُواْ عَلَيْكُمْ أَنفُسَكُمْ لَا يَضُرُّكُم مَّن ضَلَّ إِذَا ٱهْتَدَيْتُمْ﴾ وَإِنَّا سَمِعْنَا رَسُولَ اللَّهِ صَلَّى اللَّهُ عَلَيْهِ وَسَلَّمَ يَقُولُ: إِنَّ النَّاسَ إِذَا رَأَوْا الْمُنْكَرَ فَلَمْ يُنْكِرُوهُ أَوْشَكَ أَنْ يَعُمَّهُمْ اللَّهُ بِعِقَابِهِ.

أحمد

اليوم
٨٩

عَنْ حُذَيْفَةَ قَالَ: يَا مَعْشَرَ الْقُرَّاءِ! اسْتَقِيمُوا فَقَدْ سَبَقْتُمْ سَبْقًا بَعِيدًا، فَإِنْ أَخَذْتُمْ يَمِينًا وَشِمَالًا لَقَدْ ضَلَلْتُمْ ضَلَالًا بَعِيدًا.

البخاري

DAY 90

ʿAbdullāh ibn Masʿūd said: "Follow [the Qur'ān and the Prophetic Practice] and do not introduce blameworthy innovations, for you have been given what is enough, and every blameworthy innovation is a misguidance."

(Wakīʿ ibn al-Jarrāḥ, *Kitāb al-Zuhd*)

DAY 91

Yazīd ibn al-Aṣamm is reported to have said: "I heard Abū Hurayrah say: 'One of you sees a speck in his brother's eye but does not see the log in his own eye'."

(Al-Bukhārī, *al-Adab al-Mufrad*)

اليوم ٩٠

قَالَ عَبْدُ اللهِ بْنُ مَسْعُوْدٍ: اِتَّبِعُوا وَلَا تَبْتَدِعُوا فَقَدْ كُفِيْتُمْ، وَكُلُّ بِدْعَةٍ ضَلَالَةٌ.

وكيع بن الجرَّاح، كتاب الزهد

اليوم ٩١

عَنْ يَزِيدَ بْنِ الأَصَمِّ قَالَ: سَمِعْتُ أَبَا هُرَيْرَةَ يَقُولُ: يُبْصِرُ أَحَدُكُمُ الْقَذَاةَ فِي عَيْنِ أَخِيهِ، وَيَنْسَى الْجِذْلَ، أَوِ الْجِذْعَ، فِي عَيْنِ نَفْسِهِ.

البخاري، الأدب المفرد

DAY
92

Ṭaysalah ibn Mayyās said: "I was involved with a group of the Kharijites called al-Najadāt [which takes its name from their leader, Najdah ibn 'Āmir al-Ḥanafī al-Khārijī] and I committed sins which I thought were enormities. I mentioned my sins to Ibn 'Umar and he asked me to enumerate them for him. He said to me: 'These sins are not among the enormities. The enormities are nine: associating partners with Allah, unlawfully killing another person, fleeing from the enemy in battle, accusing a chaste woman of fornication, consuming usury, consuming the wealth of an orphan, doing something unlawful in the mosque, mocking others and causing one's parents to cry due to one's undutifulness.' Then Ibn 'Umar said to me: 'Do you fear the Fire and love to enter Paradise?' I said: 'Yes, by Allah!' He said: 'Is your father alive?' I said: 'I have my mother'. He said: 'By Allah! Were you to talk kindly to her and feed her, you would indeed enter Paradise as long as you avoid the enormities'."

(Al-Bukhārī, *al-Adab al-Mufrad*)

اليوم
٩٢

حَدَّثَنِي طَيْسَلَةُ بْنُ مَيَّاسٍ قَالَ: كُنْتُ مَعَ النَّجَدَاتِ، فَأَصَبْتُ ذُنُوبًا لاَ أَرَاهَا إِلاَّ مِنَ الْكَبَائِرِ، فَذَكَرْتُ ذَلِكَ لِابْنِ عُمَرَ قَالَ: مَا هِيَ؟ قُلْتُ: كَذَا وَكَذَا، قَالَ: لَيْسَتْ هَذِهِ مِنَ الْكَبَائِرِ، هُنَّ تِسْعٌ: الإِشْرَاكُ بِاللَّهِ، وَقَتْلُ نَسَمَةٍ، وَالْفِرَارُ مِنَ الزَّحْفِ، وَقَذْفُ الْمُحْصَنَةِ، وَأَكْلُ الرِّبَا، وَأَكْلُ مَالِ الْيَتِيمِ، وَإِلْحَادٌ فِي الْمَسْجِدِ، وَالَّذِي يَسْتَسْخِرُ، وَبُكَاءُ الْوَالِدَيْنِ مِنَ الْعُقُوقِ. قَالَ لِي ابْنُ عُمَرَ: أَتَفْرَقُ النَّارَ، وَتُحِبُّ أَنْ تَدْخُلَ الْجَنَّةَ؟ قُلْتُ: إِي وَاللَّهِ، قَالَ: أَحَيٌّ وَالِدُكَ؟ قُلْتُ: عِنْدِي أُمِّي، قَالَ: فَوَاللَّهِ لَوْ أَلَنْتَ لَهَا الْكَلاَمَ، وَأَطْعَمْتَهَا الطَّعَامَ، لَتَدْخُلَنَّ الْجَنَّةَ مَا اجْتَنَبْتَ الْكَبَائِرَ.

البخاري، الأدب المفرد

DAY 93

Ḥumayd ibn Nu'aym related that 'Umar [ibn al-Khaṭṭāb] and 'Uthmān ibn 'Affān were invited for food and when they left, 'Uthmān said to 'Umar: "We have attended an invitation for food I wish we did not attend." And when 'Umar asked him about the reason, he said: "I fear that this [food] was made just for boasting."

(Aḥmad)

DAY 94

Abū Rajā' reported the following: "In the pre-Islamic pagan period, when we found a nice stone, we worshipped it. And when we did not find one, we made a mound of sand, brought a she-camel whose udder was full of milk, spread its legs over the mound and milked it there until the mound was saturated with milk, then we worshipped that mound of sand for as long as we stayed in that location."

(Al-Dārimī)

اليوم ٩٣

عَنْ حُمَيْدِ بْنِ نُعَيْمٍ أَنَّ عُمَرَ وَعُثْمَانَ دُعِيَا إِلَىٰ طَعَامٍ فَلَمَّا خَرَجَا قَالَ عُثْمَانُ لِعُمَرَ: قَدْ شَهِدْنَا طَعَامًا لَوَدِدْنَا أَنْ لَمْ نَشْهَدْهُ. قَالَ: لِمَ؟ قَالَ: إِنِّي أَخَافُ أَنْ يَكُونَ صُنِعَ مُبَاهَاةً.

أحمد

اليوم ٩٤

عَنْ أَبِي رَجَاءٍ قَالَ: كُنَّا فِي الْجَاهِلِيَّةِ إِذَا أَصَبْنَا حَجَرًا حَسَنًا عَبَدْنَاهُ وَإِنْ لَمْ نُصِبْ حَجَرًا جَمَعْنَا كُثْبَةً مِنْ رَمْلٍ ثُمَّ جِئْنَا بِالنَّاقَةِ الصَّفِيِّ فَتَفَاجُّ عَلَيْهَا فَنَحْلُبُهَا عَلَى الْكُثْبَةِ حَتَّىٰ نَرْوِيَهَا ثُمَّ نَعْبُدُ تِلْكَ الْكُثْبَةَ مَا أَقَمْنَا بِذَلِكَ الْمَكَانِ.

الدَّارمي

DAY
95

Ibn Mas'ūd said: "There two traits, one which I heard from the Messenger of Allah, Allah bless him and grant him peace, and one which I have added, namely: Whoever dies believing that Allah has a peer will enter Hell; and I say: whoever dies not believing that Allah has a peer and does not associate anyone or anything with Him shall enter Paradise."

(Aḥmad)

DAY
96

Abū al-Dardā' said: "Were it not for three things, people would be just fine: succumbing to miserliness, following whims and everyone being impressed with their own opinion."

(Aḥmad)

اليوم ٩٥

قَالَ ابْنُ مَسْعُودٍ: خَصْلَتَانِ - يَعْنِي إِحْدَاهُمَا - سَمِعْتُهَا مِنْ رَسُولِ اللَّهِ صَلَّى اللَّهُ عَلَيْهِ وَسَلَّمَ وَالْأُخْرَىٰ مِنْ نَفْسِي: مَنْ مَاتَ وَهُوَ يَجْعَلُ لِلَّهِ نِدًّا دَخَلَ النَّارَ، وَأَنَا أَقُولُ: مَنْ مَاتَ وَهُوَ لَا يَجْعَلُ لِلَّهِ نِدًّا وَلَا يُشْرِكُ بِهِ شَيْئًا دَخَلَ الْجَنَّةَ.

أحمد

اليوم ٩٦

عَنْ أَبِي الدَّرْدَاءِ قَالَ: لَوْلَا ثَلَاثٌ صَلُحَ النَّاسُ: شُحٌّ مُطَاعٌ وَهَوًى مُتَّبَعٌ وَإِعْجَابُ كُلِّ ذِي رَأْيٍ بِرَأْيِهِ.

أحمد

DAY 97

ʿĀʾishah, may Allah have mercy on her, said: "Reduce the amount of sins you commit for you shall not meet Allah, glorified and exalted is He, with anything better than a small amount of sins."

(Aḥmad)

DAY 98

ʿAmmār ibn Yāsir said: ""Of the greatest of the enormities are: despairing of Allah's mercy, giving up on Allah's relief and help and feeling safe from Allah's devising."

(Al-Ṭabarānī, *Makārim al-Akhlāq*)

اليوم ٩٧

عَنْ عَائِشَةَ قَالَت: أَقِلُّوا الذُّنُوبَ فَإِنَّكُمْ لَنْ تَلْقَوُا اللَّهَ عَزَّ وَجَلَّ بِشَيْءٍ أَفْضَلَ مِنْ قِلَّةِ الذُّنُوبِ.

أحمد

اليوم ٩٨

قَالَ عَمَّارُ بْنُ يَاسِرٍ: مِنْ أَكْبَرِ الْكَبَائِرِ الْقُنُوطُ مِنْ رَحْمَةِ اللَّهِ وَالْيَأْسُ مِنْ رَوْحِ اللَّهِ عَزَّ وَجَلَّ وَالْأَمْنُ لِمَكْرِ اللَّهِ.

الطبراني، مكارم الأخلاق

DAY 99

Abū al-Dardā' said: "Indeed, knowledge is acquired through striving in learning and mildness of character is acquired through feigning mildness of character; and whoever seeks goodness shall be given it and whoever makes an effort to avoid evil shall be protected from it."

(Abū Khaythamah, *Kitāb al-'Ilm*)

DAY 100

Abū Baḥr al-'Absī reported that 'Abdullāh ibn Mas'ūd saw a man laughing at a funeral, so he said to him: "You laugh at a funeral! I will never speak a word to you from now on."

(Wakī' ibn al-Jarrāḥ, *Kitāb al-Zuhd*)

اليوم
٩٩

قَالَ أَبُو الدَّرْدَاءِ: إِنَّمَا الْعِلْمُ بِالتَّعَلُّمِ وَالْحِلْمُ بِالتَّحَلُّمِ وَمَنْ يَتَحَرَّ الْخَيْرَ يُعْطَهُ وَمَنْ يَتَوَقَّ الشَّرَّ يُوقَّهُ.

أبو خيثمة ، كتاب العلم

اليوم
١٠٠

عَنْ أَبِي بَحْرٍ الْعَبْسِيِّ أَنَّ ابْنَ مَسْعُودٍ رَأَىٰ رَجُلًا يَضْحَكُ فِي جِنَازَةٍ، فَقَالَ: تَضْحَكُ فِي جِنَازَةٍ، لَا أُكَلِّمُكَ بِكَلِمَةٍ أَبَدًا.

وكيع بن الجرَّاح ، كتاب الزهد

DAY 101

Abū al-Dardā' said: "Whoever remembers death a great deal will have less resentful envy towards others and less transgression against them."

(Aḥmad)

DAY 102

Abū 'Uthmān al-Nahdī said: "We sent a woman to 'Abdullāh ibn 'Amr to ask him: 'What is the sin that Allah never forgives?' So he answered: 'There is not a sin or deed, between the heaven and earth, that a slave commits and repents from it to Allah before death except that He accepts his repentance'."

(Ibn Abī Shaybah, *al-Muṣannaf*)

اليوم ١٠١

قَالَ أَبُو الدَّرْدَاءِ: إِنَّ مَنْ أَكْثَرَ ذِكْرَ الْمَوْتِ قَلَّ حَسَدُهُ وَبَغْيُهُ.

أحمد

اليوم ١٠٢

عَنْ أَبِي عُثْمَانَ النَّهْدِيِّ قَالَ: أَرْسَلْنَا امْرَأَةً إِلَىٰ عَبْدِ اللهِ بْنِ عَمْرٍو تَسْأَلُهُ: مَا الذَّنْبُ الَّذِي لاَ يَغْفِرُه اللهُ؟ قَالَ: مَا مِنْ ذَنْبٍ أَوْ عَمَلٍ مِمَّا بَيْنَ السَّمَاءِ إِلَىٰ الأَرْضِ يَتُوبُ مِنْهُ عَبْدٌ إِلَىٰ اللهِ تَعَالَىٰ قَبْلَ الْمَوْتِ إِلَّا تَابَ عَلَيْهِ.

ابن أبي شيبة، المصنَّف

DAY 103

It is reported that Ḥudhayfah ibn al-Yamān said: "It is enough knowledge for a person to fear Allah and it is enough lying for him to seek forgiveness from a sin and then commit it again."

(Abū Khaythamah, *Kitāb al-'Ilm*)

DAY 104

It is reported that 'Alī ibn Abī Ṭālib said: "The one who utters an obscenity and the one who spreads it share the same sin."

(Al-Bukhārī, *al-Adab al-Mufrad*)

اليوم ١٠٣

عَنْ حُذَيْفَةَ قَالَ: بِحَسْبِ الْمَرْءِ مِنَ الْعِلْمِ أَنْ يَخْشَى اللَّهَ وَبِحَسْبِهِ مِنَ الْكَذِبِ أَنْ يَسْتَغْفِرَ اللَّهَ ثُمَّ يَعُودُ.

أبو خيثمه، كتاب العلم

اليوم ١٠٤

عَنْ عَلِيٍّ بْنِ أَبِي طَالِبٍ قَالَ: الْقَائِلُ الْفَاحِشَةَ وَالَّذِي يُشِيعُ بِهَا فِي الإِثْمِ سَوَاءٌ.

البخاري، الأدب المفرد

DAY 105

'Abdullāh ibn Abī Rabī'ah reported that 'Umar ibn al-Khaṭṭāb said: "A man can introduce in his will whatever he likes while what counts is the final version of it."

(Al-Dārimī)

DAY 106

'Abd al-Raḥmān ibn Ma'qil said: "We used to tell each other that the mosque is a fortified fortress against the devil."

(Ibn Abī Shaybah, *al-Muṣannaf*)

اليوم
١٠٥

عَنْ عَبْدِ اللَّهِ بْنِ أَبِي رَبِيعَةَ أَنَّ عُمَرَ بْنَ الْخَطَّابِ قَالَ: يُحْدِثُ الرَّجُلُ فِي وَصِيَّتِهِ مَا شَاءَ وَمِلَاكُ الْوَصِيَّةِ آخِرُهَا.

الدَّارمي

اليوم
١٠٦

عَنْ عَبْدِ الرَّحْمَنِ بْنِ مَعْقِلٍ قَالَ: كُنَّا نَتَحَدَّثُ أَنَّ الْمَسْجِدَ حِصْنٌ حَصِينٌ مِنَ الشَّيْطَانِ.

ابن أبي شيبة ، المصنَّف

DAY 107

ʿAbdullāh ibn ʿAmr asked one of his nephew who had just come out of his orchid: "Are your workers at work?" His nephew responded: "I do not know!" So he said: "Were you a member of Thaqīf you would have known what your workers are doing." Then he turned towards those present and said: "When a man gets involved with his workers in his own house - in another version: in his own wealth - he becomes one of the workers of Allah, glorified and exalted is He."

(Al-Bukhārī)

DAY 108

Abū Hurayrah said: "The believer is more honourable in the sight of Allah than the angels who are with Him."

(Wakīʿ ibn al-Jarrāḥ, *Kitāb Al-Zuhd*)

اليوم ١٠٧

قَالَ عَبْدُ اللَّهِ بْنُ عَمْرٍو لِابْنِ أَخٍ لَهُ خَرَجَ مِنَ الْوَهْطِ: أَيَعْمَلُ عُمَّالُكَ؟ قَالَ: لَا أَدْرِي. قَالَ: أَمَا لَوْ كُنْتَ ثَقَفِيًّا لَعَلِمْتَ مَا يَعْمَلُ عُمَّالُكَ، ثُمَّ الْتَفَتَ إِلَيْنَا فَقَالَ: إِنَّ الرَّجُلَ إِذَا عَمِلَ مَعَ عُمَّالِهِ فِي دَارِهِ، وَقَالَ أَبُو عَاصِمٍ مَرَّةً: فِي مَالِهِ، كَانَ عَامِلاً مِنْ عُمَّالِ اللَّهِ عَزَّ وَجَلَّ.

البخاري

اليوم ١٠٨

عَنْ أَبِي هُرَيْرَةَ قَالَ: الْمُؤْمِنُ أَكْرَمُ عَلَى اللَّهِ مِنَ الْمَلَائِكَةِ الَّذِينَ عِنْدَهُ.

وقيع بن الجرّاح ، كتاب الزهد

DAY
109

ʿAbdullāh ibn Masʿūd said: "There is no respite for the believer before he meets Allah."

(Wakīʿ ibn al-Jarrāḥ *Kitāb al-Zuhd*)

DAY
110

Abū Bakr said: "I am amazed at the believer: he is rewarded for everything, even for the morsel of food he puts in his mouth."

(Wakīʿ ibn al-Jarrāḥ *Kitāb al-Zuhd*)

اليوم
١٠٩

قَالَ عَبْدُ اللَّهِ: لَا رَاحَةَ لِلْمُؤْمِنِ دُونَ لِقَاءِ اللَّهِ.

وكيع بن الجرَّاح، كتاب الزهد

اليوم
١١٠

قَالَ أَبُو بَكْرٍ: عَجِبْتُ لِلْمُؤْمِنِ أَنَّهُ يُؤْجَرُ فِي كُلِّ شَيْءٍ حَتَّىٰ فِي اللُّقْمَةِ يَرْفَعُهَا إِلَى فِيهِ.

وكيع بن الجرَّاح، كتاب الزهد

DAY 111

Abū Sufyān Ṭalḥah ibn Nāfi‘ al-Wāsiṭī related the following: "I sojourned with Jābir ibn ‘Abdullah in Makkah for six months, and one day a man asked him: 'Did you ever call anyone who faced the *qiblah* [in prayer] a disbeliever?' He responded: 'God forbid!' The man again asked: 'Did you call him an associator?' He said: 'No!'."

(Abū ‘Ubayd al-Qāsim ibn Salām, *al-Īmān*)

DAY 112

Ziyād ibn Ḥudayr ‘Umar asked me: "Do you know the things that destroy Islam?" I said: "No!" He said: "What destroys it are: the slip of the man of knowledge, the squabbling of the hypocrite using the Book of Allah and the rule of the misguiding rulers."

(a-Dārimī)

اليوم ١١١

عَنْ أَبِي سُفْيَانَ طَلْحَةَ بْنِ نَافِعٍ الوَاسِطِي قال: جَاوَرْتُ مَعَ جَابِرِ بنِ عَبْدِ اللهِ بِمكةَ ستةَ أَشْهُرٍ، فسألَهُ رجلٌ: هل كنتُمْ تُسَمُّونَ أحدًا من أهلِ القبلةِ كافرًا؟ فقال: معاذَ اللهِ! قَالَ: فَهل تُسَمُّونَهُ مُشْرِكًا؟ قَالَ: لا.

أبو عبيد القاسم ابن سلام، الإيمان

اليوم ١١٢

عَنْ زِيَادِ بْنِ حُدَيْرٍ قَالَ: قَالَ لِي عُمَرُ: هَلْ تَعْرِفُ مَا يَهْدِمُ الْإِسْلَامَ؟ قُلْتُ: لَا! قَالَ: يَهْدِمُهُ زَلَّةُ العَالِمِ وَجِدَالُ الْمُنَافِقِ بِالْكِتَابِ وَحُكْمُ الْأَئِمَّةِ الْمُضِلِّينَ.

الدَّارمي

DAY
113

Abū al-Dardā' said: "Seek refuge in Allah from the humble devotedness of the hypocrite." He was asked: "And what is that?" He said: "It is seeing the body humbly devoted while the heart is not."

(Ibn Abī Shaybah, *al-Muṣannaf*)

DAY
114

Regarding the words of Allah Most High: (... and restrain their rage...) [*Āl 'Imrān* 3: 134], Ibn 'Abbās said: "This refers to a man who verbally abuses you and you restrain your rage and do not answer back despite being able to do so."

(Al-Ṭabarānī, *Makārim al-Akhlāq*)

اليوم ١١٣

عِنْ أَبِي الدَّرْدَاءِ قال: اسْتَعِيذُوا بِاللَّهِ مِنْ خُشُوعِ النِّفَاقِ. قِيلَ لَهُ: وَمَا خُشُوعُ النِّفَاقِ؟ قَالَ: أَنْ تَرَى الْجَسَدَ خَاشِعًا وَالْقَلْبَ لَيْسَ بِخَاشِعٍ.

ابن أبي شيبة، المصنَّف

اليوم ١١٤

عَنِ ابْنِ عَبَّاسٍ فِي قَوْلِهِ: (وَالْكَاظِمِينَ الْغَيْظَ) [آل عمران: ١٣٤] يُرِيدُ الرَّجُلَ يَتَنَاوَلُكَ بِلِسَانِهِ وَأَنْتَ تَقْدِرُ أَنْ تُرَدَّ عَلَيْهِ فَتَكْظِمَ غَيْظَكَ عَنْهُ فَلَا تَرُدُّ عَلَيْهِ شَيْئًا.

الطبراني، مكارم الأخلاق

DAY 115

ʿĀṣim reported that ʿAlī [ibn Abī Ṭālib] said: "When you retire to your bed, say: 'In the name of Allah, and in the way of Allah and upon the religion of the Messenger of Allah, Allah bless him and grant him peace,' and [you say the same thing] when you place the dead person in his grave."

(Ibn Abī Shaybah, *al-Muṣannaf*)

DAY 116

Sulaym ibn Ḥanẓalah reported that ʿUmar ibn al-Khaṭṭāb used to make the following supplication: "O Allah! I seek refuge in you that you may take me to You all of a sudden or that you leave me in heedlessness or that You make me among the heedless."

(Ibn Abī Shaybah, *al-Muṣannaf*)

اليوم ١١٥

عَنْ عَاصِمٍ عَنْ عَلِيٍّ قَالَ: إِذَا أَخَذَتْ مَضْجَعَكَ فَقُلْ: بِسْمِ اللَّهِ وَفِي سَبِيلِ اللَّهِ وَعَلَى مِلَّةِ رَسُولِ اللَّهِ صَلَّى اللهُ عَلَيه وسَلَّم وَحِينَ تُدْخِلُ الْمَيِّتَ قَبْرَهُ.

ابن أبي شيبة، المصنَّف

اليوم ١١٦

عَنْ سُلَيْمِ بْنِ حَنْظَلَةَ عَنْ عُمَرَ بْنِ الْخَطَّابِ أَنَّهُ كَانَ يَقُولُ: اللَّهُمَّ إِنِّي أَعُوذُ بِكَ أَنْ تَأْخُذَنِي عَلَى غِرَّةٍ أَوْ تَذَرَنِي فِي غَفْلَةٍ أَوْ تَجْعَلَنِي مِنَ الْغَافِلِينَ.

ابن أبي شيبة، المصنَّف

DAY 117

Abū Bakr [al-Ṣiddīq] said: "When the servant mentions Allah upon starting his minor ritual ablution (*wuḍū'*), his whole body is purified; but when he performs minor ritual ablution without mentioning the name of Allah, only the parts of the body that are touched by water are purified."

(Ibn Abī Shaybah, *al-Muṣannaf*)

DAY 118

Abū Sa'īd al-Khudrī is reported to have said: "Whoever says upon finishing his minor ritual ablution: 'O Allah! Glory and praise be unto You; I bear witness that there is no deity save You; I seek Your forgiveness and repent to You,' this will be written down, sealed and raised up under the Throne; and the seal will not be broken until the Day of Judgment."

(Ibn Abi Shaybah, *al-Muṣannaf*)

اليوم
١١٧

عَنْ أَبِي بَكْرٍ قَالَ: إِذَا تَوَضَّأَ الْعَبْدُ فَذَكَرَ اسْمَ اللَّهِ حِينَ يَأْخُذُ فِي وَضُوئِهِ طَهُرَ جَسَدُهُ كُلُّهُ وَإِذَا تَوَضَّأَ وَلَمْ يَذْكُرِ اسْمَ اللَّهِ لَمْ يَطْهُرْ مِنْهُ إِلَّا مَا أَصَابَهُ الْمَاءُ.

ابن أبي شيبة، المصنَّف

اليوم
١١٨

عَنْ أَبِي سَعِيدٍ الْخُدْرِيِّ قَالَ: مَنْ قَالَ إِذَا فَرَغَ مِنْ وُضُوئِهِ: سُبْحَانَكَ اللَّهُمَّ وَبِحَمْدِكَ، أَشْهَدُ أَنْ لَا إِلَهَ إِلَّا أَنْتَ أَسْتَغْفِرُكَ وَأَتُوبُ إِلَيْكَ، خُتِمَتْ بِخَاتَمٍ ثُمَّ رُفِعَتْ تَحْتَ الْعَرْشِ فَلَمْ تُكْسَرْ إِلَى يَوْمِ الْقِيَامَةِ.

ابن أبي شيبة، المصنَّف

DAY 119

Al-Ḥasan reported that Abū al-Dardā' used to say: "Be diligent in your supplication, for whoever keeps knocking at the door is likely to have it opened for him."

(Ibn Abī Shaybah, *al-Muṣannaf*)

DAY 120

Abū Sa'īd al-Khudrī said: "When you ask Allah [for something] do it with insistence for there is nothing that can compel Him [to do anything whatsoever]."

(Ibn Abī Shaybah, *al-Muṣannaf*)

اليوم
١١٩

عَنِ الْحَسَنِ أَنَّ أَبَا الدَّرْدَاء كَانَ يَقُولُ: جِدُّوا فِي الدُّعَاءِ فَإِنَّهُ مَنْ يُكْثِرُ قَرْعَ الْبَابِ يُوشِكُ أَن يُفْتَحَ لَهُ.

ابن أبي شيبة، المصنَّف

اليوم
١٢٠

عَنْ أَبِي سَعِيدٍ قَالَ: إِذَا سَأَلْتُمُ اللَّهَ فَاعْزِمُوا فَإِنَّ اللَّهَ لاَ مُسْتَكْرِهَ لَهُ.

ابن أبي شيبة، المصنَّف

DAY 121

ʿUbādah ibn al-Ṣāmit used to make the following supplication: "O Allah! I ask you for safety and faith, forbearance and gratitude, freedom from need and chastity."

(Ibn Abī Shaybah, *al-Muṣannaf*)

DAY 122

It is reported that Abū Hurayrah said: "The degree of the deceased person will be raised and so he will ask: 'O Lord! How come my degree is raised?' And it would be said to him: 'Your offspring has asked for your forgiveness'."

(Al-Bukhārī, *al-Adab al-Mufrad*)

اليوم ١٢١

عَن عُبادَةَ بْنِ الصَّامِتِ أَنَّهُ كَانَ يَقُولُ: اللَّهُمَّ إِنِّي أَسْأَلُكَ الأَمْنَ وَالإِيمَانَ وَالصَّبْرَ وَالشُّكْرَ وَالْغِنَى وَالْعَفَافَ.

ابن أبي شيبة، المصنَّف

اليوم ١٢٢

عَنْ أَبِي هُرَيْرَةَ قَالَ: تُرْفَعُ لِلْمَيِّتِ بَعْدَ مَوْتِهِ دَرَجَتُهُ فَيَقُولُ: أَيْ رَبِّ، أَيُّ شَيْءٍ هَذِهِ؟ فَيُقَالُ: وَلَدُكَ اسْتَغْفَرَ لَكَ.

البخاري، الأدب المفرد

DAY
123

Umm al-Dardā' reported the following: "Abū al-Dardā' stood up to pray one night and then began crying, saying: 'O Allah! You have made my physical constitution well seeming, so make my character well seeming too.' In the morning, I asked him: 'O Abū al-Dardā'! Why was your supplication last night all about good character?' He said: 'O Umm al-Dardā'! The Muslim servant keeps improving his character until it becomes the cause of his entering into Paradise; or he keeps worsening his character until it becomes the cause of his entering into the Fire. Moreover, the Muslim servant can be forgiven while he is asleep.' 'How can he be forgiven while he is asleep,' I asked.' He said: 'His brother stands at night to pray and applies himself well and then asks Allah, glorified and exalted is He, and his supplication would be answered; and he would pray for his brother and his supplication would be answered too'.""

(Al-Bukhārī, *al-Adab al-Mufrad*)

اليوم
١٢٣

عَنْ أُمِّ الدَّرْدَاءِ قَالَتْ: قَامَ أَبُو الدَّرْدَاءِ لَيْلَةً يُصَلِّي، فَجَعَلَ يَبْكِي وَيَقُولُ: اللَّهُمَّ أَحْسَنْتَ خَلْقِي فَحَسِّنْ خُلُقِي، حَتَّىٰ أَصْبَحَ. قُلْتُ: يَا أَبَا الدَّرْدَاءِ، مَا كَانَ دُعَاؤُكَ مُنْذُ اللَّيْلَةِ إِلاَّ فِي حُسْنِ الْخُلُقِ؟ فَقَالَ: يَا أُمَّ الدَّرْدَاءِ! إِنَّ الْعَبْدَ الْمُسْلِمَ يَحْسُنُ خُلُقُهُ حَتَّى يُدْخِلَهُ حُسْنُ خُلُقِهِ الْجَنَّةَ، وَيَسِيءُ خُلُقُهُ حَتَّىٰ يُدْخِلَهُ سُوءُ خُلُقِهِ النَّارَ. وَالْعَبْدُ الْمُسْلِمُ يُغْفَرُ لَهُ وَهُوَ نَائِمٌ. قُلْتُ: يَا أَبَا الدَّرْدَاءِ! كَيْفَ يُغْفَرُ لَهُ وَهُوَ نَائِمٌ؟ قَالَ: يَقُومُ أَخُوهُ مِنَ اللَّيْلِ فَيَجْتَهِدُ فَيَدْعُو اللهَ عَزَّ وَجَلَّ فَيَسْتَجِيبُ لَهُ، وَيَدْعُو لأَخِيهِ فَيَسْتَجِيبُ لَهُ فِيهِ.

البخاري، الأدب المفرد

DAY 124

ʿAbdullāh ibn Masʿūd said: "Learn the legal rulings of inheritance, divorce and the pilgrimage for they are part of your religion."

(Al-Dārimī)

DAY 125

Zubayd ibn al-Ḥārith reported that when Abū Bakr al-Ṣiddīq was on his deathbed, he sent for ʿUmar ibn al-Khaṭṭāb intending to appoint him as his successor. But people protested, saying: "Are you going to appoint as our leader someone who is harsh and rude; and were he to become our leader, he would become even harsher and ruder. What are you going to say to your Lord when you meet Him about him as our leader?" Abū bakr responded by saying: "Are you threatening me with My Lord? I shall tell Him I have appointed as their leader the best of created beings." He then sent for ʿUmar,

اليوم
١٢٤

عَنْ عَبْدِ اللهِ بْنِ مَسْعُودٍ قَالَ: تَعَلَّمُوا الْفَرَائِضَ وَالطَّلَاقَ وَالْحَجَّ فَإِنَّهُ مِنْ دِينِكُمْ.

الدَّارمي

اليوم
١٢٥

عَنْ زُبَيْدِ بْنِ الْحَارِثِ أَنَّ أَبَا بَكْرٍ حِينَ حَضَرَهُ الْمَوْتُ أَرْسَلَ إِلَى عُمَرَ يَسْتَخْلِفُهُ، فَقَالَ النَّاس: تَسْتَخْلِفُ عَلَيْنَا فَظًّا غَلِيظًا، وَلَوْ قَدْ وَلِيَنَا كَانَ أَفَظَّ وَأَغْلَظَ فَمَا تَقُولُ لِرَبِّكَ إِذَا لَقِيتَهُ وَقَدِ اسْتَخْلَفْتَ عَلَيْنَا عُمَرَ؟ قَالَ أَبُو بَكْرٍ: أَبِرَبِّي تُخَوِّفُونَنِي؟ أَقُولُ: اللَّهُمَّ اسْتَخْلَفْتُ عَلَيْهِمْ خَيْرَ خَلْقِكَ. ثُمَّ أَرْسَلَ إِلَى عُمَرَ فَقَالَ:

and when he came to him, he said: "I am going to give a counsel if only you abide by it: Allah has certain rights to be fulfilled during the day which he does not accept if fulfilled at night; and He has certain rights to be fulfilled at night which he does not accept if fulfilled during the day. Moreover, He does not accept a supererogatory deed until the obligated deed is performed. And verily, those whose scales are heavy on the Day of Judgement will get heavy because, in this world, they followed the truth and felt its weight, and it befits a scale in which nothing was put on it except the truth to be heavy. And verily those whose scales are light on the Day of Judgement will be light because they followed falsehood and felt its lightness, and it befits a scale in which nothing was put in it except falsehood to be light. And indeed, Allah has mentioned the people of Paradise by reference to the good work they performed and that He has forgiven their misdeeds; so that one may say: 'I am not going to reach these ones'. And He mentioned the people of Hell by reference to the misdeeds they committed and that He has rejected their righteous deeds, so that one may say: 'I am better than these ones'. He then mentioned the verse of mercy and

إِنِّي مُوصِيكَ بِوَصِيَّةٍ إِنْ أَنْتَ حَفِظْتَهَا: إِنَّ لِلَّهِ حَقًّا بِالنَّهَارِ لَا يَقْبَلُهُ بِاللَّيْلِ وَإِنَّ لِلَّهِ حَقًّا بِاللَّيْلِ لَا يَقْبَلُهُ بِالنَّهَارِ وَإِنَّهُ لَا يَقْبَلُ نَافِلَةً حَتَّى تُؤَدِّيَ الْفَرِيضَةَ، وَإِنَّمَا ثَقُلَتْ مَوَازِينُ مَنْ ثَقُلَتْ مَوَازِينُهُ يَوْمَ الْقِيَامَةِ بِاتِّبَاعِهِمْ فِي الدُّنْيَا الْحَقَّ وَثِقَلُهُ عَلَيْهِمْ، وَحَقٌّ لِمِيزَانٍ لَا يُوضَعُ فِيهِ إِلَّا الْحَقُّ أَنْ يَكُونَ ثَقِيلاً، وَإِنَّمَا خَفَّتْ مَوَازِينُ مَنْ خَفَّتْ مَوَازِينُهُ يَوْمَ الْقِيَامَةِ بِاتِّبَاعِهِمُ الْبَاطِلَ وَخِفَّتُهُ عَلَيْهِمْ، وَحَقٌّ لِمِيزَانٍ لَا يُوضَعُ فِيهِ إِلَّا الْبَاطِلُ أَنْ يَكُونَ خَفِيفًا، وَإِنَّ اللهَ ذَكَرَ أَهْلَ الْجَنَّةِ بِصَالِحِ مَا عَمِلُوا، وَأَنَّهُ تَجَاوَزَ عَنْ سَيِّئَاتِهِمْ، فَيَقُولُ الْقَائِلُ: لَا أَبْلُغُ هَؤُلَاءِ، وَذَكَرَ أَهْلَ النَّارِ بِأَسْوَإِ مَا عَمِلُوا، وَإِنَّهُ رَدَّ عَلَيْهِمْ صَالِحَ مَا عَمِلُوا، فَيَقُولُ قَائِلٌ: أَنَا خَيْرٌ مِنْ هَؤُلَاءِ، وَذَكَرَ آيَةَ الرَّحْمَةِ وَآيَةَ

the verse of chastisement so that the believer is both desirous and fearful [of Him] and that he does hope of Allah except that which is true and that he does not throw himself in peril. If you abide by my counsel, nothing absent from you shall be more beloved to you than death; but if you ignore my counsel, nothing absent from you shall be more loathed by you than death, and you will not be able to stop it."

(Ibn Abī Shaybah, *al-Muṣannaf*)

DAY 126

Abū Bakr [al-Ṣiddīq] said: "The Muslim is rewarded for everything even in the calamity [that befalls him], breaking his shoelaces and even something he puts in the sleeve of his robe and forgets about and, as a result, gets alarmed because he thinks he had lost it, and then finds it in a utensil."

(Aḥmad)

الْعَذَابِ، لِيَكُونَ الْمُؤْمِنُ رَاغِبًا وَرَاهِبًا، لَا يَتَمَنَّى عَلَى اللهِ غَيْرَ الْحَقِّ، وَلَا يُلْقِي بِيَدِهِ إِلَى التَّهْلُكَةِ. فَإِنْ أَنْتَ حَفِظْتَ وَصِيَّتِي لَمْ يَكُنْ غَائِبٌ أَحَبَّ إِلَيْكَ مِنَ الْمَوْتِ وَإِنْ أَنْتَ ضَيَّعْتَ وَصِيَّتِي لَمْ يَكُنْ غَائِبٌ أَبْغَضَ إِلَيْكَ مِنَ الْمَوْتِ وَلَنْ تُعْجِزَهُ.

ابن أبي شيبة، المصنَّف

اليوم
١٢٦

عَنْ أَبِي بَكْرٍ الصِّدِّيقِ قَالَ: إِنَّ الْمُسْلِمَ لَيُؤْجَرُ فِي كُلِّ شَيْءٍ حَتَّى فِي النَّكْبَةِ وَانْقِطَاعِ شِسْعِهِ وَالْبِضَاعَةِ تَكُونُ فِي كُمِّهِ فَيَفْتَقِدُ بِهَا فَيَفْزَعُ لَهَا فَيَجِدُهَا فِي ضَبَّتِهِ.

أحمد

DAY 127

Ibn ʿAbbās said: "Do study and repeat this *Ḥadīth* among yourselves lest it is forgotten, for it is not like the Qur'ān which is compiled and preserved. And if you did not study and repeat this *Ḥadīth*, it will be forgotten by you; and do not say I taught *Ḥadīth* yesterday and shall not do so today. Rather, you have taught yesterday, teach it today and teach it tomorrow too."

(Al-Dārimī)

DAY 128

Sālim ibn Ḥijl reported that Abū Hurayrah, may Allah be well pleased with him, was seen crying in his illness that led to his death, so he was asked: "What is making you cry?" He replied: "You have to know that I am not crying for leaving this world of yours. I am

اليوم
١٢٧

عَنْ ابْنِ عَبَّاسٍ قَالَ: تَذَاكَرُوا هَذَا الْحَدِيثَ لَا يَنْفَلِتْ مِنْكُمْ فَإِنَّهُ لَيْسَ مِثْلَ الْقُرْآنِ مَجْمُوعٌ مَحْفُوظٌ وَإِنَّكُمْ إِنْ لَمْ تَذَاكَرُوا هَذَا الْحَدِيثَ يَنْفَلِتْ مِنْكُمْ وَلَا يَقُولَنَّ أَحَدُكُمْ حَدَّثْتُ أَمْسِ فَلَا أُحَدِّثُ الْيَوْمَ بَلْ حَدِّثْ أَمْسِ وَلْتُحَدِّثْ الْيَوْمَ وَلْتُحَدِّثْ غَدًا.

الدَّارمي

اليوم
١٢٨

عَنْ سَالِمِ بن حِجْلٍ أَنَّ أَبَا هُرَيْرَة بَكَى فِي مَرَضِهِ، فَقِيلَ لَهُ: مَا يُبْكِيكَ؟ قَالَ: أَمَا أَنِّي لا أَبْكِي عَلَى دُنْيَاكُمْ هَذِهِ،

crying because ahead of me is a long journey and my provision is scarce; and I am to face a climbing into Paradise or a descent into the Fire, and I do not know to which of the two I shall be taken. I do not know whether I will enter Paradise or be consigned to Hell."

(Aḥmad)

DAY 129

Mu'āwiyah ibn Qurrah reported that Abū al-Dardā' said: "Goodness does not lie in the fact that you have a great deal of wealth and many children. Rather, goodness lies in the fact that you have a great deal of clemency, abundant good works and that you excel people in the worship of Allah; and if you do good, you praise Allah while if you do bad, you seek forgiveness from Allah."

(Ibn Abī Shaybah, *al-Muṣannaf*)

وَلَكِنِّي أَبْكِي عَلَىٰ بُعْدِ سَفَرِي وَقِلَّةِ زَادِي، وَإِنِّي أَمْسَيْتُ فِي صُعُودٍ وَمَهْبَطَةٍ عَلَىٰ جَنَّةٍ وَنَار، وَلَا أَدْرِي إِلَىٰ أَيِّهِمَا يُؤْخَذُ بِي.

أحمد

اليوم ١٢٩

عَنْ مُعَاوِيَةَ بْنِ قُرَّةَ قَالَ: قَالَ أَبُو الدَّرْدَاءِ: لَيْسَ الْخَيْرُ أَنْ يَكْثُرَ مَالُكَ وَوَلَدُكَ، وَلَكِنَّ الْخَيْرَ أَنْ يَعْظُمَ حِلْمُكَ وَأَنْ يَكْثُرَ عَمَلُكَ وَأَنْ تُبَارِيَ النَّاسَ فِي عِبَادَةِ اللهِ، فَإِنْ أَحْسَنْتَ حَمِدْتَ اللهَ وَإِنْ أَسَأْتَ اسْتَغْفَرْتَ اللهَ.

ابن أبي شيبة، المصنَّف

DAY 130

Kathīr ʿUbayd said: "ʿĀ'ishah, may Allah be well pleased with her did not use to ask, when a child was born into her extended family, whether it was a boy or girl. All she asked was: 'Is it healthy?' and if the answer was in the affirmative, she would then say: 'Praise be to Allah, Lord of all worlds'."

(Ibn Abī Shaybah, *al-Muṣannaf*)

DAY 131

ʿAbdullāh ibn ʿAmr said: "No group of people come together and mention Allah except that Allah mentions them in a gathering more noble and honourable than their group. And no group of people come together and fail to mention Allah except that their gathering will be a bitter regret for them on the Day of Judgement."

(Ibn Abī Shaybah, *al-Muṣannaf*)

اليوم
١٣٠

قَالَ كَثِيرُ بْنُ عُبَيْدٍ: كَانَتْ عَائِشَةُ إِذَا وُلِدَ فِيهِمْ مَوْلُودٌ - يَعْنِي: فِي أَهْلِهَا - لَا تَسْأَلُ: غُلَامًا وَلَا جَارِيَةً، تَقُولُ: خُلِقَ سَوِيًّا؟ فَإِذَا قِيلَ: نَعَمْ، قَالَتِ: الْحَمْدُ لِلَّهِ رَبِّ الْعَالَمِينَ.

البخاري، الأدب المفرد

اليوم
١٣١

عَنْ عَبْدِ اللهِ بْنِ عَمْرٍو قَالَ: مَا مِنْ مَلَإٍ يَجْتَمِعُونَ فَيَذْكُرُونَ اللَّهَ إِلَّا ذَكَرَهُمُ اللَّهُ فِي مَلَإٍ أَعَزَّ مِنْ مَلَئِهِمْ وَأَكْرَمَ، وَمَا مِنْ مَلَإٍ يَتَفَرَّقُونَ لَمْ يَذْكُرُوا اللَّهَ إِلَّا كَانَ مَجْلِسُهُمْ حَسْرَةً عَلَيْهِمْ يَوْمَ الْقِيَامَةِ.

ابن أبي شيبة، المصنَّف

DAY 132

Qays reported the following: "When 'Umar [ibn al-Khaṭṭāb] went to the Levant, he was welcomed by people while he was riding his camel. They said to him: 'O Leader of the believers! Why do you not ride a horse or a mule as you are going to meet some leaders and chiefs of people', So he said: 'Do I not see you from here? Rather, the matter is from there above – and he pointed to the sky – let go of my camel!'"

(Ibn Abī Shaybah, *al-Muṣannaf*)

DAY 133

'Abd al-Malik ibn 'Umayr reported the following: "The family members of 'Abdullāh [ibn 'Umar] informed me that 'Abdullāh counselled his son 'Abd al-Raḥmān with the following advice: 'I advise you to fear Allah; confine yourself to your home, control your tongue and weep over your sins'."

(Ibn Abī Shaybah, *al-Muṣannaf*)

اليوم ١٣٢

عَنْ قَيْسٍ قَالَ: لَمَّا قَدِمَ عُمَرُ الشَّامَ اسْتَقْبَلَهُ النَّاسُ وَهُوَ عَلَى بَعِيرِهِ فَقَالُوا: يَا أَمِيرَ الْمُؤْمِنِينَ! لَوْ رَكِبْتَ بِرْذَوْنًا يَلْقَاكَ عُظَمَاءُ النَّاسِ وَوُجُوهُهُمْ، قَالَ: فَقَالَ عُمَرُ: أَلاَ أَرَاكُمْ هَاهُنَا، إِنَّمَا الأَمْرُ مِنْ هَاهُنَا، وَأَشَارَ بِيَدِهِ إِلَى السَّمَاءِ خَلُّوا سَبِيلَ جَمَلِي.

ابن أبي شيبة ، المصنَّف

اليوم ١٣٣

عَنْ عَبْدِ الْمَلِكِ بْنِ عُمَيْرٍ قَالَ: أَخْبَرَنِي آلُ عَبْدِ اللهِ أَنَّ عَبْدَ اللهِ أَوْصَى ابْنَهُ عَبْدَ الرَّحْمَنِ فَقَالَ: أُوصِيكَ بِتَقْوَى اللهِ وَلْيَسَعْكَ بَيْتُكَ وَامْلِكْ عَلَيْكَ لِسَانَكَ وَابْكِ عَلَى خَطِيئَتِكَ.

ابن أبي شيبة ، المصنَّف

DAY 134

Ibn Mas'ūd said: "There is not a single person, on the Day of Judgement, except that he would wish that he had consumed in this world just what was enough for his sustenance; and one of you will not be harmed about how the evening or morning find him as long as there is nothing that pricks his heart; and that one of you bites a live coal until it is put out is better for him than to say to something that Allah has decreed: 'I wish this did not happen!'"

(Ibn Abī Shaybah, *al-Muṣannaf*)

DAY 135

Qays reported the following: "Abū Bakr [al-Ṣiddīq] bought Bilāl [ibn Rabbāḥ] for five silver pieces and then he freed him. And so Bilal said to him: 'If you have freed me to appoint as a

اليوم ١٣٤

عَنِ ابْنِ مَسْعُودٍ قَالَ: مَا أَحَدٌ مِنَ النَّاسِ يَوْمَ الْقِيَامَةِ إِلاَّ يَتَمَنَّىٰ أَنَّهُ كَانَ يَأْكُلُ فِي الدُّنْيَا قُوتًا وَمَا يَضُرُّ أَحَدُكُمْ عَلَىٰ أيِّ حَالٍ أمْسَى وَأصْبَحَ مِنَ الدُّنْيَا أَنْ لاَ تَكُونَ فِي النَّفْسِ حَزَازَةٌ، وَلأَنْ يَعَضَّ أَحَدُكُمْ عَلَى جَمْرَةٍ حَتَّى تُطْفَأَ خَيْرٌ مِنْ أَنْ يَقُولَ لأَمْرٍ قَضَاهُ اللّهُ: لَيْتَ هَذَا لَمْ يَكُنْ.

ابن أبي شيبة، المصنَّف

اليوم ١٣٥

عَنْ قَيْسٍ قَالَ: اشْتَرَىٰ أَبُو بَكْرٍ بِلاَلاً بِخَمْسِ أَوَاقٍ ثُمَّ أَعْتَقَهُ قَالَ: فَقَالَ لَهُ بِلاَلٌ: يَا أَبَا بَكْرٍ إِنْ كُنْتَ إِنَّمَا أَعْتَقْتَنِي لِتَتَّخِذَنِي

keeper, then do so; but if you have freed me for the sake of Allah, then let me work for the sake of Allah,' upon which Abū Bakr and said: 'I have freed you for the sake of Allah'."

(Ibn Abī Shaybah, *al-Muṣannaf*)

DAY
136

Ibn 'Abbās said: "Love for the sake of Allah and hate for the sake of Allah and befriend for the sake of Allah and declare enmity for the sake of Allah, for Allah's closeness and protection is acquired through that. A man shall not savour the taste of faith, even if he performs abundant prayers and fasting, until he realises that."

(Ibn Abī Shaybah, *al-Muṣannaf*)

خَازِنًا فَاتَّخِذْنِي خَازِنًا وَإِنْ كُنْت إِنَّمَا أَعْتَقْتنِي لِلَّهِ فَدَعْنِي فَأَعْمَلُ لِلَّهِ. قَالَ: فَبَكَى أَبُو بَكْرٍ ثُمَّ قَالَ: بَلْ أَعْتَقْتُك لِلَّهِ.

ابن أبي شيبة، المصنَّف

اليوم ١٣٦

عَنِ ابْنِ عَبَّاسٍ قَالَ: أَحِبَّ فِي اللَّهِ وَأَبْغِضْ فِي اللَّهِ وَوَالِ فِي اللَّهِ وَعَادِ فِي اللَّهِ فَإِنَّمَا تُنَالُ وِلَايَةُ اللَّهِ بِذَلِكَ لَا يَجِدُ رَجُلٌ طَعْمَ الْإِيمَانِ وَإِنْ كَثُرَتْ صَلَاتُهُ وَصِيَامُهُ حَتَّى يَكُونَ كَذَلِكَ.

ابن أبي شيبة، المصنَّف

DAY 137

Anas said: "Whoever takes on a brother for the sake of Allah, Allah will build for him a castle in Paradise; and whoever gets to wear a garment at the expense of his brother, Allah will put on him a garment in the Fire; and whoever consumes food at the expense of his brother, Allah will make him eat food in the Fire; and whoever stands in a position of fame and showing off at the expense of his brother, Allah will make him stand on the Day of Judgement in a position of fame and showing off."

(Ibn Abī Shaybah, *al-Muṣannaf*)

DAY 138

Salmān [al-Fārisī] said: "When Allah created Adam, He said to him: 'There is one thing which is Mine, one thing which is yours, and one thing which is between Me and you. As for the thing which is Mine, it is that you worship

اليوم ١٣٧

عَنْ أَنَسٍ قَالَ: مَنِ اتَّخَذَ أَخًا فِي اللَّهِ بَنَى اللَّهُ لَهُ بُرْجًا فِي الْجَنَّةِ، وَمَنْ لَبِسَ بِأَخِيهِ ثَوْبًا أَلْبَسَهُ اللَّهُ ثَوْبًا فِي النَّارِ، وَمَنْ أَكَلَ بِأَخِيهِ أَكْلَةً أَكَّلَهُ اللَّهُ بِهَا أَكْلَةً فِي النَّارِ، وَمَنْ قَامَ بِأَخِيهِ مَقَامَ سُمْعَةٍ وَرِيَاءٍ أَقَامَهُ اللَّهُ يَوْمَ الْقِيَامَةِ مَقَامَ سُمْعَةٍ وَرِيَاءٍ.

ابن أبي شيبة ، المصنَّف

اليوم ١٣٨

عَنْ سَلْمَانَ قَالَ : لَمَّا خَلَقَ اللَّهُ آدَمَ قَالَ : وَاحِدَةٌ لِي وَوَاحِدَةٌ لَكَ، وَوَاحِدَةٌ بَيْنِي وَبَيْنَكَ ، فَأَمَّا الَّتِي لِي فَتَعْبُدُنِي لَا تُشْرِكُ بِي

and do not associate anyone or anything with me; as for the thing which is yours, it is that I will reward you for any good deed you perform; as for the thing which is between Me and you, it is that you ask and make supplication and I answer'."

(Ibn Abī Shaybah, *al-Muṣannaf*)

DAY
139

ʿĀʾishah said: "When Abū Bakr died, he did not leave behind any gold or silver pieces, for before he died, he took all his money and put it in public treasury."

(Aḥmad)

شَيْئًا ، وَأمَّا الَّتي لَك فَمَا عَمِلْت مِنْ شَيْءٍ جَزَيْتُك بِهِ، وَأمَّا الَّتِي بَيْنِي وَبَيْنَكَ فَمِنْك الْمَسْأَلَةَ والدُّعَاءُ وَعَلَي الإِجَابَةُ.

ابن أبي شيبة ، المصنَّف

اليوم ١٣٩

عَنْ عَائِشَةَ قَالَتْ: مَاتَ أَبُو بَكْرٍ فَمَا تَرَكَ دِينَارًا وَلَا دِرْهَمًا، وَكَانَ قَدْ أَخَذَ قَبْلَ ذَلِكَ مَالَهُ فَأَلْقَاهُ فِي بَيْتِ الْمَالِ.

أحمد

DAY 140

It is reported that a Muslim man and a Jewish man referred their dispute to 'Umar ibn al-Khaṭṭāb and, upon seeing that the claim of the Jewish man was correct, he made a judgement in his favour. The Jewish man exclaimed: "By Allah! You have made the right judgement!" Upon hearing this, 'Umar beat him with a stick, saying: "How do you know?" The Jewish man said: "We find [in our Scripture] that none judges rightly except that there is an angel on his right and another on his left who help and guide him to reach the right judgement for as long as he follows the truth. When he leaves the truth, they turn away and leave."

(Mālik, *al-Muwaṭṭa'*)

اليوم
١٤٠

عَنْ عُمَرَ بْنَ الْخَطَّابِ أَنَّه اخْتَصَمَ إِلَيْهِ مُسْلِمٌ وَيَهُودِيٌّ فَرَأَىٰ عُمَرُ أَنَّ الْحَقَّ لِلْيَهُودِيِّ فَقَضَىٰ لَهُ فَقَالَ لَهُ الْيَهُودِيُّ: وَاللهِ لَقَدْ قَضَيْتَ بِالْحَقِّ! فَضَرَبَهُ عُمَرُ بْنُ الْخَطَّابِ بِالدُّرَّةِ ثُمَّ قَالَ: وَمَا يُدْرِيكَ؟ فَقَالَ لَهُ الْيَهُودِيُّ: إِنَّا نَجِدُ أَنَّهُ لَيْسَ قَاضٍ يَقْضِي بِالْحَقِّ إِلَّا كَانَ عَنْ يَمِينِهِ مَلَكٌ وَعَنْ شِمَالِهِ مَلَكٌ يُسَدِّدَانِهِ وَيُوَفِّقَانِهِ لِلْحَقِّ مَا دَامَ مَعَ الْحَقِّ فَإِذَا تَرَكَ الْحَقَّ عَرَجَا وَتَرَكَاهُ.

مالك، الموطأ

DAY 141

Upon mentioning 'Uthmān ibn 'Affān's modesty, al-Ḥasan [al-Baṣrī] said: "Even when he was at home with locked doors, he did not take his clothes off to pour water on himself; modesty prevented him from standing straight."

(Aḥmad)

DAY 142

Sufyān ibn 'Uyaynah reported that 'Uthmān ibn 'Affān said: "I dislike to have any day or night pass without reciting the Qur'ān."

(Aḥmad)

اليوم ١٤١

عَنِ الْحَسَنِ قَالَ وَذَكَرَ عُثْمَانَ وَشِدَّةَ حَيَائِهِ فَقَالَ: إِنْ كَانَ لَيَكُونُ فِي الْبَيْتِ وَالْبَابُ عَلَيْهِ مُغْلَقٌ فَمَا يَضَعُ عَنْهُ الثَّوْبَ لِيُفِيضَ عَلَيْهِ الْمَاءَ يَمْنَعُهُ الْحَيَاءُ أَنْ يُقِيمَ صُلْبَهُ.

أحمد

اليوم ١٤٢

عَنْ سُفْيَانَ بْنِ عُيَيْنَةَ قَالَ: قَالَ عُثْمَانُ: مَا أُحِبُّ أَنْ يَأْتِيَ عَلَيَّ يَوْمٌ وَلَا لَيْلَةٌ إِلَّا أَنْظُرُ فِي اللَّهِ يَعْنِي الْقِرَاءَةَ فِي الْمُصْحَفِ.

أحمد

DAY 143

Abū Yaḥya Ḥakīm ibn Sa'd heard 'Alī saying: "Do not be hasty, quick to spread news and unable to keep a secret, for there shall be ahead of you a very painful calamity that will hit hard as well as heavy calamitous matters that will weigh on you for a long time."

(Al-Bukhārī, *al-Adab al-Mufrad*)

DAY 144

'Abd al-Raḥmān ibn al-Aswad related that his father reported that 'Abdullāh ibn Mas'ūd said: "Verily, these hearts are but receptacles, so preoccupy them with the Qur'ān and nothing else."

(Ibn Abī Shaybah, *al-Muṣannaf*)

اليوم ١٤٣

عَنْ أَبِي يَحْيَى حَكِيمِ بْنِ سَعْدٍ قَالَ: سَمِعْتُ عَلِيًّا يَقُولُ: لاَ تَكُونُوا عُجُلاً مَذَايِيعَ بُذُرًا، فَإِنَّ مِنْ وَرَائِكُمْ بَلاَءً مُبَرِّحًا مُمْلِحًا، وَأُمُورًا مُتَمَاحِلَةً رُدُحًا.

البخاري، الأدب المفرد

اليوم ١٤٤

عَنْ عَبْدِ الرَّحْمَنِ بْنِ الأَسْوَدِ عَنْ أَبِيهِ قَالَ: قَالَ عَبْدُ اللهِ بْنُ مَسْعُودٍ: إِنَّمَا هَذِهِ الْقُلُوبُ أَوْعِيَةٌ، فَأَشْغِلُوهَا بِالْقُرْآنِ وَلاَ تَشْغَلُوهَا بِغَيْرِهِ.

ابن أبي شيبة، المصنَّف

DAY 145

Zirr ibn Ḥubaysh said: "Whoever recites the last verses of *Sūrah al-Kahf* with the intention of waking up to pray at night will indeed wake up to do so." ʿAbdah [the narrator of this saying] said: "I tried it and found that it is as he said."

(Al-Dārimī)

DAY 146

It is reported that Yaḥya ibn Saʿīd said: "It has reached me that a person of good character will be the same degree of the one who stands to pray at night and fasts in hot, scorching days."

(Mālik, *al-Muwaṭṭa'*)

اليوم
١٤٥

عَنْ زِرِّ بْنِ حُبَيْشٍ قَالَ: مَنْ قَرَأَ آخِرَ سُورَةِ الْكَهْفِ لِسَاعَةٍ يُرِيدُ يَقُومُ مِنَ اللَّيْلِ قَامَهَا. قَالَ عَبْدَةُ: فَجَرَّبْنَاهُ فَوَجَدْنَاهُ كَذَلِكَ.

الدّارمي

اليوم
١٤٦

عَنْ يَحْيَى بْنِ سَعِيدٍ أَنَّهُ قَالَ: بَلَغَنِي أَنَّ الْمَرْءَ لَيُدْرِكُ بِحُسْنِ خُلُقِهِ دَرَجَةَ الْقَائِمِ بِاللَّيْلِ الظَّامِي بِالْهَوَاجِرِ.

مالك، الموطأ

DAY
147

Zayd ibn Aslam related from his father who said: "Once 'Umar ibn al-Khaṭṭāb entered in on Abū Bakr and found him holding his tongue with his hand, saying: 'This is what has got me into all kinds of trouble'."

(Ibn Abī Shaybah, *al-Muṣannaf*)

DAY
148

Abū Isḥāq related that 'Alī said: "There are a few words if were you to travel on your beast of burden you would wear them out before you find the likes of them: Let no slave have hope except in his Lord; let him fear nothing but his sin; let the one who does not know, not be shy to learn; let the man of knowledge not be shy to say: 'Allah knows!' about that which he does not know; and know that patience to faith is like the head to the body, if the heads goes, the body goes; and if patience goes, faith goes too."

(Ibn Abī Shaybah, *al-Muṣannaf*)

اليوم ١٤٧

عَنْ زَيْدِ بْنِ أَسْلَمَ عَنْ أَبِيهِ قَالَ: دَخَلَ عُمَرُ عَلَى أَبِي بَكْرٍ وَهُوَ آخِذٌ بِلِسَانِهِ هَكَذَا، يَقُولُ: هَا إِنَّ ذَا أَوْرَدَنِي الْمَوَارِدَ.

ابن أبي شيبة ، المصنَّف

اليوم ١٤٨

عَنْ أَبِي إِسْحَاقَ قَالَ: قَالَ عَلِيٌّ: كَلِمَاتٌ لَوْ رَحَلْتُمُ الْمَطِيَّ فِيهِنَّ لأَنْضَيْتُمُوهُنَّ قَبْلَ أَنْ تُدْرِكُوا مِثْلَهُنَّ: لاَ يَرْجُ عَبْدٌ إِلاَّ رَبَّهُ، وَلاَ يَخَفْ إِلاَّ ذَنْبَهُ وَلاَ يَسْتَحْيِي مَنْ لاَ يَعْلَمُ أَنْ يَتَعَلَّمَ، وَلاَ يَسْتَحْيِي عَالِمٌ إِذَا سُئِلَ عَمَّا لاَ يَعْلَمُ أَنْ يَقُولَ: اللهُ أَعْلَمُ، وَاعْلَمُوا أَنَّ مَنْزِلَةَ الصَّبْرِ مِنَ الإِيمَانِ كَمَنْزِلَةِ الرَّأْسِ مِنَ الْجَسَدِ، فَإِذَا ذَهَبَ الرَّأْسُ ذَهَبَ الْجَسَدُ، وَإِذَا ذَهَبَ الصَّبْرُ ذَهَبَ الإِيمَانُ.

ابن أبي شيبة ، المصنَّف

DAY 149

ʿAbdullāh ibn ʿAmr said: "There are four qualities, if you were to be given them, you would not be harmed by anything in this world that you may be deprived of: good character, lawful sustenance, truthful speech and preserving what has been entrusted to you."

(Al-Bukhārī, *al-Adab al-Mufrad*)

DAY 150

Zayd ibn Aslam related from his father that ʿUmar ibn al-Khaṭṭāb used to say from the pulpit: "O people! Put your homes in order and frighten these hearts before they frighten you."

(Al-Bukhārī, *al-Adab al-Mufrad*)

اليوم ١٤٩

عَنْ عَبْدِ اللهِ بْنِ عَمْرٍو قَالَ: أَرْبَعُ خِلَالٍ إِذَا أُعْطِيتَهُنَّ فَلَا يَضُرُّكَ مَا عُزِلَ عَنْكَ مِنَ الدُّنْيَا: حُسْنُ خَلِيقَةٍ، وَعَفَافُ طُعْمَةٍ، وَصِدْقُ حَدِيثٍ، وَحِفْظُ أَمَانَةٍ.

البخاري، الأدب المفرد

اليوم ١٥٠

عَنْ زَيْدِ بْنِ أَسْلَمَ، عَنْ أَبِيهِ قَالَ: كَانَ عُمَرُ يَقُولُ عَلَى الْمِنْبَرِ: يَا أَيُّهَا النَّاسُ، أَصْلِحُوا عَلَيْكُمْ مَثَاوِيكُمْ، وَأَخِيفُوا هَذِهِ الْجِنَّانَ قَبْلَ أَنْ تُخِيفَكُمْ.

البخاري، الأدب المفرد

DAY 151

Abū al-Dardā' said: "Three things are pivotal in the matter of anyone among the children of Adam: that he does not complain about his calamity to others; he does not inform others about his illness; and he does not utter any words to express his lack of faults."

(Aḥmad)

DAY 152

Abū al-Dardā' said: "What a good hermitage is a man's home: he protects therein his tongue and sight; and beware of the marketplace for it makes one talk unnecessarily and it also distracts."

(Ibn Abī Shaybah, *al-Muṣannaf*)

اليوم ١٥١

قَالَ أَبُو الدَّرْدَاءِ: ثَلَاثٌ مِنْ مِلَاكِ أَمْرِ ابْنِ آدَمَ: أَنْ لَا تَشْكُوَ مُصِيبَتَكَ وَلَا تُحَدِّثَ بِوَجَعِكَ وَلَا تُزَكِّيَ نَفْسَكَ بِلِسَانِكَ.

أحمد

اليوم ١٥٢

عَنْ أَبِي الدَّرْدَاءِ قَالَ: نِعْمَ صَوْمَعَةُ الرَّجُلِ بَيْتُهُ، يَحْفَظُ فِيهَا لِسَانَهُ وَبَصَرَهُ، وَإِيَّاكَ وَالسُّوقَ فَإِنَّهَا تُلْغِي وَتُلْهِي.

ابن أبي شيبة، المصنَّف

DAY
153

ʿAlī ibn Abī Ṭālib, may Allah be well pleased with him, said: "The greedy person is a captive of humiliation."

(Al-Sharīf al-Raḍī, *Nahj al-Balāghah*)

DAY
154

It is reported that Ibn ʿUmar said to Ḥumrān: "Make sure to meet Allah while you do not owe anything to anybody, for there are no gold or silver pieces on the Day of Judgement, rather people will be requited with their works."

(Ibn Abī Shaybah, *al-Muṣannaf*)

اليوم ١٥٣

قَالَ عَلِيُّ بْنُ أَبِي طَالِبٍ : الطَّامِعُ فِي وِثَاقِ الذُّلِّ.

الشريف الرَّضي ، نهج البلاغة

اليوم ١٥٤

عَنِ ابْنِ عُمَرَ أَنَّهُ قَالَ لِحُمْرَانَ: لاَ تَلْقَيَنَّ اللهَ بِذِمَّةٍ لاَ وَفَاءَ بِهَا فَإِنَّهُ لَيْسَ يَوْمَ الْقِيَامَةِ دِينَارٌ وَلاَ دِرْهَمٌ، إِنَّمَا يُجَازَى النَّاسُ بِأَعْمَالِهِمْ.

ابن أبي شيبة ، المصنَّف

DAY 155

Abū Mas'ūd said: "When you see your brother commit a sin, do not be the helpers of the Devil against him by saying: 'May Allah debase him,' or 'May Allah disgrace him', but rather say 'May Allah accept his repentence; may Allah forgive him'."

(Al-Ṭabarānī, *Makārim al-Akhlāq*)

DAY 156

Ṭalḥah ibn 'Ubaydullāh ibn Karīz reported that 'Umar ibn al-Khaṭṭāb said: "If one of you knew what he gets for telling his brother: 'May Allah reward you with good,' you would say it abundantly to one another."

(Ibn Abī Shaybah, *al-Muṣannaf*)

اليوم ١٥٥

عَنْ أَبِي مَسْعُودٍ قَالَ: إِذَا رَأَيْتُمْ أَخَاكُمْ قَارَفَ ذَنْبًا فَلَا تَكُونُوا أَعْوَانًا لِلشَّيْطَانِ عَلَيْهِ، تَقُولُوا: أَخْزَاهُ اللَّهُ، قَبَّحَهُ اللَّهُ، وَلَكِنْ قُولُوا: تَابَ اللَّهُ عَلَيْهِ، غَفَرَ لَهُ.

الطبراني، مكارم الأخلاق

اليوم ١٥٦

عَنْ طَلْحَةَ بْنِ عُبَيْدِ اللهِ بْنِ كَرِيزٍ قَالَ: قَالَ عُمَرُ: لَوْ يَعْلَمُ أَحَدُكُمْ مَا لَهُ فِي قَوْلِهِ لِأَخِيهِ: جَزَاكَ اللَّهُ خَيْرًا، لَأَكْثَرَ مِنْهَا بَعْضُكُمْ لِبَعْضٍ.

ابن أبي شيبة، المصنَّف

DAY 157

It is reported that Sa'īd ibn al-Musayyab said: "Upon breaking the front of his shoe, 'Umar ibn al-Khaṭṭāb said: 'Verily, we are unto Allah, and unto Him we shall return!' So he was asked: 'O Leader of the believers! [You say this] even about your shoe?' He said: 'Yes! Anything that befalls the believer and he dislikes is a calamity'."

(Ibn Abī Shaybah, *al-Muṣannaf*)

DAY 158

It is reported that al-Mughīrah ibn Shu'bah said: "A man said: 'May Allah preserve this ruler! Your chamberlain knows some men and gives them preference when it comes to who sees you'. He said: 'Allah shall pardon him, for acquaintance does indeed benefit even with a rabid dog or a mad, bolting camel'."

(Al-Bukhārī, *al-Adab al-Mufrad*)

عَنْ سَعِيدِ بْنِ الْمُسَيَّبِ قَالَ: انْقَطَعَ قِبَالُ نَعْلِ عُمَرَ فَقَالَ: إِنَّا لِلَّهِ
وَإِنَّا إِلَيْهِ رَاجِعُونَ، فَقَالُوا: يَا أَمِيرَ الْمُؤْمِنِينَ، أَفِي قِبَالِ نَعْلِكَ؟
قَالَ: نَعَمْ، كُلُّ شَيْءٍ أَصَابَ الْمُؤْمِنَ يَكْرَهُهُ فَهُوَ مُصِيبَةٌ.

ابن أبي شيبة، المصنَّف

عَنِ الْمُغِيرَةِ بْنِ شُعْبَةَ: قَالَ رَجُلٌ: أَصْلَحَ اللهُ الْأَمِيرَ إِنَّ أَذَنَكَ
يَعْرِفُ رِجَالاً فَيُؤْثِرُهُمْ بِالإِذْنِ. قَالَ: عَذَرَهُ اللهُ، إِنَّ الْمَعْرِفَةَ
لَتَنْفَعُ عِنْدَ الْكَلْبِ الْعَقُورِ وَعِنْدَ الْجَمَلِ الصَّؤُولِ.

البخاري، الأدب المفرد

DAY 159

Sa'īd ibn Jubayr said: "I saw Ibn 'Abbās holding his tongue and saying [addressing his tongue]: 'Say something good and you will benefit; or remain silent and you shall be safe before a time comes when you will bitterly regret it'."

(Aḥmad)

DAY 160

'Abdullāh ibn Mas'ūd, may Allah be well pleased with him said: "People will remain righteous and close-knit as long as they get their knowledge from the Companions of Muhammad, Allah bless him and grant him peace, as well as from their most distinguished scholars; and they will perish when they start getting their knowledge from the less distinguished people amongst them."

('Abd al-Razzāq, *al-Muṣannaf*)

اليوم ١٥٩

عَنْ سَعِيدِ بْنِ جُبَيْرٍ قَالَ: رَأَيْتُ ابْنَ عَبَّاسٍ آخِذًا بِلِسَانِهِ وَهُوَ يَقُولُ: قُلْ خَيْرًا تَغْنَمْ أَوِ اصْمُتْ تَسْلَمْ قَبْلَ أَنْ تَنْدَمَ.

أحمد

اليوم ١٦٠

قَالَ ابْنُ مَسْعُودٍ: لَا يَزَالُ النَّاسُ صَالِحِينَ مُتَمَاسِكِينَ مَا أَتَاهُمُ الْعِلْمَ مِنْ أَصْحَابِ مُحَمَّدٍ صَلَّى اللهُ عَلَيْهِ وَسَلَّمَ وَمِنْ أَكَابِرِهِمْ، فَإِذَا أَتَاهُمْ مِنْ أَصَاغِرِهِمْ هَلَكُوا.

عبد الرزّاق، المصنّف

DAY 161

Al-Aḥnaf [ibn Qays] reported that ʿUmar [ibn al-Khaṭṭāb] said: "Acquire deep understanding of the *Dīn* before you become leaders [of your people]."

(Ibn Abī Shaybah, *al-Muṣannaf*)

DAY 162

ʿAlī [ibn Abī Ṭālib] said: "Make an effort to acquire knowledge, and when you do acquire it, keep it tight and do not taint it with laughter or play, lest [people's] hearts reject it."

(Al-Dārimī)

اليوم ١٦١

عَنِ الأَحْنَفِ قَالَ: قَالَ عُمَرُ: تَفَقَّهُوا قَبْلَ أَنْ تُسَوَّدُوا.

ابن أبي شيبة، المصنَّف

اليوم ١٦٢

قَالَ عَلِيُّ ابْنُ أَبِي طَالِبٍ: تَعَلَّمُوا الْعِلْمَ فَإِذَا عَلِمْتُمُوهُ فَاكْظِمُوا عَلَيْهِ وَلَا تَشُوبُوهُ بِضَحِكٍ وَلَا بِلَعِبٍ فَتَمُجَّهُ الْقُلُوبُ.

الدّارمي

DAY 163

Abū al-Dardā' said: "Indeed, you will never become a man of knowledge until you first become a learner, and you will never be a man of knowledge unless and until you apply what you have learnt."

(Wakī' ibn al-Jarrāḥ, *Kitāb al-Zuhd*)

DAY 164

'Abdullāh ibn Mas'ūd said: "Strive to be a man of knowledge or a student of knowledge and do not strive to be anything in between."

(Abū Khaythamah, *Kitāb al-'Ilm*)

اليوم
١٦٣

عَنْ أَبِي الدَّرْدَاءِ قَالَ: إِنَّكَ لَنْ تَكُونَ عَالِمًا حَتَّىٰ تَكُونَ مُتَعَلِّمًا، وَلَنْ تَكُونَ عَالِمًا حَتَّىٰ تَكُونَ بِمَا عَلِمْتَ عَامِلًا.

وكيع بن الجرَّاح، كتاب الزهد

اليوم
١٦٤

قَالَ عَبْدُ اللهِ: أُغْدُ عَالِمًا أَوْ مُتَعَلِّمًا وَلَا تَغْدُ بَيْنَ ذَلِكَ.

أبو خيثمه، كتاب العلم

DAY
165

Salmān [al-Fārisī] is reported to have said: "Knowledge that is not taught is like wealth that is not spent from."

(Al-Zuhayr ibn Ḥarb, *Kitāb al-ʿIlm*)

DAY
166

ʿAbdullāh ibn Sufyān reported from his uncle that he heard ʿUmar ibn al-Khaṭṭāb say: "Preserve knowledge through writing."

(Ibn Abī Shaybah, *al-Muṣannaf*)

اليوم ١٦٥

عَنْ سَلْمَانَ قَالَ: عِلْمٌ لَا يُقَالُ بِهِ كَكَنْزٍ لَا يُنْفَقُ مِنْهُ.

الزهير ابن حرب ، كتاب العلم

اليوم ١٦٦

عَنْ عَبْدِ الْمَلِكِ بْنِ عَبْدِ اللهِ بْنِ سُفْيَانَ عَنْ عَمِّهِ أَنَّهُ سَمِعَ عُمَرَ بْنَ الْخَطَّابِ يَقُولُ: قَيِّدُوا الْعِلْمَ بِالْكِتَابِ.

ابن أبي شيبة ، المصنَّف

DAY 167

Al-Qāsim reported that ʿAbdullāh said: "Do not be hasty in praising people or dispraising them, for you may like a man today and dislike him tomorrow, or dislike him today and like him tomorrow. And verily, the servants do slight each other and Allah forgives all sins on the Day of Judgement. Allah is also more compassionate towards His servant when He meets him than the mother of a child whose bedding she spreads on a plain ground and then smoothens it with her hand such that if a scorpion bites, it will bite her, or if there is a thorn in it, it will prick her."

(Ibn Abī Shaybah, *al-Muṣannaf*)

اليوم
١٦٧

عَنِ الْقَاسِمِ، قَالَ: قَالَ عَبْدُ اللهِ: لاَ تَعْجَلُوا بِحَمْدِ النَّاسِ وَلا بِذَمِّهِمْ فَإِنَّ الرَّجُلَ يُعْجِبُكَ الْيَوْمَ وَيَسُوؤُكَ غَدًا وَيَسُوؤُكَ الْيَوْمَ وَيُعْجِبُكَ غَدًا، وَإِنَّ الْعِبَادَ يُغَيِّرُونَ وَاللهُ يَغْفِرُ الذُّنُوبَ يَوْمَ الْقِيَامَةِ، وَاللهُ أَرْحَمُ بِعَبْدِهِ يَوْمَ يَأْتِيهِ مِنْ أُمٍّ وَاحِدٍ فَرَشَتْ لَهُ فِي أَرْضٍ قِيٍّ ثُمَّ قَامَتْ تَلْتَمِسُ فِرَاشَهُ بِيَدِهَا فَإِنْ كَانَتْ لَدْغَةٌ كَانَتْ بِهَا وَإِنْ كَانَتْ شَوْكَةٌ كَانَتْ بِهَا.

ابن أبي شيبة، المصنَّف

DAY 168

Al-Ḥasan reported that ʿUmar ibn al-Khaṭṭāb said: "Those who are led fulfil the rights of their leader as long as the latter fulfils the right of Allah; and if he strays far from that, they will stray far from that too."

(Ibn Abī Shaybah, *al-Muṣannaf*)

DAY 169

ʿAmir al-Shaʿbī reported that ʿUmar ibn al-Khaṭṭāb said: "Sufficient for a man is his religion, while his self-respect lies in his good character and his stock is his reason."

(Ibn Abī Shaybah, *al-Muṣannaf*)

اليوم
١٦٨

عَنِ الْحَسَنِ قَالَ: قَالَ عُمَرُ: الرَّعِيَّةُ مُؤَدِّيَةٌ إِلَى الإِمَامِ مَا أَدَّى الإِمَامُ إِلَى اللَّهِ، فَإِذَا رَتَعَ رَتَعُوا.

ابن أبي شيبة ، المصنَّف

اليوم
١٦٩

عَنْ عَامِرٍ قَالَ: قَالَ عُمَرُ: حَسْبُ الرَّجُل دِينُهُ، وَمُرُوءَتُهُ خُلُقُهُ، وَأَصْلُهُ عَقْلُهُ.

ابن أبي شيبة ، المصنَّف

DAY 170

'Ubaydullāh ibn 'Adī ibn al-Khiyār reported that 'Umar ibn al-Khaṭṭāb said: "When the servant humbles himself to Allah, Allah raises his wisdom and says to him: 'Rise, may Allah make you rise!' And so he feels small within but in the eyes of people he is great. And when the servant becomes haughty and exceeds his limits, Allah breaks him down to earth and says to him: 'Be disgraced! May Allah disgrace you!' And so he feels quite great in his eyes while he is very small in people's eyes, so much so that he is more despicable in Allah's eyes than a pig."

(Ibn Abī Shaybah, *al-Muṣannaf*)

اليوم
١٧٠

عَنْ عُبَيْدِ اللَّهِ بْنِ عَدِيِّ بْنِ الْخِيَارِ، قَالَ: قَالَ عُمَرُ: إِنَّ الْعَبْدَ إِذَا تَوَاضَعَ لِلَّهِ رَفَعَ اللَّهُ حِكْمَتَهُ، وَقَالَ: انْتَعِشْ نَعَشَكَ اللَّهُ، فَهُوَ فِي نَفْسِهِ صَغِيرٌ وَفِي أَنْفُسِ النَّاسِ كَبِيرٌ، وَإِنَّ الْعَبْدَ إِذَا تَعَظَّمَ وَعَدَا طَوْرَهُ وَهَصَهُ اللَّهُ إِلَى الأَرْضِ، وَقَالَ اخْسَأْ خَسَأَكَ اللَّهُ، فَهُوَ فِي نَفْسِهِ كَبِيرٌ وَفِي أَنْفُسِ النَّاسِ صَغِيرٌ حَتَّى لَهُوَ أَحْقَرُ عِنْدَهُ مِنْ خِنْزِيرٍ.

ابن أبي شيبة، المصنَّف

DAY 171

It is reported that Ibn ʿUmar said: "Whoever fears his Lord and maintains ties with his kinship will have his lifespan augmented, his wealth increased and his family members will love him."

(Ibn Abī Shaybah, *al-Muṣannaf*)

DAY 172

Sālim ibn ʿAbdullāh reported from his father that ʿUmar ibn al-Khaṭṭāb used to say to his children: "When you reach the morning, disperse and do not stay together in one house, for I fear that you may stop talking to each other or that an evil thing may happen between you."

(Al-Bukhārī, *al-Adab al-Mufrad*)

اليوم
١٧١

عَنِ ابْنِ عُمَرَ قَالَ: مَنِ اتَّقَىٰ رَبَّهُ وَوَصَلَ رَحِمَهُ نُسِيءَ لَهُ فِي عُمْرِهِ وَثَرَا مَالُهُ وَأَحَبَّهُ أَهْلُهُ.

ابن أبي شيبة، المصنَّف

اليوم
١٧٢

عَنْ سَالِمِ بْنِ عَبْدِ اللهِ عَنْ أَبِيهِ، كَانَ عُمَرُ يَقُولُ لِبَنِيهِ: إِذَا أَصْبَحْتُمْ فَتَبَدَّدُوا، وَلَا تَجْتَمِعُوا فِي دَارٍ وَاحِدَةٍ، فَإِنِّي أَخَافُ عَلَيْكُمْ أَنْ تَقَاطَعُوا، أَوْ يَكُونَ بَيْنَكُمْ شَرٌّ.

البخاري، الأدب المفرد

DAY 173

Muhammad ibn Shihāb reported that ʿUmar ibn al-Khaṭṭāb said: "Do not get involved in that which does not concern you, stay away from your enemy and take as a bosom friend only a trustworthy person, for the trustworthy person has no equal. And do not keep the company of an immoral person lest he teaches his immorality, and do not divulge your secret to him; and consult about your affairs only with those who fear Allah a great deal."

(Ibn Abī Shaybah, *al-Muṣannaf*)

DAY 174

Zayd ibn Ṣūḥān reported that ʿUmar said [to a group of people]: "What prevents you from stopping a man when you see him violating people's good names?" They said: "We do not do so to escape his sharp tongue." So he said: "That's the least you can do as you are witnesses."

(Ibn Abī Shaybah, *al-Muṣannaf*)

اليوم
١٧٣

عَنْ مُحَمَّدِ بْنِ شِهَابٍ، قَالَ: قَالَ عُمَرُ: لَا تَعْتَرِضْ فِيمَا لا يَعْنِيك وَاعْتَزِلْ عَدُوَّك وَاحْتَفِظْ مِنْ خَلِيلِك إلَّا الأَمِين، فَإِنَّ الأَمِينَ لَا يُعَادِلُهُ شَيْءٌ. لَا تَصْحَبَ الْفَاجِرَ فَيُعَلِّمُك مِنْ فُجُورِهِ وَلَا تُفْشِ إلَيْهِ بِسِرِّك وَاسْتَشِرْ فِي أَمْرِكَ الَّذِينَ يَخْشَوْنَ اللَّهَ.

ابن أبي شيبة ، المصنَّف

اليوم
١٧٤

عَنْ زَيْدِ بْنِ صُوحَانَ، قَالَ: قَالَ عُمَرُ: مَا يَمْنَعُكُمْ إذَا رَأَيْتُمْ الرَّجُلَ يَخْرِقُ أَعْرَاضَ النَّاسِ أَنْ لَا تُغَيِّرُوا عَلَيْهِ؟ قَالُوا: نَتَّقِي لِسَانَهُ. قَالَ: ذَاكَ أَدْنَى أَنْ تَكُونُوا شُهَدَاءَ.

ابن أبي شيبة ، المصنَّف

DAY
175

ʿAbdullāh ibn al-Zubayr said: "I have never seen any two women who are more generous than ʿĀ'ishah and Asmā' and their generosity was different. As for ʿĀ'ishah she used to save up and, when she had saved up something [decent], she distributed it [on the poor]. And as for Asmā', she never saved up anything for the morrow."

(Al-Bukhārī, *al-Adab al-Mufrad*)

DAY
176

Abū Ḥāzim reported that Abū Hurayrah said: "Whoever donates old clothes [to the poor], Allah will clothe him for it with silk clothes [on the Day of Judgement]; and whoever donates new clothes [to the poor], Allah will clothe him for it with brocade clothes [on the Day of Judgement]."

(Ibn Abī Shaybah, *al-Muṣannaf*)

اليوم
١٧٥

عَنْ عَبْدِ اللَّهِ بْنِ الزُّبَيْرِ قَالَ: مَا رَأَيْتُ امْرَأَتَيْنِ أَجْوَدَ مِنْ عَائِشَةَ وَأَسْمَاءَ: أَمَّا عَائِشَةُ فَكَانَتْ تَجْمَعُ الشَّيْءَ إِلَى الشَّيْءِ، حَتَّىٰ إِذَا كَانَ اجْتَمَعَ عِنْدَهَا قَسَمَتْ، وَأَمَّا أَسْمَاءُ فَكَانَتْ لَا تُمْسِكُ شَيْئًا لِغَدٍ.

البخاري، الأدب المفرد

اليوم
١٧٦

عَنْ أَبِي حَازِمٍ قَالَ: قَالَ أَبُو هُرَيْرَةَ: مَنْ كَسَا خَلِقًا كَسَاهُ اللَّهُ بِهِ حَرِيرًا، وَمَنْ كَسَا جَدِيدًا كَسَاهُ اللَّهُ بِهِ إِسْتَبْرَقًا.

ابن أبي شيبة، المصنَّف

DAY 177

It is related that Ibn ʿAbbās said: "There is not a single Muslim who has Muslim parents and he starts the day by treating them well, out of seeking reward from Allah, except that Allah opens for him two gates – i.e. of Paradise – and if it is one, then it is just one. And if he angers one of them, Allah will not be pleased with him until they become pleased with him." Then he was asked: "Even if it was them who wronged him?" He replied: "Even if it was them who wronged him."

(Al-Bukhārī, *al-Adab al-Mufrad*)

DAY 178

It is reported that Abū Mūsā al-Ashʿarī said: "It is part of glorifying Allah to honour any grey-haired Muslim, the memoriser of the Qur'ān who is neither extreme nor lax about and the just ruler."

(Al-Bukhārī, *al-Adab al-Mufrad*)

اليوم ١٧٧

عَنِ ابْنِ عَبَّاسٍ قَالَ: مَا مِنْ مُسْلِمٍ لَهُ وَالِدَانِ مُسْلِمَانِ يُصْبِحُ إِلَيْهِمَا مُحْتَسِبًا إِلَّا فَتَحَ لَهُ اللَّهُ بَابَيْنِ يَعْنِي: مِنَ الْجَنَّةِ وَإِنْ كَانَ وَاحِدًا فَوَاحِدٌ، وَإِنْ أَغْضَبَ أَحَدَهُمَا لَمْ يَرْضَى اللَّهُ عَنْهُ حَتَّى يَرْضَى عَنْهُ، قِيلَ: وَإِنْ ظَلَمَاهُ؟ قَالَ: وَإِنْ ظَلَمَاهُ.

البخاري، الأدب المفرد

اليوم ١٧٨

عَنِ أَبِي مُوسَى الأَشْعَرِيِّ قَالَ: إِنَّ مِنَ إِجْلَالِ اللَّهِ إِكْرَامَ ذِي الشَّيْبَةِ الْمُسْلِمِ وَحَامِلِ الْقُرْآنِ غَيْرِ الْغَالِي فِيهِ وَلَا الْجَافِي عَنْهُ، وَإِكْرَامَ ذِي السُّلْطَانِ الْمُقْسِطِ.

البخاري، الأدب المفرد

DAY 179

It is related that ʿAbdullah ibn Masʿūd said: "There are no two Muslims except that there is a covering protection between them from Allah, glorified and exalted is He. But if one of them says to the other a word which entails severance of relationship, then he has broken Allah's covering protection; and if one of them says to the other: 'You are an unbeliever,' then one of them becomes an unbeliever."

(Al-Bukhārī, *al-Adab al-Mufrad*)

DAY 180

Umm al-Ḥasan reported that she was at the house of Umm Salamah, the wife of the Prophet, Allah bless him and grant him peace, when some needy people came in. So she said: "Shall I tell them to leave?" Umm Salamah replied: "We have not been commanded to behave in this way; give them a date each."

(Ibn Abī Shaybah, *al-Muṣannaf*)

اليوم
١٧٩

عَنْ عَبْدِ اللَّهِ قَالَ: مَا مِنْ مُسْلِمَيْنِ إِلَّا بَيْنَهُمَا مِنَ اللَّهِ عَزَّ وَجَلَّ سِتْرٌ فَإِذَا قَالَ أَحَدُهُمَا لِصَاحِبِهِ كَلِمَةَ هَجْرٍ فَقَدْ خَرَقَ سِتْرَ اللَّهِ، وَإِذَا قَالَ أَحَدُهُمَا لِلْآخَرِ: أَنْتَ كَافِرٌ، فَقَدْ كَفَرَ أَحَدُهُمَا.

البخاري، الأدب المفرد

اليوم
١٨٠

عَنْ أُمِّ الْحَسَنِ أَنَّهَا كَانَتْ عِنْدَ أُمِّ سَلَمَةَ زَوْجِ النَّبِيِّ صَلَّى اللَّهُ عَلَيْهِ وَسَلَّمَ، فَجَاءَ مَسَاكِينُ فَقَالَتْ: أُخْرِجُهُنَّ؟ فَقَالَتْ أُمُّ سَلَمَةَ: مَا بِهَذَا أُمِرْنَا أَبِدِّيهِنَّ بِتَمْرَةٍ تَمْرَةٍ.

ابن أبي شيبة، المصنَّف

DAY 181

It is reported that ʿAlī ibn Abī Ṭālib said: "That I gather a few of my brothers over a measure or two of food is more beloved to me than me going to your marketplace and emancipating a slave."

(Al-Bukhārī, *al-Adab al-Mufrad*)

DAY 182

It is reported that Abū Hurayrah said: "The most miserly of people is the one who fails to give the greeting of peace to people, and the loser is the one who does not return the greeting of peace. And if a tree comes between you and your brother and you are able to greet him with the greeting of peace first, do so."

(Al-Bukhārī, *al-Adab al-Mufrad*)

اليوم
١٨١

عَنْ عَلِيٍّ قَالَ: لأَنْ أَجْمَعَ نَفَرًا مِنْ إِخْوَانِي عَلَى صَاعٍ أَوْ صَاعَيْنِ مِنْ طَعَامٍ أَحَبُّ إِلَيَّ مِنْ أَنْ أَخْرُجَ إِلَى سُوقِكُمْ فَأُعْتِقَ رَقَبَةً.

البخاري، الأدب المفرد

اليوم
١٨٢

عَنْ أَبِي هُرَيْرَةَ قَالَ: أَبْخَلُ النَّاسِ مَنْ بَخِلَ بِالسَّلَامِ، وَالْمَغْبُونُ مَنْ لَمْ يَرُدَّهُ، وَإِنْ حَالَتْ بَيْنَكَ وَبَيْنَ أَخِيكَ شَجَرَةٌ، فَإِنِ اسْتَطَعْتَ أَنْ تَبْدَأَهُ بِالسَّلَامِ لَا يَبْدَؤُكَ فَافْعَلْ.

البخاري، الأدب المفرد

DAY 183

'Ubayd al-Kindī reported from his father that he heard 'Alī ibn Abī Ṭālib say to Ibn al-Kawwā': "Do you know what the people of old have said? [They said:]: 'Love your beloved one in moderation for, one day, he may become loathed by you; and hate the one you hate in moderation for, one day, he may become beloved to you'."

(Al-Bukhārī, *al-Adab al-Mufrad*)

DAY 184

It is reported that'Umar ibn al-Khaṭṭāb said: "Let your love not turn into infatuation nor your hatred into utter wastage." He was asked: "How so?" He said: "When you love someone and you cling to them like the clinging of a child; and when you hate someone, you wish him or her to be hurt."

(Al-Bukhārī, *al-Adab al-Mufrad*)

اليوم ١٨٣

عَنْ عُبَيْدٍ الْكِنْدِيُّ عَنْ أَبِيهِ قَالَ: سَمِعْتُ عَلِيًّا يَقُولُ لِابْنِ الْكَوَّاءِ: هَلْ تَدْرِي مَا قَالَ الأَوَّلُ؟ أَحْبِبْ حَبِيبَكَ هَوْنًا مَا، عَسَى أَنْ يَكُونَ بَغِيضَكَ يَوْمًا مَا، وَأَبْغِضْ بَغِيضَكَ هَوْنًا مَا، عَسَى أَنْ يَكُونَ حَبِيبَكَ يَوْمًا مَا.

البخاري، الأدب المفرد

اليوم ١٨٤

عَنْ عُمَرَ بْنِ الْخَطَّابِ قَالَ: لَا يَكُنْ حُبُّكَ كَلَفًا وَلَا بُغْضُكَ تَلَفًا. فَقُلْتُ: كَيْفَ ذَاكَ؟ قَالَ: إِذَا أَحْبَبْتَ كَلِفْتَ كَلَفَ الصَّبِيِّ، وَإِذَا أَبْغَضْتَ أَحْبَبْتَ لِصَاحِبِكَ التَّلَفَ.

البخاري، الأدب المفرد

DAY
185

ʿAbdullāh ibn ʿĀmir reported that he heard ʿUthmān ibn ʿAffān say: "Indeed, the wealthiest person in my sight is the one who does not harm others with either his weapon or hand."

(Ibn Abī Shaybah, *al-Muṣannaf*)

DAY
186

Mūsā ibn Yasār reported that his uncle related that Salmān al-Fārisī wrote to Abū al-Dardā' the following: "Knowledge is like streams of water; people come to them and more than one person benefits from them. And verily, wisdom that is not communicated is like a body without a soul; and a knowledge that is not conveyed is like a treasure that is not spent from. And verily, the simile of the man of knowledge is that of a man who carries a lamp in a dark alley; anyone who passes by him can see his way clearly, and everyone prays for him."

(Al-Dārimī)

اليوم ١٨٥

عَنْ عَبْدِ اللَّهِ بْنِ عَامِرٍ قَالَ: سَمِعْتُ عُثْمَانَ يَقُولُ: إِنَّ أَعْظَمَكُمْ عِنْدِي غِنَاءً مَنْ كَفَّ سِلَاحَهُ وَيَدَهُ.

ابن أبي شيبة، المصنَّف

اليوم ١٨٦

عَنْ مُوسَى بْنِ يَسَارٍ عَنْ عَمِّهِ قَالَ بَلَغَنِي أَنَّ سَلْمَانَ كَتَبَ إِلَى أَبِي الدَّرْدَاءِ: إِنَّ الْعِلْمَ كَالْيَنَابِيعِ يَغْشَاهُنَّ النَّاسُ فَيَخْتَلِجُهُ هَذَا وَهَذَا فَيَنْفَعُ اللَّهُ بِهِ غَيْرَ وَاحِدٍ وَإِنَّ حِكْمَةً لَا يُتَكَلَّمُ بِهَا كَجَسَدٍ لَا رُوحَ فِيهِ وَإِنَّ عِلْمًا لَا يُخْرَجُ كَكَنْزٍ لَا يُنْفَقُ مِنْهُ وَإِنَّمَا مَثَلُ الْعَالِمِ كَمَثَلِ رَجُلٍ حَمَلَ سِرَاجًا فِي طَرِيقٍ مُظْلِمٍ يَسْتَضِيءُ بِهِ مَنْ مَرَّ بِهِ وَكُلٌّ يَدْعُو لَهُ بِالْخَيْرِ.

الدَّارمي

DAY 187

Abū al-Dardā' said: "Seek knowledge! But if you fail to seek it, then show love towards the men of knowledge; and if you fail to show love towards them, at least do not hate them."

(Aḥmad)

DAY 188

'Abdullāh ibn Mas'ūd said: "You are living at a time in which there are abundant *fuqahā'* and few orators, but there shall come a time after you when there will be few *fuqahā'* and abundant orators."

(Abū Khaythamah, *Kitāb al-'Ilm*)

اليوم
١٨٧

قَالَ أَبُو الدَّرْدَاءِ: اُطْلُبُوا العِلْمَ، فَإِنْ لَمْ تَطْلُبُوهُ فَأَحِبُّوا أَهْلَهُ، فَإِنْ لَمْ تُحِبُّوهُمْ فَلَا تَبْغَضُوهُمْ.

أحمد

اليوم
١٨٨

سَمِعْتُ ابْنَ مَسْعُودٍ يَقُولُ: إِنَّكُمْ فِي زَمَانٍ كَثِيرٌ فُقَهَاؤُهُ، قَلِيلٌ خُطَبَاؤُهُ، وَسَيَأْتِي مِنْ بَعْدِكُمْ زَمَانٌ قَلِيلٌ فُقَهَاؤُهُ كَثِيرٌ خُطَبَاؤُهُ.

أبو خيثمه، كتاب العلم

DAY
189

ʿAlī ibn Abī Ṭālib said: "Shall I not inform you who the *faqīh* is, I mean the real *faqīh*? It is the one who does not make people despair of Allah's mercy, does not make them feel safe from Allah's chastisement, does not give dispensations regarding disobediences of Allah; and he does not leave the Qur'ān in preference to other things. Verily, there is no good in knowledge in which there is no real understanding; verily, there is no good in a recitation [of the Qur'ān] in which there is no reflection; and verily, there is no good in worship in which there is no meditation."

(Abū Khaythamah, *Kitāb al-ʿIlm*)

DAY
190

It is reported that Abū ʿUbaydah ibn al-Jarrāḥ used to march with the army and say: "How many a person who wears clean clothes but soils his religion; how many a person honours himself while in reality he is humiliating

اليوم ١٨٩

قَالَ عَلِيّ بن أَبِي طَالِبٍ: أَلَا أُخْبِرُكُمْ بِالْفَقِيهِ حَقِّ الْفَقِيهِ مَنْ لَمْ يُقَنِّطِ النَّاسَ مِنْ رَحْمَةِ اللَّهِ، وَلَمْ يُؤْمِنْهُمْ مِنْ عَذَابِ اللَّهِ، وَلَمْ يُرَخِّصْ لَهُمْ فِي مَعَاصِي اللَّهِ، وَلَمْ يَتْرُكِ الْقُرْآنَ رَغْبَةً عَنْهُ إِلَىٰ غَيْرِه. أَلَا لَا خَيْرَ فِي عِلْمٍ لَيْسَ فِيهِ تَفَهُّمٌ، أَلَا لَا خَيْرَ فِي قِرَاءَةٍ لَيْسَ فِيهَا تَدَبُّرٌ، أَلَا لَا خَيْرَ فِي عِبَادَةٍ لَيْسَ فِيهَا تَفَكُّرٌ.

أبو خيثمه ، كتاب العلم

اليوم ١٩٠

عَنْ أَبِي عُبَيْدَةَ بْنِ الْجَرَّاحِ أَنَّهُ كَانَ يَسِيرُ فِي الْعَسْكَرِ وَيَقُولُ: أَلَا رُبَّ مُبَيِّضٍ لِثِيَابِهِ مُدَنِّسٍ لِدِينِهِ، أَلَا رُبَّ مُكْرِمٍ لِنَفْسِهِ

himself. Verily, hasten to replace your old sins with new good deeds, for were one of you to sin as much as what is between the earth and the sky and then does one good deed, it will tower over all his sins and erase them."

(Aḥmad)

DAY 191

Abū al-Aḥwas reported that ʿAbdullāh said: "Be used to doing good, for all goodness lies in making it a habit."

(Ibn Abī Shaybah, *al-Muṣannaf*)

DAY 192

It is reported that Ibn ʿUmar said: "A man will not be counted among the men of knowledge until he does not resentfully envy those who are more knowledgeable than him, look down on those who have less knowledge than him or seek a recompense for his knowledge."

(Ibn Abī Shaybah, *al-Muṣannaf*)

وَهُوَ لَهَا مُهِينٌ، أَلَا بَادِرُوا السَّيِّئَاتِ الْقَدِيمَاتِ بِالْحَسَنَاتِ الْحَدِيثَاتِ، فَلَوْ أَنَّ أَحَدَكُمْ أَخْطَأَ مَا بَيْنَهُ وَبَيْنَ السَّمَاءِ وَالْأَرْضِ ثُمَّ عَمِلَ حَسَنَةً لَعَلَتْ فَوْقَ سَيِّئَاتِهِ حَتَّىٰ تَقْهَرَهُنَّ.

أحمد

اليوم ١٩١

عَنْ أَبِي الأَحْوَصِ قَالَ: قَالَ عَبْدُ اللَّهِ: تَعَوَّدُوا الْخَيْرَ فَإِنَّمَا الْخَيْرُ فِي الْعَادَةِ.

ابن أبي شيبة، المصنَّف

اليوم ١٩٢

عَنِ ابْنِ عُمَرَ قَالَ: لَا يَكُونُ رَجُلٌ مِنْ أَهْلِ الْعِلْمِ حَتَّىٰ لَا يَحْسُدَ مَنْ فَوْقَهُ وَلَا يُحَقِّرَ مَنْ دُونَهُ وَلَا يَبْتَغِي بِعِلْمِهِ ثَمَنًا.

ابن أبي شيبة، المصنَّف

DAY 193

Abū al-Dardā' said: "Earning money lawfully is scarce; so whoever earns money unlawfully and spends it on what is lawful – and whoever earns money unlawfully and spends it on what is unlawful – that is the incurable disease. And whoever earns money lawfully and spend it on what is lawful, that washes away sins just as water washes away dirt from a rock all dust."

(Aḥmad)

DAY 194

It is reported that Ibn 'Umar said: "No dose is greater in reward in the sight of Allah than a dose of rage that the servant suppresses out of seeking Allah's Countenance."

(Ibn Mājah)

اليوم ١٩٣

قَالَ أَبُو الدَّرْدَاءِ: إِنَّ كَسْبَ المَالِ مِنْ سَبِيلِ الحَلَالِ قَلِيلٌ، فَمَنْ كَسَبَ مَالًا مِنْ غَيْرِ حِلِّهِ فَوَضَعَهُ فِي حَقِّهِ وَمَنْ كَسِبَ مَالًا مِنْ غَيْرِ حِلِّهِ فَوَضَعَهُ فِي غَيْرِ حَقِّهِ فَذَلِكَ الدَّاءُ العُضَالُ. وَمَنْ كَسَبَ مَالًا مِنْ حِلِّهِ فَوَضَعَهُ فِي حَقِّهِ فَذَلِكَ يَغْسِلُ الذُّنُوبَ كَمَا يَغْسِلُ المَاءُ التُّرَابَ عَنِ الصَّفَا.

أحمد

اليوم ١٩٤

عَنِ ابْنِ عُمَرَ قَالَ: مَا مِنْ جَرْعَةٍ أَعْظَمَ عِنْدَ اللهِ أَجْرًا مِنْ جَرْعَةِ غَيْظٍ كَظَمَهَا عَبْدٌ ابْتِغَاءَ وَجْهِ اللهِ.

إبن ماجه

DAY
195

It is reported from Maʿan that ʿAbdullāh ibn Masʿud said: "Do not be divided amongst yourselves lest you perish."

(Ibn Abī Shaybah, *al-Muṣannaf*)

DAY
196

It is reported that ʿAbdullāh ibn ʿUmar said: "Verily, one of the real messes that is inescapable for whoever gets himself fall in it, is the unlawful killing of another person."

(al-Bukhārī)

اليوم
١٩٥

عَنْ مَعَنْ قَالَ: قَالَ عَبْدُ اللَّهِ: لاَ تَفْتَرِقُوا فَتَهْلَكُوا.

ابن أبي شيبة، المصنَّف

اليوم
١٩٦

عَنْ عَبْدِ اللَّهِ بْنِ عُمَرَ، قَالَ: إِنَّ مِنْ وَرَطَاتِ الْأُمُورِ الَّتِي لَا مَخْرَجَ لِمَنْ أَوْقَعَ نَفْسَهُ فِيهَا، سَفْكَ الدَّمِ الْحَرَامِ بِغَيْرِ حِلِّهِ.

البخاري

DAY 197

'Uthmān ibn Abī Rawwād reported that he heard al-Zuhrī say: "I entered in on Anas ibn Mālik, while he was in Damascus, and found him crying, and so I asked him: 'Why are you crying?' He said: 'Of the thing that I witnessed, I do not know anything except this prayer but even this prayer has now been neglected'."

(al-Bukhārī)

DAY 198

It is related from Qays that 'Amr ibn al-'Āṣ was walking one day with a few of his students when they passed by a swollen, dead mule, so he said: "By Allah! That one of you eats of this until his belly is full is better for him than consuming the flesh of a Muslim."

(Al-Bukhārī, *al-Adab al-Mufrad*)

اليوم ١٩٧

عَنْ عُثْمَانَ بْنِ أَبِي رَوَّادٍ، قَالَ: سَمِعْتُ الزُّهْرِيَّ يَقُولُ: دَخَلْتُ عَلَىٰ أَنَسِ بْنِ مَالِكٍ بِدِمَشْقَ وَهُوَ يَبْكِي، فَقُلْتُ: مَا يُبْكِيكَ؟ فَقَالَ: لَا أَعْرِفُ شَيْئًا مِمَّا أَدْرَكْتُ إِلَّا هَذِهِ الصَّلَاةَ، وَهَذِهِ الصَّلَاةُ قَدْ ضُيِّعَتْ.

البخاري

اليوم ١٩٨

عَنْ قَيْسٍ قَالَ: كَانَ عَمْرُو بْنُ الْعَاصِ، يَسِيرُ مَعَ نَفَرٍ مِنْ أَصْحَابِهِ، فَمَرَّ عَلَىٰ بَغْلٍ مَيِّتٍ قَدِ انْتَفَخَ، فَقَالَ: وَاللَّهِ، لأَنْ يَأْكُلَ أَحَدُكُمْ هَذَا حَتَّىٰ يَمْلأَ بَطْنَهُ، خَيْرٌ مِنْ أَنْ يَأْكُلَ لَحْمَ مُسْلِمٍ.

البخاري، الأدب المفرد

DAY 199

ʿAbdullāh ibn Abī al-Hudhayl related that ʿAbdullāh ibn Masʿūd, along with other people, went to visit someone who was sick and, while there, one of them who went with him started looking at a woman of the house, so Ibn Masʿūd said to him: "That your eyes both pop out is better than what you are doing."

(Al-Bukhārī, *al-Adab al-Mufrad*)

DAY 200

Ṣafwān ibn Muḥriz said: "I hosted Jundub al-Bajalī and, while at my house, I heard him say: 'The example of the one who admonishes people and forgets himself is like that of a lamp, it shines for people to allow them to see the way but burns itself in the process'."

(Aḥmad)

اليوم
١٩٩

عَنْ عَبْدِ اللَّهِ بْنِ أَبِي الْهُذَيْلِ قَالَ: دَخَلَ عَبْدُ اللَّهِ بْنُ مَسْعُودٍ عَلَى مَرِيضٍ يَعُودُهُ، وَمَعَهُ قَوْمٌ، وَفِي الْبَيْتِ امْرَأَةٌ، فَجَعَلَ رَجُلٌ مِنَ الْقَوْمِ يَنْظُرُ إِلَى الْمَرْأَةِ، فَقَالَ لَهُ عَبْدُ اللَّهِ: لَوِ انْفَقَأَتْ عَيْنُكَ كَانَ خَيْرًا لَكَ.

البخاري، الأدب المفرد

اليوم
٢٠٠

صَفْوَانُ بْنُ مُحْرِزٍ، قَالَ: نَزَلَ عَلَيَّ جُنْدُبٌ الْبَجَلِيُّ، فَسَمِعْتُهُ يَقُولُ: مَثَلُ الَّذِي يَعِظُ النَّاسَ وَيَنْسَى نَفْسَهُ مَثَلُ الْمِصْبَاحِ يُضِيءُ لِغَيْرِهِ وَيَحْرِقُ نَفْسَهُ.

أحمد

DAY
201

ʿAbdullāh ibn Masʿūd said: "I presume that a man forgets the knowledge he has learnt due to the sins he commits."

(Abū Khaythamah, *Kitāb al-ʿIlm*)

DAY
202

Al-Aswad reported that ʿAbdullāh ibn Masʿūd said: "The believer sees his sins as if they are on the precipice of a mountain, he fears they may fall on him while the immoral person sees his sins as if they were flies on his nose which he just waves away and they fly away."

(Aḥmad)

اليوم
٢٠١

قَالَ عَبْدُ اللَّهِ: إِنِّي لَأَحْسَبُ الرَّجُلَ يَنْسَى الْعِلْمَ كَانَ يَعْلَمُهُ لِلْخَطِيئَةِ يَعْمَلُهَا.

أبو خيثمة، كتاب العلم

اليوم
٢٠٢

عَنْ الْأَسْوَدِ قَالَ: قَالَ عَبْدُ اللَّهِ: إِنَّ الْمُؤْمِنَ يَرَى ذُنُوبَهُ كَأَنَّهُ فِي أَصْلِ جَبَلٍ يَخَافُ أَنْ يَقَعَ عَلَيْهِ وَإِنَّ الْفَاجِرَ يَرَى ذُنُوبَهُ كَذُبَابٍ وَقَعَ عَلَى أَنْفِهِ فَقَالَ بِهِ هَكَذَا فَطَارَ.

أحمد

DAY
203

Anas reported that Salmān al-Fārisī fell ill and, when he visited him, he found him weeping, so he asked him: "Why are you weeping, O my brother, are you not one of the Companions of the Messenger of Allah, Allah bless him and grant him peace? Are you not this? Are you not that?" So Salmān said: "I am not weeping due to either of two things: out of greed for this world or dislike of the next. However, the Messenger of Allah, Allah bless him and grant him peace, entrusted me with something, and I think I have betrayed that?" "What was it that he entrusted you with?" he asked. Salmān said: "He entrusted me that it is enough for one [in this world] to have like the provision of a rider [who is travelling by]. And I do not see except that I have violated that. As for you, O Saʿd, fear Allah when you judge between people, when you divide [estates or wealth] and when you are about to decide something." Thabit said: "It has reached me that, when he died, he left only twenty odd silver pieces which he had received from the public treasury."

(Ibn Mājah)

اليوم
٢٠٣

عَنْ أَنَسٍ قَالَ: اشْتَكَى سَلْمَانُ فَعَادَهُ سَعْدُ فَرَءاهُ يَبْكِي، فَقَالَ لَهُ سَعْدٌ: مَا يُبْكِيكَ يَا أَخِي أَلَيْسَ قَدْ صَحِبْتَ رَسُولَ اللَّهِ صَلَّى اللَّهُ عَلَيْهِ وَسَلَّمَ؟ أَلَيْسَ أَلَيْسَ؟ قَالَ سَلْمَانُ: مَا أَبْكِي وَاحِدَةً مِنَ اثْنَتَيْنِ مَا أَبْكِي ضِنًّا لِلدُّنْيَا وَلَا كَرَاهِيَةً لِلْآخِرَةِ وَلَكِنْ رَسُولُ اللَّهِ صَلَّى اللَّهُ عَلَيْهِ وَسَلَّمَ عَهِدَ إِلَيَّ عَهْدًا فَمَا أُرَانِي إِلَّا قَدْ تَعَدَّيْتُ قَالَ: وَمَا عَهِدَ إِلَيْكَ؟ قَالَ عَهِدَ إِلَيَّ أَنَّهُ يَكْفِي أَحَدَكُمْ مِثْلُ زَادِ الرَّاكِبِ وَلَا أُرَانِي إِلَّا قَدْ تَعَدَّيْتُ وَأَمَّا أَنْتَ يَا سَعْدُ فَاتَّقِ اللَّهَ عِنْدَ حُكْمِكَ إِذَا حَكَمْتَ وَعِنْدَ قَسْمِكَ إِذَا قَسَمْتَ وَعِنْدَ هَمِّكَ إِذَا هَمَمْتَ. قَالَ ثَابِتٌ: فَبَلَغَنِي أَنَّهُ مَا تَرَكَ إِلَّا بِضْعَةً وَعِشْرِينَ دِرْهَمًا مِنْ نَفَقَةٍ كَانَتْ عِنْدَهُ.

إبن ماجه

DAY
204

Abū Hurayrah said: "There is no good in excessive talk."

(Ibn Abī Shaybah, *al-Muṣannaf*)

DAY
205

Ismāʿīl ibn Umayyah reported that ʿUmar ibn al-Khaṭṭāb said: "Indeed, there is in solitude ease and comfort from the evil companions."

(Wakīʿ ibn al-Jarrāḥ, *Kitāb al-Zuhd*)

اليوم ٢٠٤

عَنْ أَبِي هُرَيْرَةَ قَالَ: لَا خَيْرَ فِي فُضُولِ الْكَلَامِ.

ابن أبي شيبة ، المصنّف

اليوم ٢٠٥

عَنْ إِسْمَاعِيلَ بْنِ أُمَيَّةَ قَالَ: قَالَ عُمَرُ بْنُ الْخَطَّابِ: إِنَّ فِي الْعُزْلَةِ رَاحَةً مِنْ خِلَاطِ السُّوءِ.

وكيع بن الجرَّاح ، كتاب الزهد

DAY 206

Maysarah al-Nahdī reported that ʿAlī ibn Abī Ṭālib passed by a group of people who were playing chess, so he said to them: "(What are these statues unto which you are cleaving?)."

(Ibn Abī Shaybah, *al-Muṣannaf*)

DAY 207

Ibrāhīm al-Taymī related from his father who said: "We were sitting with ʿUmar ibn al-Khaṭṭāb when a man came in and this prompted another man to start praising him in his presence. So ʿUmar said: 'You have killed the man, may Allah kill you! You praise him in his face about his religion!'"

(Ibn Abī Shaybah, *al-Muṣannaf*)

اليوم ٢٠٦

عَنْ مَيْسَرَةَ النَّهْدِيِّ، قَالَ: مَرَّ عَلِيٌّ عَلَى قَوْمٍ يَلْعَبُونَ بِالشِّطْرَنْجِ، فَقَالَ: ﴿مَا هَٰذِهِ ٱلتَّمَاثِيلُ ٱلَّتِيٓ أَنتُمْ لَهَا عَٰكِفُونَ﴾.

ابن أبي شيبة، المصنَّف

اليوم ٢٠٧

عَنْ إِبْرَاهِيمَ التَّيْمِيِّ، عَنْ أَبِيهِ قَالَ: كُنَّا قُعُودًا عِنْدَ عُمَرَ بْنِ الْخَطَّابِ، فَدَخَلَ عَلَيْهِ رَجُلٌ فَسَلَّمَ عَلَيْهِ، فَأَثْنَى عَلَيْهِ رَجُلٌ مِنَ الْقَوْمِ فِي وَجْهِهِ، فَقَالَ له عُمَرُ: عَقَرْتَ الرَّجُلَ عَقَرَكَ اللَّهُ، تُثْنِي عَلَيْهِ فِي وَجْهِهِ فِي دِينِهِ.

ابن أبي شيبة، المصنَّف

DAY 208

Sufyān related that ʿUmar asked Kaʿb: "Who are the masters of knowledge?" He said: "Those who practise what they know." He asked him again: "So what has taken knowledge out of the hearts of the savants?" He said: "Greed!"

(al-Dārimī)

DAY 209

Abū Idrīs related that he heard Abū al-Dardā' say: "Shall I not tell you about that which is better for you than giving alms and fasting? It is reconciling between people; verily, rancour is the eraser [of the *Dīn*].""

(Al-Bukhārī, *al-Adab al-Mufrad*)

اليوم ٢٠٨

عَنْ سُفْيَانَ أَنَّ عُمَرَ قَالَ لِكَعْبٍ: مَنْ أَرْبَابُ الْعِلْمِ؟ قَالَ: الَّذِينَ يَعْمَلُونَ بِمَا يَعْلَمُونَ. قَالَ: فَمَا أَخْرَجَ الْعِلْمَ مِنْ قُلُوبِ الْعُلَمَاءِ؟ قَالَ: الطَّمَعُ!

الدَّارمي

اليوم ٢٠٩

روى أَبُو إِدْرِيسَ أَنَّهُ سَمِعَ أَبَا الدَّرْدَاءِ يَقُولُ: أَلَا أُحَدِّثُكُمْ بِمَا هُوَ خَيْرٌ لَكُمْ مِنَ الصَّدَقَةِ وَالصِّيَامِ؟ صَلَاحُ ذَاتِ الْبَيْنِ، أَلَا وَإِنَّ الْبُغْضَةَ هِيَ الْحَالِقَةُ.

البخاري، الأدب المفرد

DAY 210

It is reported that Muʿādh ibn Jabal said: "When you love a brother, do not wrangle with him, do not treat him badly and do not spy around about him, for you may fall upon an enemy of his who may say something which is false about him and thus cause a rift between you two."

(Al-Bukhārī, *al-Adab al-Mufrad*)

DAY 211

It is reported that ʿAbdullāh ibn ʿAbbās said: "When you are about to mention the faults of your companion, remember your own faults."

(Aḥmad)

اليوم ٢١٠

عَنْ مُعَاذِ بْنِ جَبَلٍ أَنَّهُ قَالَ: إِذَا أَحْبَبْتَ أَخًا فَلاَ تُمَارِهِ وَلاَ تُشَارِّهِ وَلاَ تَسْأَلْ عَنْهُ، فَعَسَى أَنْ تُوَافِيَ لَهُ عَدُوًّا فَيُخْبِرَكَ بِمَا لَيْسَ فِيهِ، فَيُفَرِّقَ بَيْنَكَ وَبَيْنَهُ.

ابن أبي شيبة، المصنَّف

اليوم ٢١١

عَنِ ابْنِ عَبَّاسٍ قَالَ: إِذَا أَرَدْتَ أَنْ تَذْكُرَ عُيُوبَ صَاحِبِكَ فَاذْكُرْ عُيُوبَ نَفْسِكَ.

أحمد

DAY 212

Abū al-Aḥwas reported that ʿAbdullāh ibn Masʿūd said: "The meanest of the believer's character traits is obscenity."

(Ibn Abī Shaybah, *al-Muṣannaf*)

DAY 213

Abū Maʿmar reported that Abū Bakr al-Ṣiddīq said: "He has disbelieved in Allah the one who claims an unknown lineage or disavows a lineage even when it is exact."

(Ibn Abī Shaybah, *al-Muṣannaf*)

اليوم ٢١٢

عَنْ أَبِي الأَحْوَصِ عَنْ عَبْدِ اللَّهِ قَالَ: أَلأَمُ أَخْلَاقِ الْمُؤْمِنِ: الْفُحْشُ.

ابن أبي شيبة ، المصنَّف

اليوم ٢١٣

عَنْ أَبِي مَعْمَرٍ قَالَ: قَالَ أَبُو بَكْرٍ: كَفَرَ بِاللَّهِ مَنِ ادَّعَى نَسَبًا لَا يُعْلَمُ، وَتَبَرَّأَ مِنْ نَسَبٍ، وَإِنْ دَقَّ.

ابن أبي شيبة ، المصنَّف

DAY 214

Maymūn ibn Abī Shabīb reported that ʿUmar ibn al-Khaṭṭāb said: "You will not reach the true nature of faith until you abstain from lying when you are jesting."

(Ibn Abī Shaybah, *al-Muṣannaf*)

DAY 215

It is reported that ʿAbdullāh ibn Masʿūd said: "Lying is not good either in times of seriousness or times of jest; nor is it good that one promises something to his child and then breaks his promise."

(Al-Bukhārī, *al-Adab al-Mufrad*)

اليوم ٢١٤

عَنْ مَيْمُونِ بْنِ أَبِي شَبِيبٍ عَنْ عُمَرَ قَالَ: لاَ تَبْلُغُ حَقِيقَةَ الإِيمَانِ حَتَّى تَدَعَ الْكَذِبَ فِي الْمِزَاحِ.

ابن أبي شيبة، المصنَّف

اليوم ٢١٥

عَنْ عَبْدِ اللهِ قَالَ: لاَ يَصْلُحُ الْكَذِبُ فِي جِدٍّ وَلاَ هَزْلٍ، وَلاَ أَنْ يَعِدَ أَحَدُكُمْ وَلَدَهُ شَيْئًا ثُمَّ لاَ يُنْجِزُ لَهُ.

البخاري، الأدب المفرد

DAY 216

Rajā' ibn Ḥayawah related that Abū al-Darda' gathered the people of Damascus and said the following to them: "Hear this from a brother who wishes you well: Why do you amass that which you do not consume, hope for that which you will never attain and build that which you shall not inhabit? Where are those who came before you? Those who amassed a great deal, hoped a lot and built strong buildings: what they had amassed has turned into nothing, their long hopes have turned to be mere delusions and their houses have become graves."

(Ibn Abī Shaybah, *al-Muṣannaf*)

DAY 217

Abū al-Aḥwaṣ reported that 'Abdullāh said: "With every happiness there is sorrow."

(Ibn Abī Shaybah, *al-Muṣannaf*)

اليوم ٢١٦

عَنْ رَجَاءِ بْنِ حَيْوَةَ قَالَ: جَمَعَ أَبُو الدَّرْدَاءِ أَهْلَ دِمَشْقَ، فَقَالَ: اسْمَعُوا مِنْ أَخٍ لَكُمْ نَاصِحٍ: أَتَجْمَعُونَ مَا لَا تَأْكُلُونَ، وَتُؤَمِّلُونَ مَا لَا تُدْرِكُونَ، وَتَبْنُونَ مَا لَا تَسْكُنُونَ، أَيْنَ الَّذِينَ كَانُوا مِنْ قَبْلِكُمْ، فَجَمَعُوا كَثِيرًا وَأَمَّلُوا بَعِيدًا وَبَنَوْا شَدِيدًا، فَأَصْبَحَ جَمْعُهُمْ بُورًا، وَأَصْبَحَ أَمَلُهُمْ غُرُورًا، وَأَصْبَحَتْ دِيَارُهُمْ قُبُورًا.

ابن أبي شيبة، المصنَّف

اليوم ٢١٧

عَنْ أَبِي الأَحْوَصِ قَالَ: قَالَ عَبْدُ اللهِ: مَعَ كُلِّ فَرْحَةٍ تَرْحَةٌ.

ابن أبي شيبة، المصنَّف

DAY 218

Shaqīq related that ʿUmar ibn al-Khaṭṭāb wrote the following: "This world is verdant and sweet. Whoever takes it while observing what is due in it shall be blessed in it; and whoever takes it otherwise shall be like someone who eats but he is never satiated."

(Ibn Abī Shaybah, *al-Muṣannaf*)

DAY 219

ʿArjafah al-Sulamī related that Abū Bakr al-Ṣiddīq said: "Weep and If you cannot, then feign [the state of the person who is] crying."

(Ibn Abī Shaybah, *al-Muṣannaf*)

اليوم ٢١٨

عَنْ شَقِيقٍ قَالَ: كَتَبَ عُمَرُ: إِنَّ الدُّنْيَا خَضِرَةٌ حُلْوَةٌ، فَمَنْ أَخَذَهَا بِحَقِّهَا كَانَ قَمِنًا أَنْ يُبَارَكَ لَهُ فِيهِ، وَمَنْ أَخَذَهَا بِغَيْرِ ذَلِكَ كَانَ كَالآكِلِ الَّذِي لاَ يَشْبَعُ.

ابن أبي شيبة، المصنَّف

اليوم ٢١٩

عَنْ عَرْفَجَةَ السُّلَمِيِّ قَالَ: قَالَ أَبُو بَكْرٍ: ابْكُوا فَإِنْ لَمْ تَبْكُوا فَتَبَاكَوْا.

ابن أبي شيبة، المصنَّف

DAY 220

Ṭāriq ibn Shihāb related that when 'Umar [ibn al-Khaṭṭāb] went to the Levant, the soldiers came to him and [saw that] he was wearing a loincloth, leather socks and a turban, holding his camel's head while it was treading on water. Those present said: "O Commander of the Believers! Will you meet army chiefs and Levantine patriarchs in this state?" And 'Umar replied: "Verily, we are people who were honoured by Islam and we are not going to get any honour through anything else apart from it."

(Ibn Abī Shaybah, *al-Muṣannaf*)

DAY 221

When the treasures of the allies of Chosroes were brought before 'Umar [ibn al-Khaṭṭāb], and he saw so much gold and silver that bedazzled the eye, he cried. The narrator adds that 'Abd al-Rahman exclaimed: "O Commander of the Believers! Why are you crying? This is a day of

اليوم ٢٢٠

عَنْ طَارِقِ بْنِ شِهَابٍ، قَالَ: لَمَّا قَدِمَ عُمَرُ الشَّامَ أَتَتْهُ الْجُنُودُ وَعَلَيْهِ إِزَارٌ وَخُفَّانِ وَعِمَامَةٌ وَهُوَ آخِذٌ بِرَأْسِ بَعِيرٍ يَخُوضُ الْمَاءَ، فَقَالُوا: يَا أَمِيرَ الْمُؤْمِنِينَ، تَلْقَاكَ الْجُنُودُ وَبَطَارِقَةُ الشَّامِ وَأَنْتَ عَلَى هَذِ الْحَالِ، فَقَالَ عُمَرُ: إِنَّا قَوْمٌ أَعَزَّنَا اللهُ بِالإِسْلَامِ فَلَنْ نَلْتَمِسَ الْعِزَّ بِغَيْرِهِ.

ابن أبي شيبة، المصنَّف

اليوم ٢٢١

عَنْ إِبْرَاهِيمَ بْنِ عَبْدِ الرَّحْمَنِ بْنِ عَوْفٍ قَالَ: لَمَّا أُتِيَ عُمَرُ بِكُنُوزِ آلِ كِسْرَى فَإِذَا مِنَ الصَّفْرَاءِ وَالْبَيْضَاءِ مَا يَكَادُ أَنْ يَحَارَ مِنْهُ الْبَصَرُ. قَالَ: فَبَكَى عُمَرُ عِنْدَ ذَلِك، قَالَ فَقَالَ عَبْدُ الرَّحْمَنِ: مَا يُبْكِيكَ يَا أَمِيرَ الْمُؤْمِنِينَ؟ إِنَّ هَذَا الْيَوْمَ يَوْمُ شُكْرٍ وَسُرُورٍ

gratitude, delight and joy." 'Umar responded: "No group of people has an abundance of these except that Allah cast enmity and hatred amongst them."

(Ibn Abī Shaybah, *al-Muṣannaf*)

DAY 222

Al-Ḥasan reported that 'Umar [ibn al-Khaṭṭāb] was once walking along with his son, 'Abdullāh ibn 'Umar when he saw a weak and frail girl who was repeatedly walking and then falling to the ground. 'Umar exclaimed: "What a poor girl! Who knows this girl?". His son submitted: "By Allah, she is one of your own girls." Astonishingly 'Umar asked: "Who is she?" His son explained: "She is my daughter." 'Umar said: "Woe unto you, O 'Abdullāh ibn 'Umar, you are killing her of malnutrition!" 'Abdullāh replied: "What can we do? You have deprived us of what you have." 'Umar looked at him and then said: "What I have? Why do you not gain a livlihood for your daughters as other people do? By Allah, I do not have for you anything except your due share [from the public treasury] just like the rest of other Muslims."

(Ibn Abī Shaybah, *al-Muṣannaf*)

وَفَرِح ، فَقَالَ عُمَرُ : مَا كَثُرَ هَذَا عِنْدَ قَوْمٍ إِلاَّ أَلْقَىٰ اللهُ بَيْنَهُمْ الْعَدَاوَةَ وَالْبَغْضَاء.

ابن أبي شيبة ، المصنَّف

اليوم
٢٢٢

عَنِ الْحَسَنِ قَالَ: كَانَ عُمَرُ يَمْشِي فِي طَرِيقٍ وَمَعَهُ عَبْدُ اللهِ بْنُ عُمَرَ فَرَأَىٰ جَارِيَةً مَهْزُولَةً تَطِيشُ مَرَّةً وَتَقُومُ أُخْرَىٰ فَقَالَ: هَا بُؤْسَ لِهَذِهِ هَاهْ ! مَنْ يَعْرِفُ تَيَّاهُ. فَقَالَ عَبْدُ اللهِ: هَذِهِ وَاللهِ إِحْدَىٰ بَنَاتِكَ. قَالَ: بَنَاتِي؟ قَالَ : نَعَم ! قَالَ: مَنْ هِيَ؟ قَالَ: بِنْتُ عَبْدِ اللهِ بْنِ عُمَرَ. قَالَ: وَيْلَكَ يَا عَبْدَ اللهِ بْنَ عُمَرَ، أَهْلَكْتَهَا هَزْلًا. قَالَ: مَا نَصْنَعُ؟ مَنَعْتَنَا مَا عِنْدَكَ. فَنَظَرَ إِلَيْهِ فَقَالَ: مَا عِنْدِي؟ عَزَّكَ أَنْ تَكْسِبَ لِبَنَاتِكَ كَمَا تَكْسِبُ الْأَقْوَامُ؟ لَا وَاللهِ مَا لَكَ عِنْدِي إِلَّا سَهْمُكَ مَعَ الْمُسْلِمِينَ.

ابن أبي شيبة ، المصنَّف

DAY
223

ʿUmar ibn al-Khaṭṭāb said in one of his sermons: "Take yourselves to task before you are called to account; assess yourselves before you are assessed; and be prepared for the Grand Assembly. Nothing would be concealed about you when your record would be presented."

(Ibn Abī Shaybah, *al-Muṣannaf*)

DAY
224

ʿUmar [ibn al-Khaṭṭāb] said: "Keep the company of those who repent often for they have the softests of hearts."

(Ibn Abī Shaybah, *al-Muṣannaf*)

اليوم ٢٢٣

عَنْ عُمَرَ بْنِ الْخَطَّابِ أَنَّهُ قَالَ فِي خُطْبَتِهِ: حَاسِبُوا أَنْفُسَكُمْ قَبْلَ أَنْ تُحَاسَبُوا وَزِنُوا أَنْفُسَكُمْ قَبْلَ أَنْ تُوزَنُوا وَتَزَيَّنُوا لِلْعَرْضِ الأَكْبَرِ يَوْمَ تُعْرَضُونَ لاَ تَخْفَى مِنْكُمْ خَافِيَةٌ.

ابن أبي شيبة ، المصنَّف

اليوم ٢٢٤

قَالَ عُمَرُ: جَالِسُوا التَّوَّابِينَ فَإِنَّهُمْ أَرَقُّ شَيْءٍ أَفْئِدَةً.

ابن أبي شيبة ، المصنَّف

DAY
225

ʿUmar [ibn al-Khaṭṭāb] said: "For me, had it not been for walking in the way of Allah, placing my forehead on the ground [in prayer] and keeping the company of people who pluck the most wholesome of speech like dates are plucked, then I would have wished to join Allah."

(Ibn Abī Shaybah, *al-Muṣannaf*)

DAY
226

ʿUmar [ibn al-Khaṭṭāb] said: "Whoever wants the truth, let him show himself."

(Ibn Abī Shaybah, *al-Muṣannaf*)

اليوم ٢٢٥

قَالَ عُمَرُ: لَوْلَا أنْ أَسِيرَ فِي سَبِيلِ اللهِ أَوْ أَضَعَ جَبِينِي لِلَّهِ فِي التُّرَابِ أَوْ أُجَالِسَ قَوْمًا يَلْتَقِطُونَ طَيِّبَ الْكَلَامِ كَمَا يُلْتَقَطُ التَّمْرُ، لَأَحْبَبْتُ أَنْ أَكُونَ قَدْ لَحِقْتُ بِاللَّهِ.

ابن أبي شيبة، المصنَّف

اليوم ٢٢٦

قَالَ عُمَرُ: مَنْ أَرَادَ الْحَقَّ فَلْيَنْزِلْ بِالْبِرَازِ، يَعْنِي يُظْهِرُ أَمْرَهُ.

ابن أبي شيبة، المصنَّف

DAY
227

Sufyān reported that ʿUmar [ibn al-Khaṭṭāb] wrote to Abū Mūsā [al-Ashʿarī]: "Verily, you will not obtain the works of the Afterlife through anything better than the renouncement of this world."

(Ibn Abī Shaybah, *al-Muṣannaf*)

DAY
228

ʿAlī ibn Abī Ṭālib, may Allah be well pleased with him, said: "Greed is a perpetual bondage."

(Al-Sharīf al-Raḍī, *Nahj al-Balāghah*)

اليوم ٢٢٧

عَنْ سُفْيَانَ قَالَ: كَتَبَ عُمَرُ إِلَى أَبِي مُوسَى: إِنَّكَ لَنْ تَنَالَ عَمَلَ الْآخِرَةِ بِشَيْءٍ أَفْضَلَ مِنَ الزُّهْدِ فِي الدُّنْيَا.

ابن أبي شيبة، المصنَّف

اليوم ٢٢٨

قَالَ عَلِيُّ بْنُ أَبِي طَالِبٍ: الطَّمَعُ رِقٌّ مُؤَبَّدٌ.

الشّريف الرَّضِيّ، نهج البلاغة

DAY 229

ʿUmar [ibn al-Khaṭṭāb] said: "Were a lamb to perish because it got lost by the banks of the Euphrates, I would be afraid that Allah may ask me about it."

(Ibn Abī Shaybah, *al-Muṣannaf*)

DAY 230

Ḥudhayfah [ibn al-Yamān] related the following: "I entered in on ʿUmar [ibn al-Khaṭṭāb] and found him sitting on a log of wood, talking to himself. So I drew close to him and asked him: "O Commander of the Believers, what is worrying you?" He gestured with his hands and pointed at something. I asked him again: "What is worrying you? By Allah, if we saw you doing anything wrong, we would set you right." He replied: "By Allah, besides Whom there is no other god, would you set me right if you

اليوم ٢٢٩

قَالَ عُمَرُ: لَوْ هَلَكَ حَمْلٌ مِنْ وَلَدِ الضَّأْنِ ضَيَاعًا بِشَاطِئِ الْفُرَاتِ خَشِيتُ أَنْ يَسْأَلَنِي اللهُ عَنْهُ.

ابن أبي شيبة، المصنَّف

اليوم ٢٣٠

عَنْ حُذَيْفَةَ قَالَ: دَخَلْتُ عَلَى عُمَرَ وَهُوَ قَاعِدٌ عَلَى جِذْعٍ فِي دَارِهِ وهو يُحَدِّث نَفْسَهُ، فدَنَوتُ منه فقُلتُ: مَا الذي أهمَّكَ يَا أميرُ المُؤمِنِينَ؟ فقال عمر: هكذا بيده - وأشارَ بِهَا. قلتُ: مَا الَّذي يُهِمُّك؟ واللهِ لَوْ رَأَيْنَا مِنْكَ أمرًا نُنكِرُهُ لَقَوَّمْنَاكَ. فَقَالَ عُمَرُ: ءاللهِ لا إِلهَ إِلَّا هُوَ، لو رَأَيتُمْ مِنِّي أَمرًا تُنْكِرُونَهُ لقَوَّمْتُمُوهُ؟

see any wrongdoing from me?" I told him: "By Allah besides Whom there is no other god, if we find you doing anything wrong, we would set you right." This delighted 'Umar a great deal and so he said: "All praise be to Allah Who made among you - the Prophet's Companions - those who would set me right if they saw anything wrong from me."

(Ibn Abī Shaybah, *al-Muṣannaf*)

DAY
231

'Alī [ibn Abī Ṭālib] said: "Blessed are all the anonymous servants who know people but who are not known by them, those known by Allah Who bestow on them His good pleasure. Those are the lamps of guidance from whom Allah removes every dark sedition and enters in His tremendous mercy. Those are not tattlers who announce other people's secrets nor are they harsh or show-offs."

(Ibn Abī Shaybah, *al-Muṣannaf*)

فَقُلتُ: ءاللهِ الَّذي لا إلهَ إلاّ هُوَ، لو رَأينا مِنكَ أمْرًا نُنكِرُهُ لقَوَّمْناكَ، ففَرِحَ بذلكَ فرحًا شَدِيدًا، وقالَ الحمْدُ للهِ الَّذي جَعَلَ فِيْكُمْ - أَصْحابَ مُحَمَّدٍ - مَنْ الَّذي إذا رأىٰ مِنِّي أمرًا يُنكِرُهُ قوَّمَنِي.

ابن أبي شيبة، المصنَّف

اليوم
٢٣١

قَالَ عَلِيٌّ: طُوبىٰ لِكُلِّ عَبْدٍ نُومَةٍ عَرَفَ النَّاسَ وَلَمْ يَعْرِفْهُ النَّاسُ، وَعَرَفَهُ اللهُ مِنْهُ بِرِضْوَانٍ، أُولَئِكَ مَصَابِيحُ الْهُدىٰ، يُجْلي عَنْهُمْ كُلَّ فِتْنَةٍ مُظْلِمَةٍ وَيُدْخِلُهُمُ اللهُ فِي رَحْمَتِهِ، لَيْسَ أُولئِكَ بِالْمَذَايِيعِ الْبُذْرِ وَلاَ بِالْجُفَاةِ الْمُرَائِينَ.

ابن أبي شيبة، المصنَّف

DAY 232

ʿAṭāʾ ibn Abī Rabāḥ related that whenever ʿAlī ibn Abī Ṭālib dispatched a military expedition, he appointed a man as its leader and then advised him thus: "I counsel you to hold fast to Godfearingness, [and it is] inevitable that you will meet Him, nor is there any ultimate end except to Him; He further owns this life of the world in the Hereafter. Seek also that which brings you near to Allah, for what is with Allah is a tremendous substitute to the life of this world."

(Ibn Abī Shaybah, *al-Muṣannaf*)

DAY 233

ʿAbdullāh ibn Masʿūd said: "The limpidity of this world has gone and nothing of it remains except its turpidity, hence death is [in such a case] a gift for every Muslim."

(Ibn Abī Shaybah, *al-Muṣannaf*)

اليوم ٢٣٢

عَنْ عطَاءٍ بنِ أَبِي رَبَاح، قَالَ: كَانَ عَلِيُّ بْنِ أَبِي طَالِبٍ إذا بعث سَرِيَّةً وَلَّى أمْرَهَا رَجُلاً فَأَوْصَاهُ، فقَالَ: أُوْصِيكَ بِتَقْوَىٰ اللهِ، لاَ بُدَّ لَكَ مِنْ لِقَاءِهِ، وَلَا مُنْتَهَى لَكَ دُونَهُ وَهُوَ يَمْلِكُ الدُّنْيَا فِي الآخِرَةِ. وَعَلَيْكَ بِالَّذِي يُقَرِّبُكَ إِلَى اللهِ فَإِنَّ فِيمَا عِنْدَ اللهِ خَلَفًا مِنَ الدُّنْيَا.

ابن أبي شيبة، المصنَّف

اليوم ٢٣٣

قَالَ عَبْدُ اللهِ بنِ مَسْعُودٍ: ذَهَبَ صَفْوُ الدُّنْيَا وَبَقِيَ كَدَرُهَا، فَالْمَوْتُ تُحْفَةٌ لِكُلِّ مُسْلِمٍ.

ابن أبي شيبة، المصنَّف

DAY 234

ʿAbdullāh ibn Masʿūd is reported to have said: "A person has enough knowledge if he has fear of Allah, while he has enough ignorance if he is conceited about his own works."

(Ibn Abī Shaybah, *al-Muṣannaf*)

DAY 235

ʿAbdullāh ibn Masʿūd is reported to have said: "Whoever wants the Hereafter will [inevitably] harm this world [of his]; and whoever wants this world will [inevitably] harm [his salvation in] the Hereafter. O people! Do cause harm to that which is evanescent for the sake of what is everlasting."

(Ibn Abī Shaybah, *al-Muṣannaf*)

اليوم
٢٣٤

عَنِ ابْنِ مَسْعُودٍ أَنَّهُ قَالَ: بِحَسْبِ الْمَرْءِ مِنَ الْعِلْمِ أَنْ يَخْشَى اللَّهَ وَبِحَسْبِهِ جَهْلًا أَنْ يُعْجَبَ بِعَمَلِهِ.

ابن أبي شيبة ، المصنَّف

اليوم
٢٣٥

عَنْ عَبْدِ اللَّهِ بْنِ مَسْعُود قَالَ: مَنْ أَرَادَ الآخِرَةِ أَضَرَّ بِالدُّنْيَا وَمَنْ أَرَادَ الدُّنْيَا أَضَرَّ بِالآخِرَةِ يَاقَوْمْ فَأَضِرُّوا بِالْفَانِي لِلْبَاقِي.

ابن أبي شيبة ، المصنَّف

DAY 236

ʿAbdullāh ibn Masʿūd said: "I wish I knew that Allah has forgiven one of my sins, after that I would not care which of the Children of Adam gave birth to me."

(Ibn Abī Shaybah, *al-Muṣannaf*)

DAY 237

ʿAbdullāh ibn Masʿūd said: "Verily, I do not fear for you unintentional mistakes; what I fear for you are deliberate sins. And verily, I do not fear for you that you think little of your works; what I fear for you is that you think that you have done a great deal of them."

(Ibn Abī Shaybah, *al-Muṣannaf*)

اليوم
٢٣٦

قَالَ عَبْدُ اللَّهِ: لَوَدِدْتُ أَنِّي أَعْلَمُ أَنَّ اللَّهَ غَفَرَ لِي ذَنْبًا مِنْ ذُنُوبِي وَإِنِّي لَا أُبَالِي أَيَّ وَلَدِ آدَمَ وَلَدَنِي.

ابن أبي شيبة، المصنَّف

اليوم
٢٣٧

قَالَ عَبْدُ اللَّهِ: إِنِّي لَا أَخَافُ عَلَيْكُمْ فِي الْخَطَإِ وَلَكِنِّي أَخَافُ عَلَيْكُمْ فِي الْعَمْدِ. إِنِّي لَا أَخَافُ عَلَيْكُمْ أَنْ تَسْتَقِلُّوا أَعْمَالَكُمْ وَلَكِنِّي أَخَافُ عَلَيْكُمْ أَنْ تَسْتَكْثِرُوهَا.

ابن أبي شيبة، المصنَّف

DAY
238

ʿAbdullāh ibn Masʿūd said: "Say [only] that which is good and you shall be known for it; and act on it [i.e. that which is good] and you shall become of the people of goodness; and do not be hasty or tattlers who divulge other's secrets."

(Ibn Abī Shaybah, *al-Muṣannaf*)

DAY
239

ʿAbdullāh ibn Masʿūd is reported to have said: "Seek knowledge and you shall become knowlegeable, and once you become knowlegeable, act on what you know."

(Ibn Abī Shaybah, *al-Muṣannaf*)

اليوم ٢٣٨

قَالَ عَبْدُ اللَّهِ: قُولُوا خَيْرًا تُعْرَفُوا بِهِ، وَاعْمَلُوا بِهِ تَكُونُوا مِنْ أَهْلِهِ، وَلَا تَكُونُوا عُجُلًا مَذَايِيعَ بُذْرًا.

ابن أبي شيبة، المصنَّف

اليوم ٢٣٩

عَنْ عَبْدِ اللَّهِ، قَالَ: تَعَلَّمُوا تَعَلَّمُوا، فَإِذَا عَلِمْتُمْ فَاعْمَلُوا.

ابن أبي شيبة، المصنَّف

DAY 240

ʿAbdullāh ibn Masʿūd said: "The peak of humility is to accept a place of less honour in a gathering and to first greet with the greeting of peace whomever you meet."

(Ibn Abī Shaybah, *al-Muṣannaf*)

DAY 241

ʿAbdullāh ibn Masʿūd said: "Enough wretchedness, or disappointment, for a man to spend the night while Satan has urinated in his ear, such that he reaches the morning without making remembrance of Allah."

(Ibn Abī Shaybah, *al-Muṣannaf*)

اليوم ٢٤٠

قَالَ عَبْدُ اللَّهِ : إِنَّ مِنْ رَأْسِ التَّوَاضُعِ أَنْ تَرْضَى بِالدُّونِ مِنْ شَرَفِ الْمَجْلِسِ وَأَنْ تَبْدَأَ بِالسَّلَامِ مَنْ لَقِيتَ .

ابن أبي شيبة ، المصنَّف

اليوم ٢٤١

قَالَ عَبْدُ اللَّهِ : كَفَى بِالْمَرْءِ مِنَ الشَّقَاءِ، أَوْ مِنَ الْخَيْبَةِ، أَنْ يَبِيتَ وَقَدْ بَالَ الشَّيْطَانُ فِي أُذُنِهِ فَيُصْبِحُ وَلَمْ يَذْكُرِ اللَّهَ.

ابن أبي شيبة ، المصنَّف

DAY 242

ʿAbdullāh ibn Masʿūd is reported to have said: "[People are of different categories: there is] the one who is prosperous in this world and also in the Hereafter; the one who is destitute in this world and also in the Hereafter; and the one who is prosperous in this world but destitute in the Hereafter, such that he gets a break and people shall get a break from him."

(Ibn Abī Shaybah, *al-Muṣannaf*)

DAY 243

ʿAbdullāh ibn Masʿud said: "Indeed, I detest the man who is idle: neither engaged in the occupations of this world nor in the occupations of the Afterlife."

(Ibn Abī Shaybah, *al-Muṣannaf*)

اليوم
٢٤٢

عَنْ عَبْدِ اللهِ بْنِ مَسْعُودٍ، قَالَ: مُوَسَّعٌ عَلَيْهِ فِي الدُّنْيَا مُوَسَّعٌ عَلَيْهِ فِي الآخِرَةِ مَقْتُورٌ عَلَيْهِ فِي الدُّنْيَا مَقْتُورٌ عَلَيْهِ فِي الآخِرَةِ مُوَسَّعٌ عَلَيْهِ فِي الدُّنْيَا مَقْتُورٌ عَلَيْهِ فِي الآخِرَةِ، مُسْتَرِيحٌ وَمُسْتَرَاحٌ مِنْهُ.

ابن أبي شيبة، المصنَّف

اليوم
٢٤٣

قَالَ عَبْدُ اللهِ: إِنِّي لَأَمْقُتُ الرَّجُلَ أَنْ أَرَاهُ فَارِغًا لَيْسَ فِي شَيْءٍ مِنْ عَمَلِ الدُّنْيَا وَلَا عَمَلِ الآخِرَةِ.

ابن أبي شيبة، المصنَّف

DAY
244

ʿAbdullah ibn Masʿūd said: "By Him besides Whom there is no other god, the believing servant is not given anything better than having a good opinion of Allah. And by Him besides Whom there is no other god, when the believing servant does have a good opinion of Allah, He will grant it to him, for indeed all goodness is in His Hand."

(Ibn Abī Shaybah, *al-Muṣannaf*)

DAY
245

ʿAbdullāh ibn Masʿūd said: "Check people at their deathbeds. If you see the servant die in a good state according to what you see, then expect good for him; but if you see him die in a bad state, according to what you see, then do fear for him. This is because if the servant is damned, even if people admire some of his

اليوم ٢٤٤

قَالَ عَبْدُ اللَّهِ: وَالَّذِي لَا إِلَهَ غَيْرُه، مَا أُعْطِيَ عَبْدٌ مُؤْمِنٌ مِنْ شَيْءٍ أَفْضَلَ مِنْ أَنْ يُحْسِنَ بِاللَّهِ ظَنَّهُ، وَالَّذِي لَا إِلَهَ غَيْرُهُ، لَا يُحْسِنُ عَبْدٌ مُؤْمِنٌ بِاللَّهِ ظَنَّهُ إِلَّا أَعْطَاهُ ذَلِكَ، فَإِنَّ الْخَيْرَ كُلَّهُ بِيَدِهِ.

ابن أبي شيبة، المصنَّف

اليوم ٢٤٥

قَالَ عَبْدُ اللَّهِ: انْظُرُوا النَّاسَ عِنْدَ مَضَاجِعِهِمْ، فَإِذَا رَأَيْتُمُ الْعَبْدَ يَمُوتُ عَلَى خَيْرِ مَا تَرَوْنَهُ فَارْجُوا لَهُ الْخَيْرَ، وَإِذَا رَأَيْتُمُوهُ يَمُوتُ عَلَى شَرِّ مَا تَرَوْنَهُ فَخَافُوا عَلَيْهِ فَإِنَّ الْعَبْدَ إِذَا كَانَ شَقِيًّا وَإِنْ أَعْجَبَ النَّاسَ بَعْضُ عَمَلِهِ قُيِّضَ لَهُ شَيْطَانٌ فَأَرْدَاهُ وَأَهْلَكَهُ

work, then a satan is sent to him to mislead and destroy him until the damnation which is destined for him overtakes him. But if he is felicitous, even if people dislike some of his works, then an angel is sent to him to guide and show him the right course until the felicity which is destined for him overtakes him."

(Ibn Abī Shaybah, *al-Muṣannaf*)

DAY
246

Abū'l-Dardā' said: "Those whose tongues are still moist with the rememberance of Allah shall enter Paradise laughing."

(Ibn Abī Shaybah, *al-Muṣannaf*)

حَتَّىٰ يُدْرِكَهُ الشَّقَاءُ الَّذِي كُتِبَ عَلَيْهِ، وَإِذَا كَانَ سَعِيدًا وَإِنْ كَانَ النَّاسُ يَكْرَهُونَ بَعْضَ عَمَلِهِ قُيِّضَ لَهُ مَلَكٌ فَأَرْشَدَهُ وَسَدَّدَهُ حَتَّىٰ تُدْرِكَهُ السَّعَادَةُ الَّتِي كُتِبَتْ لَهُ.

ابن أبي شيبة ، المصنَّف

اليوم
٢٤٦

عَنْ أَبِي الدَّرْدَاءِ قَالَ : إِنَّ الَّذِينَ لاَ تَزَالُ أَلْسِنَتُهُمْ رَطْبَةً مِنْ ذِكْرِ اللَّهِ يَدْخُلُونَ الْجَنَّةَ وَهُمْ يَضْحَكُونَ.

ابن أبي شيبة ، المصنَّف

DAY 247

Abū'l-Dardā' said to his son: "O my son! Let the mosque be your home for I heard the Messenger of Allah (blessings and peace be upon him) say: 'Mosques are the homes of the godfearing and whoever takes the mosque as his home, Allah guarantees for him comfort, mercy and safe crossing of the Bridge over Hell to Paradise'."

(Ibn Abī Shaybah, *al-Muṣannaf*)

DAY 248

Salmān [al-Fārisī] said: "When the servant raises his hands to ask Allah for something good, Allah is reticent to leave him empty-handed."

(Ibn Abī Shaybah, *al-Muṣannaf*)

اليوم ٢٤٧

قَالَ أَبُو الدَّرْدَاءِ لِابْنِهِ: يَا بُنَيِّ! لِيَكُنِ الْمَسْجِدُ بَيْتَكَ، فَإِنِّي سَمِعْتُ رَسُولَ اللهِ صَلَّى اللهُ عَلَيْهِ وَسَلَّمَ يَقُولُ: الْمَسَاجِدُ بُيُوتُ الْمُتَّقِينَ، فَمَنْ يَكُنِ الْمَسْجِدُ بَيْتَهُ ضَمِنَ اللهُ لَهُ بِالرَّوْحِ وَالرَّحْمَةِ وَالْجَوَازِ عَلَى الصِّرَاطِ إِلَى الْجَنَّةِ.

ابن أبي شيبة ، المصنَّف

اليوم ٢٤٨

عَنْ سَلْمَانَ، قَالَ: إِنَّ اللهَ يَسْتَحْيِي أَنْ يَبْسُطَ إِلَيْهِ عَبْدٌ يَدَيْهِ يَسْأَلُهُ بِهِمَا خَيْرًا فَيَرُدُّهُمَا خَائِبَتَيْنِ.

ابن أبي شيبة ، المصنَّف

DAY 249

Ḥumayd ibn Hilāl reported that ʿAbdullāh ibn ʿUmar used to said: "Leave that which has nothing to do with you; do not speak about that which does not concern you; and preserve your tongue just as you preserve your wealth."

(Ibn Abī Shaybah, *Muṣannaf*)

DAY 250

Abū Mūsa [al-Ashʿarī] is reported to have said: "Verily, what destroyed those who came before you are these gold and silver pieces and they will destroy you too."

(Ibn Abī Shaybah, *al-Muṣannaf*)

اليوم ٢٤٩

عَنْ حُمَيْدِ بْنِ هِلالٍ قَالَ: كَانَ عَبْدُ اللهِ بْنُ عَمْرٍو يَقُولُ: دَعْ مَا لَسْتَ مِنْهُ فِي شَيْءٍ وَلَا تَنْطِقْ فِيمَا لَا يَعْنِيكَ وَاخْزُنْ لِسَانَكَ كَمَا تَخْزُنُ نَفَقَتَكَ.

ابن أبي شيبة، المصنَّف

اليوم ٢٥٠

عَنْ أَبِي مُوسَىٰ قَالَ: إِنَّمَا أَهْلَكَ مَنْ كَانَ قَبْلَكُمْ هَذَا الدِّينَارُ وَالدِّرْهَمُ وَهُمَا مُهْلِكَاكُمْ.

ابن أبي شيبة، المصنَّف

DAY
251

Abū'l-Aswad reported that Abū Mūsā [al-Ash'arī] assembled all the memorisers of the Qur'ān according to different recitations and said: "Let no one enter in on you except those who have collected the Qur'ān." He said: "We entered in on him and we were about three-hundred men. He admonished us and said: "You are the Qur'ān experts of this land, and you are this and you are that, so let not the passage of time change you, making your hearts harden just as the hearts of the People of the Book grew hard."

(Ibn Abī Shaybah, *al-Muṣannaf*)

DAY
252

Ḥudhayfah [ibn al-Yamān] is reported to have said: "If Allah had no created beings who sinned in the past, He would have created other sinning beings whom He would then forgive on the Day of Judgement."

(Ibn Abī Shaybah, *al-Muṣannaf*)

اليوم ٢٥١

عن أَبِي الأَسْوَدِ قَالَ: جَمَعَ أَبُو مُوسَىٰ الْقُرَّاءَ فَقَالَ: لَا يَدْخُلَنَّ عَلَيْكُمْ إِلَّا مَنْ جَمَعَ الْقُرْآنَ. قَالَ: فَدَخَلْنَا زُهَاءَ ثَلَاثِمِائَةِ رَجُلٍ فَوَعَظَنَا وَقَالَ: أَنْتُمْ قُرَّاءُ هَـٰذَا الْبَلَدِ وَأَنْتُمْ فَلَا يَطُولَنَّ عَلَيْكُمُ الْأَمَدُ فَتَقْسُو قُلُوبُكُمْ كَمَا قَسَتْ قُلُوبُ أَهْلِ الْكِتَابِ.

ابن أبي شيبة، المصنَّف

اليوم ٢٥٢

عَنْ حُذَيْفَةَ أَنَّهُ قَالَ: لَوْ أَنَّهُ لَمْ يُمْسِ لِلَّهِ عَزَّ وَجَلَّ خَلْقٌ يَعْصُونَ فِيمَا مَضَىٰ لَخَلَقَ خَلْقاً يَعْصُونَ فَيَغْفِرَ لَهُمْ يَوْمَ الْقِيَامَةِ.

ابن أبي شيبة، المصنَّف

DAY
253

Abū Wā'il is reported to have said: "Allah protects the servant on the Day of Judgement and conceals him with His Hand and then asks him: "Do you know what is in here?" The servant would say: "Yes, O Lord!" Upon which Allah would say: "I make you a witness that I have forgiven you."

(Ibn Abī Shaybah, *al-Muṣannaf*)

DAY
254

It is reported from 'Abdullāh ibn Mas'ud that a man who had committed a sin came to him and so he asked him about what he had done. But he was then distracted from him and turned to the people who were with him to address them. When he looked again at that man, he saw that the man was crying. Upon which he said to him: "This is the right

اليوم
٢٥٣

عَنْ أَبِي وَائِلٍ قَالَ: إِنَّ اللهَ يَسْتُرُ الْعَبْدَ يَوْمَ الْقِيَامَةِ، فَيَسْتُرُهُ بِيَدِهِ، فَيَقُولُ: تَعْرِفُ مَا هَاهُنَا؟ فَيَقُولُ: نَعَمْ يَا رَبِ. فَيَقُولُ: أُشْهِدُكَ أَنِّي قَدْ غَفَرْتُ لَكَ.

ابن أبي شيبة ، المصنَّف

اليوم
٢٥٤

عَنْ عَبْدِ اللهِ بْنِ مَسْعُودٍ قَالَ: أَتَاهُ رَجُلٌ قَدْ أَلَمَّ بِذَنْبٍ فَسَأَلَهُ عَنْهُ، فَلَهَى عَنْهُ، وَأَقْبَلَ عَلَى الْقَوْمِ يُحَدِّثُهُمْ ، فَحَانَتْ إِلَيْهِ نَظْرَةٌ مِنْ عَبْدِ اللهِ، فَإِذَا عَيْنُ الرَّجُلِ تُهْرَاقُ، فَقَالَ: هَذَا أَوَانُ هَمِّكَ

moment for the concern you came to ask me about: Paradise has seven gates. All of which open and close except for the gate of repentance [which never closes and] which is under the charge of an angel; so strive in doing good works and do not despair."

(Ibn Abī Shaybah, *al-Muṣannaf*)

DAY 255

It is reported that ʿAbdullāh ibn Masʿūd said: "There is not a single instructor of good conduct except that he likes that his instruction is acted upon and Allah's instruction of good conduct is the Qur'ān."

(al-Dārimī)

مَا جِئْتَ تَسْأَلُنِي عَنْهُ: إِنَّ لِلْجَنَّةِ سَبْعَةُ أَبْوَابٍ كُلُّهَا تُفْتَحُ وَتُغْلَقُ غَيْرُبَابِ التَّوْبَةِ، مُوَكَّلٌ بِهِ مَلَكٌ، فَاعْمَلْ وَلَا تَيْأَسْ.

ابن أبي شيبة ، المصنَّف

اليوم
٢٥٥

عَنْ ابْنِ مَسْعُودٍ قَالَ: لَيْسَ مِنْ مُؤَدِّبٍ إِلَّا وَهُوَ يُحِبُّ أَنْ يُؤْتَى أَدَبُهُ وَإِنَّ أَدَبَ اللهِ الْقُرْآنُ.

الدّارمي

DAY 256

Iyās ibn ʿĀmir said: "ʿAlī ibn Abī Ṭālib held [one day] my hand and said: 'If you live [long enough then you shall see] that those who teach the Qur'ān are of three categories: one category consists of those who do it for the sake of Allah; one category consists of those who do it for the sake of argumentation and one category consists of those who do it for the sake of this world, and whoever seeks [this world] through it shall get it.'"

(al-Dārimī)

DAY 257

When his students came to visit him, ʿAbdullāh ibn Masʿūd asked them: "Do you sit with one another?" They replied: "Yes, we have not abandoned this practice." Then he asked

اليوم
٢٥٦

قَالَ إِيَاسُ بْنُ عَامِرٍ: أَخَذَ عَلِيُّ بْنُ أَبِي طَالِبٍ بِيَدِي ثُمَّ قَالَ إِنَّكَ إِنْ بَقِيتَ سَيَقْرَأُ الْقُرْآنَ ثَلاثَةُ أَصْنَافٍ: فَصِنْفٌ للهِ وَصِنْفٌ لِلْجِدَالِ وَصِنْفٌ لِلدُّنْيَا، وَمَنْ طَلَبَ بِهِ أَدْرَكَ.

الدارمي

اليوم
٢٥٧

قَالَ عَبْدُ اللهِ لِأَصْحَابِهِ حِينَ قَدِمُوا عَلَيْهِ: هَلْ تَجَالَسُونَ؟ قَالُوا: لَيسَ نَتْرُكُ ذاكَ. قَالَ: فَهَلْ تَزَاوَرُونَ؟ قَالُوا: نَعَمْ يَا أَبَا عَبْدِ الرَّحْمَنِ،

them: "Do you visit one another?" They said: "Yes, O Abū 'Abd al-Raḥmān, whenever one of us misses his brother for a while, he goes looking for him even as far as the end of Kufah". And so he said: "You shall be fine as long as you keep doing this."

(al-Dārimī)

DAY
258

Ibn 'Abbās said: "Are you not afraid to be chastised or swallowed up by the earth when you say [on equal footing]: 'the Messenger of Allah (blessings and peace be upon him) said and so-and-so said'".

(al-Dārimī)

إِنَّ الرَّجُلَ مِنَّا لَيَفْقِدُ أَخَاهُ فَيَمْشِي فِي طَلَبِهِ إِلَىٰ أَقْصَى الْكُوفَةِ حَتَّىٰ يَلْقَاهُ. قَالَ: فَإِنَّكُمْ لَنْ تَزَالُوا بِخَيْرٍ مَا فَعَلْتُمْ ذَلِكَ.

الدَّارمي

اليوم ٢٥٨

قَالَ ابْنُ عَبَّاسٍ: أَمَا تَخَافُونَ أَنْ تُعَذَّبُوا أَوْ يُخْسَفَ بِكُمْ أَنْ تَقُولُوا: قَالَ رَسُولُ اللَّهِ صَلَّىٰ اللهُ عَلَيْهِ وَسَلَّمَ وَقَالَ فُلَانٌ.

الدَّارمي

DAY
259

ʿAlī [ibn Abī Ṭālib] said: "Faith starts in the heart as a white dot, and the more faith increases the whiter it becomes until the whole heart becomes white. Hypocrisy, on the other hand, starts in the heart as a black dot, and the more hypocrisy increases the darker it becomes until the whole heart becomes black. By Him in Whose Hand is my soul! Were you to split the heart of the believer open, you would certainly find it white; and were you to split the heart of the hypocrite open, you would certainly find it black."

(Ibn Abī Shaybah, *al-Muṣannaf*)

DAY
260

It is reported that Abū Hurayrah said: "The weak believer is like a new soft shoot of a plant that is tossed up and down by the wind." The narrator asked him: "What about the strong

اليوم ٢٥٩

قَالَ عَلِيٌّ: الْإِيمَانُ يَبْدَأُ نُقْطَةً بَيْضَاءَ فِي الْقَلْبِ، كُلَّمَا ازْدَادَ الْإِيمَانُ ازْدَادَتْ بَيَاضًا حَتَّىٰ يَبْيَضَّ الْقَلْبُ كُلُّهُ. وَالنِّفَاقُ يَبْدَأُ نُقْطَةً سَوْدَاءَ فِي الْقَلْبِ، كُلَّمَا ازْدَادَ النِّفَاقُ ازْدَادَتْ سَوَادًا، حَتَّىٰ يَسْوَدَّ الْقَلْبُ كُلُّهُ، وَالَّذِي نَفْسِي بِيَدِهِ لَوْ شَقَقْتُمْ عَنْ قَلْبِ مُؤْمِنٍ لَوَجَدْتُمُوهُ أَبْيَضَ، وَلَوْ شَقَقْتُمْ عَنْ قَلْبِ مُنَافِقٍ لَوَجَدْتُمُوهُ أَسْوَدَ.

ابن أبي شيبة، المصنَّف

اليوم ٢٦٠

عَنْ أَبِي هُرَيْرَةَ قَالَ: مَثَلُ الْمُؤْمِنِ الضَّعِيفِ كَمَثَلِ الْخَامَةِ مِنَ الزَّرْعِ تُمِيلُهَا الرِّيحُ مَرَّةً وَتُقِيمُهَا مَرَّةً. قَالَ: قُلْتُ: فَالْمُؤْمِنُ الْقَوِيُّ؟

believer?" He said: "He is like a palm tree that provides its goodness at every moment, and there is also the same under its shade, and it is not swayed by the wind."

(Ibn Abī Shaybah, *al-Muṣannaf*)

DAY 261

It is reported that Abū Hurayrah said: "Faith is pure, and so when a person commits fornication, faith leaves him; but if he regrets what he has done and repents, faith comes back to him."

(Ibn Abī Shaybah, *al-Muṣannaf*)

DAY 262

Ibn 'Umar said: "Verily modesty and faith are bound together, so when one of them goes, the other one goes too."

(Ibn Abī Shaybah, *al-Muṣannaf*)

قَالَ: مِثْلُ النَّخْلَةِ تُؤْتِي أُكُلَهَا كُلَّ حِينٍ فِي ظِلِّهَا ذَلِكَ وَلَا تُمِيلُهَا الرِّيحُ.

ابن أبي شيبة، المصنَّف

اليوم ٢٦١

عَنْ أَبِي هُرَيْرَةَ قَالَ: الْإِيمَانُ نَزِهٌ، فَمَنْ زَنَا فَارَقَهُ الْإِيمَانُ، فَإِنْ لَامَ نَفْسَهُ وَرَاجَعَ، رَاجَعَهُ الْإِيمَانُ.

ابن أبي شيبة، المصنَّف

اليوم ٢٦٢

قَالَ ابْنُ عُمَرَ: إِنَّ الْحَيَاءَ وَالإِيمَانَ قُرِنَا جَمِيعًا، فَإِذَا رُفِعَ أَحَدُهُمَا رُفِعَ الآخَرُ.

ابن أبي شيبة، المصنَّف

DAY 263

It is reported that Ḥudhayfah said: "There are four kinds of hearts: the layered heart, that is the heart of the hypocrite; the overshadowed heart, and that is the heart of the unbeliever; the pure heart, and that is the heart of the believer; and the heart in which there is hypocrisy and faith. The latter is like an abscess, which is supplied by pus and blood; or it is like a tree which is irrigated by clean and dirty water and it is therefore affected by the water which has an overwhelming effect."

(Ibn Abī Shaybah, *al-Muṣannaf*)

DAY 264

It is reported that ʿAlī [ibn Abī Ṭālib] said: "Islam consists of a tripod: faith, the prayer and the community. Thus, no prayer is accepted without faith. So whoever has faith must

اليوم ٢٦٣

عَنْ حُذَيْفَةَ قَالَ: الْقُلُوبُ أَرْبَعَةٌ: قَلْبٌ مُصَفَّحٌ فَذَلِكَ قَلْبُ الْمُنَافِقِ، وَقَلْبٌ أَغْلَفُ فَذَلِكَ قَلْبُ الْكَافِرِ، وَقَلْبٌ أَجْرَدُ فَكَأَنَّ فِيهِ سِرَاجًا يُزْهِرُ فَذَاكَ قَلْبُ الْمُؤْمِنِ، وَقَلْبٌ فِيهِ نِفَاقٌ وَإِيمَانٌ فَمَثَلُهُ كَمَثَلِ قُرْحٍ يَمُدُّهَا قَيْحٌ وَدَمٌ وَمَثَلُهُ كَمَثَلِ شَجَرَةٍ يَسْقِيهَا مَاءٌ خَبِيثٌ وَمَاءٌ طَيِّبٌ فَإِنَّ مَا غَلَبَ غَلَبَ عَلَيْهِ.

ابن أبي شيبة ، المصنَّف

اليوم ٢٦٤

عَنْ عَلِيٍّ قَالَ: إِنَّ الْإِسْلَامَ ثَلَاثُ أَثَافٍ: الْإِيمَانُ وَالصَّلَاةُ وَالْجَمَاعَةُ. فَلَا تُقْبَلُ صَلَاةٌ إِلَّا بِالْإِيمَانِ، فَمَنْ آمَنَ صَلَّى

certainly pray and whoever prays must certainly keep within the community. And whoever leaves the community as much as a cubit has removed the noose of Islam from his neck."

(Ibn Abī Shaybah, *al-Muṣannaf*)

DAY 265

ʿAmmār [ibn Yāsir] is reported to have said: "Whoever combines three things has obtained faith: to rein in one's ego; to spend on others even when in possession of very little; and to give the greeting of peace to everyone."

(Ibn Abī Shaybah, *al-Muṣannaf*)

وَمَن صَلَّىٰ جامعَ ومَنْ فَارَقَ الجَماعَةَ قَيْدَ شِبْرٍ فقَدْ خَلعَ رِبْقَةَ الإِسْلَامِ مِنْ عُنُقِهِ.

ابن أبي شيبة ، المصنَّف

اليوم ٢٦٥

عَنْ عمَّارٍ قَالَ : ثَلاثٌ مَنْ جَمعَهُنَّ جَمعَ الإِيمَانَ: الإِنْصَافُ مِنْ نَفْسِكَ وَالإِنْفاقُ مِنَ الإِقْتَارِ وَبَذْلُ السَّلامِ لِلْعَالَمِ.

ابن أبي شيبة ، المصنَّف

DAY 266

Abū Bakr al-Ṣiddīq said: "If I were to catch a drunkard, I would love that Allah conceals him [such that others do not know about his drinking], and if I were to catch a thief, I would love that Allah conceals him [such that others do not know about his stealing]."

(Ibn Abī Shaybah, *al-Muṣannaf*)

DAY 267

Muʿādh ibn Jabal said: "The Child of Adam does not do any work that is likely to save him from Allah's chastisement more than the remembrance of Allah."

(Mālik, *Muwaṭṭa'*)

اليوم
٢٦٦

قال أَبُو بَكْرٍ الصِّدِّيق: لَوْ أَخَذْتُ شَارِبًا لَأَحْبَبْتُ أَنْ يَسْتُرَهُ اللَّهُ وَلَوْ أَخَذْتُ سَارِقًا لَأَحْبَبْتُ أَنْ يَسْتُرَهُ اللَّهُ.

ابن أبي شيبة ، المصنَّف

اليوم
٢٦٧

قَالَ مُعَاذُ بْنُ جَبَلٍ: مَا عَمِلَ ابْنُ آدَمَ مِنْ عَمَلٍ أَنْجَى لَهُ مِنْ عَذَابِ اللَّهِ مِنْ ذِكْرِ اللَّهِ.

ابن أبي شيبة ، المصنَّف

DAY 268

Sa'īd ibn Mawhab related that he went with Salmān [al-Fārisī] to visit a sick friend of his from Kindah. And Salmān said to him: "When Allah inflicts the believer with a tribulation and then relieves him of it, that would count as an expiation for his [past] sins and he would then be taken to task for any subsequent sins. When, on the other hand, Allah inflicts the impudent person with a tribulation and then relieves him of it, he is like a camel who has been fettered by its owners, and it does not know why they have done so, and then it is released by them and it does not know why they have done so either."

(Ibn Abī Shaybah, *al-Muṣannaf*)

اليوم
٢٦٨

عَنْ سَعِيدِ بْنِ مَوْهَبٍ قَالَ: انْطَلَقْت مَعَ سَلْمَانَ إِلَىٰ صَدِيقٍ لَهُ يَعُودُهُ مِنْ كِنْدَةَ، فَقَالَ: إِنَّ الْمُؤْمِنَ يُصِيبُهُ اللهُ بِالْبَلاَءِ ثُمَّ يُعَافِيهِ فَيَكُونُ كَفَّارَةً لِسَيِّئَاتِهِ وَيُسْتَعْتَبُ فِيمَا بَقِيَ وَإِنَّ الْفَاجِرَ يُصِيبُهُ اللهُ بِالْبَلاَءِ ثُمَّ يُعَافِيهِ فَيَكُونُ كَالْبَعِيرِ عَقَلَهُ أَهْلُهُ لاَ يَدْرِي لِمَ عَقَلُوهُ ثُمَّ أَرْسَلُوهُ فَلاَ يَدْرِي لِمَ أَرْسَلُوهُ.

ابن أبي شيبة، المصنَّف

DAY 269

Muʿādh said: "When Allah tests the servant with illness, He says to the angel on his left side: 'Stop recording [his bad deeds]' and to the angel on his right side: 'Write for my servant the good deeds he used to do'."

(Ibn Abī Shaybah, *al-Muṣannaf*)

DAY 270

ʿAbdullāh ibn Masʿūd said: "Verily, the pain [that the believing servant suffers] is not rewarded but it is an expiation of sins."

(Ibn Abī Shaybah, *al-Muṣannaf*)

اليوم ٢٦٩

عَنْ مُعَاذٍ قَال: إِذَا ابْتَلَى اللهُ الْعَبْدَ بِالسَّقَمِ قَالَ لِصَاحِبِ الشِّمَالِ ارْفَعْ وَقَالَ لِصَاحِبِ الْيَمِينِ اكْتُبْ لِعَبْدِي مَا كَانَ يَعْمَلُ.

ابن أبي شيبة ، المصنَّف

اليوم ٢٧٠

قَالَ عَبْدُ اللهِ بن مسعود: إِنَّ الْوَجَعَ لَا يُكْتَبُ بِهِ الأَجْرُ وَلَكِنْ تُكَفَّرُ بِهِ الْخَطَايَا.

ابن أبي شيبة ، المصنَّف

DAY 271

ʿĀʾishah said: "No person is pricked by a thorn or suffers anything more serious than that except that Allah removes his sins."

(Ibn Abī Shaybah, *al-Muṣannaf*)

DAY 272

Abū Wāʾil related that ʿAbdullāh ibn Masʿūd used to hold a session of exhortation for people every Thursday. Then a man said to him: "O Abū ʿAbd al-Raḥmān, I wish that you would hold such a session every day", to which he replied: "In truth, what prevents me from doing so is that I do not like to bore you; and indeed, I present exhortation to you as the Prophet, Allah bless him and grant him peace, used to present it to us, out of fear to bring boredom on us."

(al-Bukhārī)

اليوم ٢٧١

عَنْ عَائِشَةَ قَالَتْ: مَا شِيكَ امْرُؤٌ بِشَوْكَةٍ فَمَا فَوْقَهَا إِلاَّ حَطَّ اللَّهُ بِهَا عَنْهُ خَطَايَاهُ.

ابن أبي شيبة، المصنَّف

اليوم ٢٧٢

عَنْ أَبِي وَائِلٍ، قَالَ: كَانَ عَبْدُ اللَّهِ يُذَكِّرُ النَّاسَ فِي كُلِّ خَمِيسٍ، فَقَالَ لَهُ رَجُلٌ: يَا أَبَا عَبْدِ الرَّحْمَنِ، لَوَدِدْتُ أَنَّكَ ذَكَّرْتَنَا كُلَّ يَوْمٍ. قَالَ: أَمَا إِنَّهُ يَمْنَعُنِي مِنْ ذَلِكَ أَنِّي أَكْرَهُ أَنْ أُمِلَّكُمْ، وَإِنِّي أَتَخَوَّلُكُمْ بِالْمَوْعِظَةِ كَمَا كَانَ النَّبِيُّ صَلَّى اللَّهُ عَلَيْهِ وَسَلَّمَ يَتَخَوَّلُنَا بِهَا مَخَافَةَ السَّآمَةِ عَلَيْنَا.

البخاري

DAY
273

It is reported that ʿAbdullāh ibn ʿAbbās, may Allah be pleased with both father and son, said: "O Muslims! Why do you ask the People of the Book when the Book that was revealed to His Prophet, Allah bless him and grant him peace, is the most recent Revelation from Allah? You are still reciting it [as it was revealed] without any added embellishment while Allah has informed that the People of the Book have altered what Allah had sent down to them and changed the Book with their own hands, saying {*'This is from Allah Himself,' to buy a paltry price thereby*} [*al-Baqarah* 2: 79]. Does the knowledge that has come to you not stop you from asking them questions? By Allah! We have not seen any man from amongst them ask you about the Book that has been revealed to you."

(al-Bukhārī)

اليوم
٢٧٣

عَنْ عَبْدِ اللَّهِ بْنِ عَبَّاسٍ قَالَ: يَا مَعْشَرَ الْمُسْلِمِينَ! كَيْفَ تَسْأَلُونَ أَهْلَ الْكِتَابِ وَكِتَابُكُمُ الَّذِي أُنْزِلَ عَلَىٰ نَبِيِّهِ صَلَّىٰ اللَّهُ عَلَيْهِ وَسَلَّمَ أَحْدَثُ الأَخْبَارِ بِاللَّهِ، تَقْرَءُونَهُ لَمْ يُشَبْ، وَقَدْ حَدَّثَكُمُ اللَّهُ أَنَّ أَهْلَ الْكِتَابِ بَدَّلُوا مَا كَتَبَ اللَّهُ وَغَيَّرُوا بِأَيْدِيهِمُ الْكِتَابَ، فَقَالُوا: (هَٰذَا مِنْ عِندِ ٱللَّهِ لِيَشْتَرُوا۟ بِهِۦ ثَمَنًا قَلِيلًا ۖ)، أَفَلَا يَنْهَاكُمْ مَا جَاءَكُمْ مِنَ الْعِلْمِ عَنْ مُسَاءَلَتِهِمْ، لَا وَاللَّهِ مَا رَأَيْنَا مِنْهُمْ رَجُلًا قَطُّ يَسْأَلُكُمْ عَنِ الَّذِي أُنْزِلَ عَلَيْكُمْ.

البخاري

DAY
274

A woman asked 'Ā'ishah: "Should one of us make up the missed prayer after becoming pure from menstruation?" So she replied: "Do you belong to the Ḥarūriyyah sect [one of the Kharijite groups]? The Prophet, Allah bless him and grant him peace, never commanded us to do it."

(al-Bukhārī)

DAY
275

It is reported from 'Ā'ishah that she said: "The believing women used to pray the *Ṣubḥ* prayer with the Prophet (blessings and peace be upon him) wrapped up in their sheets and then after that return to their families without being recognized by anyone."

(Muslim)

اليوم ٢٧٤

سَأَلَتْ امْرَأَةٌ عَائِشَةَ: أَتَجْزِي إِحْدَانَا صَلَاتَهَا إِذَا طَهُرَتْ؟ فقالَتْ: أحَرُورِيَّةٌ أنْتِ؟ كُنَّا نَحِيضُ مَعَ النَّبِيِّ صَلَّىٰ اللهُ عَلَيْهِ وَسَلَّمَ فَلَا يَأْمُرُنَا بِهِ، أوْ قالَتْ: فَلَا نَفْعَلُهُ.

البخاري

اليوم ٢٧٥

عَنْ عَائِشَةَ قَالَتْ: كُنَّ نساءُ المُؤْمِناتِ يُصلِّينَ معَ النَّبيِّ صلَّىٰ اللهُ عليهِ وسلَّمَ صلاةَ الصُّبحِ، مُتلفِّعاتٍ بِمُروطِهِنَّ، ثمَّ يرجِعنَ إلىٰ أَهْلِهِنَّ، وما يَعرفُهُنَّ أحَدٌ.

مسلم

DAY 276

It is reported that ʿĀ'ishah (may Allah be well pleased with her) said: "What an evil thing that you have equated us [i.e. women] with dogs and donkeys [i.e. regarding that which nullifies the prayer]! It happened to me that the Messenger of Allah (blessings and peace be upon him) would be praying while I was lying down between him and the *qiblah*, and whenever he wanted to prostrate he touched my feet and I withdrew them [to make space for him to prostrate]."

(Aḥmad)

DAY 277

ʿUbayd ibn ʿUmayr reported that it reached ʿĀ'ishah that ʿAbdullāh ibn ʿAmr commanded women, when they take major ritual ablution (*ghusl*), to loosen their hair and so she said: "I am astonished that ʿAbdullāh ibn ʿAmr

اليوم ٢٧٦

عَنْ عَائِشَةَ قَالَتْ: بِئْسَمَا عَدَلْتُمُونَا بِالكَلْبِ وَالحِمَارِ، لَقَدْ رَأَيْتُنِي وَرَسُولُ اللهِ صَلَّى اللهُ عَلَيْهِ وَسَلَّمَ يُصَلِّي وَأَنَا مُضْطَجِعَةٌ بَيْنَهُ وَبَيْنَ القِبْلَةِ، فَإِذَا أَرَادَ أَنْ يَسْجُدَ غَمَزَ رِجْلَيَّ، فَقَبَضْتُهُمَا.

أحمد

اليوم ٢٧٧

عَنْ عُبَيْدِ بْنِ عُمَيْرٍ قَالَ بَلَغَ عَائِشَةَ أَنَّ عَبْدَ اللهِ بْنَ عَمْرٍو يَأْمُرُ النِّسَاءَ إِذَا اغْتَسَلْنَ أَنْ يَنْقُضْنَ رُءُوسَهُنَّ فَقَالَتْ: يَا عَجَبًا لِابْنِ

commands women, when they take major ritual ablution (*ghusl*), to loosen their hair; why does he not ask them to shave their hair too? I and the Messenger of Allah (blessings and peace be upon him) used to wash for major ritual purity from the same utensil and I did no more than pour water three times on my hair."

(Muslim)

DAY 278

It is reported that 'Urwah [ibn al-Zubayr] said to 'Ā'ishah: "I do not reckon that the one who does not go between Ṣafā and Marwah has done anything wrong, and I consider it insignificant if I do not go between them. And so she said: "O nephew! Evil is what you have said! The Messenger of Allah (blessings and peace be upon him) went between Ṣafā and Marwah as did the Muslims and so it has become something that should be emulated. Only in the pre-Islamic period when the rebellious ones invoked Manāt, they did not go between Ṣafā and Marwah. When Islam came,

عَمْرٍو هذا يَأْمُرُ النِّسَاءَ إِذَا اغْتَسَلْنَ أَنْ يَنْقُضْنَ رُءُوسَهُنَّ أَفَلَا يَأْمُرُهُنَّ أَنْ يَحْلِقْنَ رُءُوسَهُنَّ لَقَدْ كُنْتُ أَغْتَسِلُ أَنَا وَرَسُولُ اللهِ صَلَّى اللهُ عَلَيْهِ وَسَلَّمَ مِنْ إِنَاءٍ وَاحِدٍ وَلَا أَزِيدُ عَلَى أَنْ أُفْرِغَ عَلَى رَأْسِي ثَلَاثَ إِفْرَاغَاتٍ.

مسلم

اليوم ٢٧٨

عَنْ عُرْوَةَ قَالَ: قُلتُ لِعَائِشَةَ: ما أَرَى عَلَى أَحَدٍ لَمْ يَطُفْ بَيْنَ الصَّفَا وَالْمَرْوَةِ شيئًا، وَما أُبَالِي أَنْ لَا أَطُوفَ بَيْنَهُمَا. قَالَتْ: بِئْسَ ما قُلْتَ، يا ابْنَ أُخْتِي، طَافَ رَسولُ اللهِ صَلَّى اللهُ عَلَيْهِ وسلَّمَ، وَطَافَ المُسْلِمُونَ، فَكَانَتْ سُنَّةً وإِنَّمَا كانَ مَنْ أَهَلَّ لِمَنَاةَ الطَّاغِيَةِ الَّتِي بِالمُشَلَّلِ، لا يَطُوفُونَ بَيْنَ الصَّفَا وَالْمَرْوَةِ، فَلَمَّا كانَ

we asked the Prophet, blessings and peace be upon him, about it and Allah, glorified and exalted is He, revealed the following verse: [*Verily, Safa and Marwa[h] are sites of Allah's worship. So whoever makes pilgrimage to the Sacred House or the lesser visitation, there is no wrong or harm in making many a rounds between them*] (*al-Baqarah* 2: 158). Had it been as you contend, Allah would have said: [*There is no sin in making many a rounds between them*]."

(Muslim)

DAY 279

ʿAlī [ibn Abī Ṭālib] (may Allah be well pleased with him) said: "When the following verse was revealed: "*... and if you reveal what is in your hearts or conceal it, Allah shall reckon with you for it: He forgives whomever He wills, and punishes whomever He wills, and Allah has absolute power to do anything*" (*al-Baqarah* 2: 284), we were saddened. We said: one of us says something to himself and is taken to task for it, not knowing what Allah shall forgive and what He

الإِسْلَامُ سَأَلْنَا النَّبِيَّ صَلَّى اللهُ عَلَيْهِ وسلَّم عن ذلك؟ فأنْزَلَ اللهُ عَزَّ وَجَلَّ: (إِنَّ الصَّفَا وَالْمَرْوَةَ مِن شَعَائِرِ اللهِ فَمَنْ حَجَّ الْبَيْتَ أَوِ اعْتَمَرَ فَلَا جُنَاحَ عَلَيْهِ أَن يَطَّوَّفَ بِهِمَا)، ولو كَانَتْ كما تَقُولُ لَكَانَتْ: فلا جُنَاحَ عليه أنْ لا يَطَّوَّفَ بِهِمَا.

مسلم

اليوم
٢٧٩

قَالَ عَلِيُّ بْنُ أَبِي طَالِبٍ: لَمَّا نَزَلَتْ هَذِهِ الآيَةُ (وَإِن تُبْدُواْ مَا فِي أَنفُسِكُمْ أَوْ تُخْفُوهُ يُحَاسِبْكُم بِهِ اللَّهُ فَيَغْفِرُ لِمَن يَشَاءُ وَيُعَذِّبُ مَن يَشَاءُ وَاللَّهُ عَلَى كُلِّ شَيْءٍ قَدِيرٌ) الآيَةَ أَحْزَنَتْنَا. قُلْنَا يُحَدِّثُ أَحَدُنَا نَفْسَهُ فَيُحَاسَبُ بِهِ لا نَدْرِي مَا يُغْفَرُ مِنْهُ

shall not. And so this other verse was revealed which abrogated it: [*Allah does not tax any soul but what it can bear: it shall have all it earns, and but pay for what it commits. 'O Lord, take us not to task if we forget, or make an honest mistake...'*] (*al-Baqarah* 2: 286)."

(al-Tirmidhī)

DAY 280

It is related that 'Ā'ishah said: "The Messenger of Allah (blessings and peace be upon him) recited: [*It is He who has sent you down the Book: Some of its verses are unmistakably plain, which are the basis of the Book; while others are subtle of understanding between nuances. As for those in whose hearts is perverseness, they pursue only the subtle of it, seeking to sow doubts, and seeking to interpret it as they please while no one knows its true interpretation but Allah and those firmly grounded in its knowledge: they say, 'We believe in it, each of these kinds of verses is from our Lord.' Yet*

وَلَا مَا لَا يُغْفَرُ، فَنَزَلَتْ هَذِهِ الْآيَةُ بَعْدَهَا فَنَسَخَتْهَا (لَا يُكَلِّفُ ٱللَّهُ نَفْسًا إِلَّا وُسْعَهَا ۚ لَهَا مَا كَسَبَتْ وَعَلَيْهَا مَا ٱكْتَسَبَتْ ۗ رَبَّنَا لَا تُؤَاخِذْنَآ إِن نَّسِينَآ أَوْ أَخْطَأْنَا).

الترمذي

اليوم ٢٨٠

عَنْ عَائِشَةَ قَالَتْ: قَرَأَ رَسُولُ اللهِ صَلَّى اللهُ عَلَيهِ وَسَلَّمَ (هُوَ ٱلَّذِىٓ أَنزَلَ عَلَيْكَ ٱلْكِتَـٰبَ مِنْهُ ءَايَـٰتٌ مُّحْكَمَـٰتٌ هُنَّ أُمُّ ٱلْكِتَـٰبِ وَأُخَرُ مُتَشَـٰبِهَـٰتٌ ۖ فَأَمَّا ٱلَّذِينَ فِى قُلُوبِهِمْ زَيْغٌ فَيَتَّبِعُونَ مَا تَشَـٰبَهَ مِنْهُ ٱبْتِغَآءَ ٱلْفِتْنَةِ وَٱبْتِغَآءَ تَأْوِيلِهِۦ ۗ وَمَا يَعْلَمُ تَأْوِيلَهُۥٓ إِلَّا ٱللَّهُ ۗ وَٱلرَّٰسِخُونَ فِى ٱلْعِلْمِ يَقُولُونَ ءَامَنَّا بِهِۦ كُلٌّ مِّنْ

none remember and heed but those of insight and mind] (*Āl ʿImrān* 3: 7). And so, if you see those who dispute about it, then they are the ones meant by Allah, gloried and exalted is He, in these verses, and so beware of them."

(Aḥmad)

DAY 281

It is related that ʿĀ'ishah, may Allah be well pleased with her, said: "If anyone tells you that the Prophet (blessings and peace be upon him) concealed anything that he was commanded to communicate to others, then he has lied. Then she recited Allah's words (*O Messenger: Convey everything that has been sent down to you from your Lord*) [*al-Mā'idah* 5: 67]".

(al-Bukhārī)

عِندِ رَبِّنَاۗ وَمَا يَذَّكَّرُ إِلَّآ أُوْلُواْ ٱلۡأَلۡبَٰبِ)، فَإِذَا رَأَيْتُمُ الَّذِينَ يُجَادِلُونَ فِيهِ فَهُمُ الَّذِينَ عَنَى اللهُ عَزَّ وَجَلَّ فَاحْذَرُوهُمْ.

أحمد

اليوم
٢٨١

عَنْ عَائِشَةَ قَالَتْ: مَن حَدَّثَكَ أَنَّهُ صَلَّى اللهُ عَلَيْهِ وَسَلَّمَ كَتَمَ شَيْئًا مِمَّا أُمِرَ بِتَبلِيغِهِ فَقَدْ كَذَبَ، ثُمَّ قَرَأَتْ: (يَا أَيُّهَا الرَّسُولُ بَلِّغْ مَا أُنْزِلَ إِلَيْكَ مِنْ رَبِّكَ) [المائدة: ٦٧].

البخاري

DAY 282

It is related that 'Ā'ishah, may Allah be well pleased with her, said: "May Allah have mercy on the believing women who had migrated in the first phase. When Allah revealed, "*And let them pitch their head covers fast down over their collars...*" (*al-Nūr* 24: 31), they tore their sheets and made scarves out of them."

(al-Bukhārī)

DAY 283

'Ā'ishah, may Allah be well pleased with her, said: "After '*When the victorious help of Allah come...*' (*al-Naṣr* 110: 1) was revealed to him, the Messenger of Allah, blessings and peace be upon him, never prayed any prayer except that he said during it: "Glory be to You, O our Lord,. All praise is Yours; O Allah, forgive me."

(al-Bukhārī)

اليوم ٢٨٢

عَنْ عَائِشَةَ قَالَتْ: يَرحَمُ اللَّهَ نِسَاءَ المُهَاجِرَاتِ الأُوَّلَ، لَمَّا أَنْزَلَ اللَّهُ: (وَلْيَضْرِبْنَ بِخُمُرِهِنَّ عَلَىٰ جُيُوبِهِنَّ) شَقَّقْنَ أَكْنُفَ مُرُوطِهُنَّ فَاخْتَمَرْنَ بِهَا.

البخاري

اليوم ٢٨٣

عَنْ عَائِشَةَ قَالَتَ: ما صَلَّىٰ رسولُ اللَّهِ صَلَّىٰ اللَّهُ عَلَيْهِ وَسَلَّمَ صَلاةً بَعْدَ أَنْ نَزَلَتْ عليه: (إِذَا جَآءَ نَصْرُ ٱللَّهِ وَٱلْفَتْحُ) إِلَّا يَقُولُ فِيهَا: سُبْحَانَكَ رَبَّنَا وبِحَمْدِكَ، اللَّهُمَّ اغْفِرْ لِي.

البخاري

DAY 284

It is related that 'Ā'ishah, may Allah be well pleased with her, said: "The household of Muhammad, blessings and peace be upon him, never had their fill of wheat bread for three consecutive days since he came to Madinah and until he passed on."

(al-Bukhārī)

DAY 285

It is reported that 'Ā'ishah, may Allah be well pleased with her, said: "The Prophet (blessings and peace be upon him) was never given a choice between two things except that he chose the easiest of the two as long as he did not commit a sin by doing so, for he would be the farthest person from it if it was a sin; and by Allah, he never avenged himself for anything he was subjected to unless the sanctities of Allah were violated, for then he took revenge for Allah's sake."

(al-Bukhārī)

اليوم ٢٨٤

عَنْ عَائِشَةَ قَالَتْ: مَا شَبِعَ آلُ مُحَمَّدٍ صَلَّى اللَّهُ عَلَيْهِ وَسَلَّمَ مُنْذُ قَدِمَ الْمَدِينَةَ مِنْ طَعَامِ بُرٍّ ثَلَاثَ لَيَالٍ تِبَاعًا حَتَّى قُبِضَ.

البخاري

اليوم ٢٨٥

عَنْ عَائِشَةَ قَالَتْ: مَا خُيِّرَ النَّبِيُّ صَلَّى اللَّهُ عَلَيْهِ وَسَلَّمَ بَيْنَ أَمْرَيْنِ إِلَّا اخْتَارَ أَيْسَرَهُمَا مَا لَمْ يَأْثَمْ، فَإِذَا كَانَ الْإِثْمُ كَانَ أَبْعَدَهُمَا مِنْهُ، وَاللَّهِ مَا انْتَقَمَ لِنَفْسِهِ فِي شَيْءٍ يُؤْتَى إِلَيْهِ قَطُّ حَتَّى تُنْتَهَكَ حُرُمَاتُ اللَّهِ فَيَنْتَقِمُ لِلَّهِ.

البخاري

DAY 286

ʿAbdullāh ibn Masʿūd (may Allah be well pleased with him) said: "Faith ultimately culminates in scrupulousness; and the best [practice] of religion is that one's mind is never bereft of remembrance of Allah, glorious and majestic is He. And whoever accepts whatever Allah sends down from heaven to earth shall enter Paradise if Allah wills; and whoever desires Paradise without any lingering doubt, then let him not fear the rebuke of any censoring person [regarding religion]."

(Al-Bayhaqī, *al-Zuhd al-Kabīr*)

DAY 287

Ibn Masʿūd (may Allah be well pleased with him) said: "There shall come a time when, if one of you could find death to buy in exchange for a price, he would do so; and there

اليوم
٢٨٦

قَالَ ابْنُ مَسْعُودٍ: يَنْتَهِي الْإِيمَانُ إِلَى الْوَرَعِ، وَمِنْ أَفْضَلِ الدِّينِ أَنْ لَا يَزَالَ بَالُهُ غَيْرُ خَالٍ عَنْ ذِكْرِ اللهِ عَزَّ وَجَلَّ، وَمَنْ رَضِيَ بِمَا أَنْزَلَ اللهُ مِنَ السَّمَاءِ إِلَى الْأَرْضِ دَخَلَ الْجَنَّةَ إِنْ شَاءَ اللهُ، وَمَنْ أَرَادَ الْجَنَّةَ لَا شَكَّ فِيهَا فَلَا يَخَفْ فِي اللهِ لَوْمَةَ لَائِمٍ.

البيهقي، الزهد الكبير

اليوم
٢٨٧

قَالَ ابْنُ مَسْعُودٍ: إِنَّهُ سَيَأْتِي عَلَيْكُمْ زَمَانٌ لَوْ وَجَدَ فِيهِ أَحَدُكُمُ الْمَوْتَ يُبَاعُ بِثَمَنٍ لَاشْتَرَاهُ، وَإِنَّهُ سَيَأْتِي

shall come a time when a man would be envied for his lack of wealth and children just as he is envied today for his abundance of wealth and children."

(Abū Mas'ūd al-Mūṣilī, *Kitāb al-Zuhd*)

DAY 288

Abdullah ibn Mas'ūd (may Allah be well pleased with him) said: "This [Straight] Path is attended – it is attended by the satans – who call out: 'O slave of Allah, come here: this is the way' to bar [people] from the way of Allah; so hold fast to the rope of Allah for, indeed, the rope of Allah is the Qur'an." .

(al-Suyūṭī, *al-Durr al-Manthūr*)

عَلَيْكُمْ زَمَانٌ يُغْبَطُ فِيهِ الرَّجُلُ بِخِفَّةِ الْحَالِ كَمَا يُغْبَطُ فِيهِ الْيَوْمَ بِكَثْرَةِ الْمَالِ وَالْوَلَدِ.

أبو مسعود بن عمران، كتاب الزهد

اليوم ٢٨٨

عَنْ ابْنِ مَسْعُودٍ قَالَ: إِنَّ هَذَا الصِّرَاطَ مُحْتَضَرٌ تَحْضُرُهُ الشَّيَاطِينُ، يُنَادُونَ يَا عَبْدَ اللهِ هَلُمَّ هَذَا هُوَ الطَّرِيقُ لِيَصُدُّوا عَنْ سَبِيلِ اللهِ، فَاعْتَصِمُوا بِحَبْلِ اللهِ فَإِنَّ حَبْلَ اللهِ الْقُرْآنُ.

السيوطي، الدرُّ المنثور

DAY
289

'Umar ibn al-Khaṭṭāb (may Allah be well pleased with him) said: "O people! Seek the reward of your deeds solely from Allah, for whoever does so shall have inscribed for him the reward of his deeds as well as the reward of seeking his reward solely from Allah."

(al-'Aynī, *'Umdat al-Qārī*)

DAY
290

'Umar ibn al-Khaṭṭāb (may Allah be well pleased with him) said: "Whoever looks intently at the entrance hall of someone's house before being given permission to enter has committed an immoral act."

(al-Bukhārī, *al-Adab al-Mufrad*)

اليوم
٢٨٩

قَالَ عُمَرُ: يَا أَيُّهَا النَّاسُ إِحْتَسِبُوا أَعمَالَكُمْ فَإِنَّ مَنْ إِحْتَسَبَ عَمَلَهُ كُتِبَ لَهُ أَجْرُ عَمَلِهِ وَأَجْرُ حِسْبَتِهِ.

العيني، عُمْدةُ القاري

اليوم
٢٩٠

عَنْ عُمَرَ بْنِ الخَطَّابِ قَالَ: مَنْ مَلأَ عَيْنَيْهِ مِنْ قَاعَةِ بَيْتٍ قَبْلَ أَنْ يُؤْذَنَ لَهُ فَقَدْ فَسَقَ.

البخاري، الأدب المفرد

DAY 291

'Umar ibn al-Khaṭṭāb (may Allah be well pleased with him) said: "Uprightness is that you are steadfast in complying to commands and prohibitions and that you do not play fast and loose like foxes."

(al-Baghawī, *Tafsīr al-Baghawī*)

DAY 292

Abū al-Dardā' (may Allah be well pleased with him) said: "Worship Allah as if you see Him, and consider yourselves [already] among the dead; and know that a modicum [of wealth] which suffices you [from asking others] is much better than a great deal [of wealth] which distracts you; and realise also that righteousness never perishes and that sinning is never forgotten."

(Ibn Abī Shaybah, *al-Muṣannaf*)

اليوم ٢٩١

قَالَ عُمَرُ: الاِسْتِقَامَةُ أَنْ تَسْتَقِيمَ عَلَى الأَمْرِ وَالنَّهْيِ وَلَا تَرُوغُ رَوَغَانَ الثَّعَالِبِ.

البغوي، تفسير البغوي

اليوم ٢٩٢

قَالَ أَبُو الدَّرْدَاءِ: اعْبُدُوا اللهَ كَأَنَّكُمْ تَرَوْنَهُ وَعُدُّوا أَنْفُسَكُمْ مِنَ الْمَوْتَىٰ وَاعْلَمُوا أَنَّ قَلِيلًا يُغْنِيكُمْ خَيْرٌ مِنْ كَثِيرٍ يُلْهِيكُمْ وَاعْلَمُوا أَنَّ الْبِرَّ لَا يَبْلَىٰ وَأَنَّ الإِثْمَ لَا يُنْسَىٰ.

ابن أبي شيبة، المصنَّف

DAY 293

ʿAbdullāh ibn Masʿūd (may Allah be well pleased with him) urged his son: "O my dear son, weep upon remembering your sinful deeds."

(Wakīʿ ibn al-Jarrāḥ, *Kitāb al-Zuhd*)

DAY 294

ʿAlqamah related that ʿAbdullāh ibn Masʿūd (may Allah be well pleased with him) said: "The believer may commit a sin and, because of it, he suffers at his death so that it may serve as an expiation for his sin. And the wicked person may do a good deed and, because of it, he gets some relief at his death so that his good deed is rewarded in this world."

(Wakīʿ ibn al-Jarrāḥ, *Kitāb al-Zuhd*)

اليوم ٢٩٣

قَالَ عَبْدُ اللَّهِ لِابْنِهِ: يَا بُنَيَّ ابْكِ مِنْ ذِكْرِ خَطِيئَتِكَ.

وكيع بن الجرَّاح، كتاب الزهد

اليوم ٢٩٤

عَنْ عَلْقَمَةَ قَالَ: قَالَ عَبْدُ اللَّهِ: إِنَّ الْمُؤْمِنَ لَيَعْمَلُ السَّيِّئَةَ فَيُشَدَّدُ عَلَيْهِ بِهَا عِنْدَ مَوْتِهِ لِيَكُونَ بِهَا، وَإِنَّ الْفَاجِرَ لَيَعْمَلُ الْحَسَنَةَ فَيُخَفَّفُ بِهَا عَلَيْهِ عِنْدَ مَوْتِهِ لِيَكُونَ بِهَا.

وكيع بن الجرَّاح، كتاب الزهد

DAY
295

ʿAlī ibn Abī Ṭālib, may Allah be well pleased with him, said: "Beware of letting greed force you to use means which lead you to destruction."

(Ibn Abī al-Dunyā, *al-Qanāʿah wa'l-Taʿaffuf*)

DAY
296

ʿAmar ibn al-Khaṭṭāb (may Allah be well pleased with him) said: " Deliberateness is good in all matters except when it comes to the Hereafter."

(Wakīʿ ibn al-Jarrāḥ, *Kitāb al-Zuhd*)

اليوم ٢٩٥

قَالَ عَلِيُّ بْنُ أَبِي طَالِبٍ: إِيَّاكَ أَنْ تَرْجُفَ بِكَ مَطَايَا الطَّمَعِ فَتُورِدَكَ مَنَاهِلَ الهَلَكَةِ.

ابن أبي الدنيا، القناعة والتّعفّف

اليوم ٢٩٦

قَالَ عُمَرُ: التُّؤَدَةُ فِي كُلِّ شَيْءٍ خَيْرٌ إِلَّا مَا كَانَ فِي أَمْرِ الآخِرَةِ.

وكيع بن الجرّاح، كتاب الزهد

DAY 297

ʿAbdullāh ibn Masʿūd (may Allah be well pleased with him) said: "All people know how to talk well. However, he has attained his share [of goodness] the one whose deeds conform to his words whereas the one whose deeds contradict his words has not done anything but censures himself."

(Wakīʿ ibn al-Jarrāḥ, *Kitāb al-Zuhd*)

DAY 298

ʿAlī ibn Abī Ṭālib (may Allah be well pleased with him) said: "Acquire knowledge and you shall be known for it; act upon it and you shall be among the men of knowledge, for there shall come a time when nine out of ten people will deny the truth, and none shall escape from this except those who are unknown amongst

اليوم ٢٩٧

قَالَ عَبْدُ اللهِ: إِنَّ النَّاسَ قَدْ أَحْسَنُوا الْقَوْلَ كُلُّهُمْ، فَمَنْ وَافَقَ قَوْلُهُ فِعْلَهُ فَذَلِكَ الَّذِي أَصَابَ حَظَّهُ، وَمَنْ خَالَفَ قَوْلُهُ فِعْلَهُ فَإِنَّمَا وَبَّخَ نَفْسَهُ.

وكيع بن الجرَّاح، كتاب الزهد

اليوم ٢٩٨

قَالَ عَلِيٌّ: تَعَلَّمُوا الْعِلْمَ تُعْرَفُوا بِهِ وَاعْمَلُوا بِهِ تَكُونُوا مِنْ أَهْلِهِ، فَإِنَّهُ سَيَأْتِي مِنْ بَعْدِكُمْ زَمَانٌ يُنْكَرُ فِيهِ الْحَقَّ تِسْعَةُ أَعْشَارِهِمْ لَا يَنْجُو مِنْهُ إِلَّا كُلُّ نُوَمَةٍ،

people: those indeed are the leaders of guidance and the shining lamps of knowledge; neither do I propagate iniquities nor divulge other people's secrets."

(Wakīʿ ibn al-Jarrāḥ, *Kitāb al-Zuhd*)

DAY
299

ʿAbdullāh ibn Masʿūd (may Allah be well pleased with him) said: "Do not acquire knowledge with the following intentions: to wrangle with insolent people; to argue with the jurists; or to draw people's attention to you. Rather, intend with your words and deeds that which is with Allah for it is everlasting while everything else is evanescent."

(al-Dārimī)

أُولَئِكَ أَئِمَّةُ الْهُدَى وَمَصَابِيحُ الْعِلْمِ، لَيْسُوا بِالْعُجُلِ الْمَذَايِيعِ الْبُذْرِ.

وكيع بن الجرَّاح، كتاب الزهد

اليوم ٢٩٩

قَالَ ابْنُ مَسْعُودٍ: لَا تَعَلَّمُوا الْعِلْمَ لِثَلَاثٍ: لِتُمَارُوا بِهِ السُّفَهَاءَ أَوْ لِتُجَادِلُوا بِهِ الْفُقَهَاءَ أَوْ لِتَصْرِفُوا بِهِ وُجُوهَ النَّاسِ إِلَيْكُمْ، وَابْتَغُوا بِقَوْلِكُمْ وَفِعْلِكُمْ مَا عِنْدَ اللَّهِ، فَإِنَّهُ يَبْقَى وَيَذْهَبُ مَا سِوَاهُ.

الدَّارمي

DAY 300

Tamīm al-Dārī related that, during Umar's reign, people started erecting high buildings, so 'Umar ibn al-Khaṭṭāb (RA) addressed them as follows: "O Arabs, [humble yourselves] to the ground, [humble yourselves] to the ground. There is no Islam without a community, and there is no community without leadership, just as there is no leadership if there is no compliance. And so, whoever has been made a leader by his people and he has deep understanding, then he shall bring prosperity for himself and for them. And whoever is made a leader by his people while he has no deep understanding, then he shall destroy himself and destroy them."

(al-Dārimī)

اليوم
٣٠٠

عَنْ تَمِيمٍ الدَّارِيِّ قَالَ: تَطَاوَلَ النَّاسُ فِي الْبِنَاءِ فِي زَمَنِ عُمَرَ فَقَالَ عُمَرُ: يَا مَعْشَرَ الْعُرَيْبِ الْأَرْضَ الْأَرْضَ، إِنَّهُ لَا إِسْلَامَ إِلَّا بِجَمَاعَةٍ وَلَا جَمَاعَةَ إِلَّا بِإِمَارَةٍ وَلَا إِمَارَةَ إِلَّا بِطَاعَةٍ فَمَنْ سَوَّدَهُ قَوْمُهُ عَلَى الْفِقْهِ كَانَ حَيَاةً لَهُ وَلَهُمْ وَمَنْ سَوَّدَهُ قَوْمُهُ عَلَى غَيْرِ فِقْهٍ كَانَ هَلَاكًا لَهُ وَلَهُمْ.

الدَّارمي

DAY 301

ʿAbdullāh ibn Masʿūd (may Allah be well pleased with him) said: "By Allah besides whom there is no other deity! There is nothing on the face of the earth that is more deserving of a prolonged restraint than the tongue."."

(Wakīʿ ibn al-Jarrāḥ, *Kitāb al-Zuhd*)

DAY 302

ʿAbdullāh ibn Masʿūd (may Allah be well pleased with him) said: "The most beloved speech to Allah is for the servant to say: 'O Allah! I confess my sin and acknowledge Your blessing, so forgive me for none forgives sins except You.'"

(Wakīʿ ibn al-Jarrāḥ, *Kitāb al-Zuhd*)

اليوم ٣٠١

قَالَ عَبْدُ اللَّهِ: وَاللَّهِ الَّذِي لَا إِلَهَ غَيْرُهُ، مَا عَلَىٰ ظَهْرِ الْأَرْضِ شَيْءٌ أَحَقُّ بِطُولِ السِّجْنِ مِنَ اللِّسَانِ.

وكيع بن الجرّاح، كتاب الزهد

اليوم ٣٠٢

قَالَ عَبْدُ اللَّهِ: إِنَّ مِنْ أَحَبِّ الْكَلَامِ إِلَىٰ اللَّهِ أَنْ يَقُولَ الْعَبْدُ: اللَّهُمَّ أَعْتَرِفُ بِالذَّنْبِ وَأَبُوءُ بِالنِّعْمَةِ فَاغْفِرْ لِي إِنَّهُ لَا يَغْفِرُ الذُّنُوبَ إِلَّا أَنْتَ.

وكيع بن الجرّاح، كتاب الزهد

DAY 303

ʿUmar ibn al-Khaṭṭāb (may Allah be well pleased with him) said: "When Allah bestows on you the affection of a dignified fellow Muslim, cling on to it as much as you can."

(Wakīʿ ibn al-Jarrāḥ, *Kitāb al-Zuhd*)

DAY 304

ʿAbdullāh ibn Masʿūd (may Allah be well pleased with him) said: "Safety lies in two things just as destruction lies in two things too. Safety lies in [sincere] intention and sound mind while destruction lies in despair and conceitedness."

(Wakīʿ ibn al-Jarrāḥ, *Kitāb al-Zuhd*)

اليوم ٣٠٣

قَالَ عُمَرُ بْنُ الْخَطَّابِ: إِذَا رَزَقَكَ اللهُ وُدَّ امْرِئٍ مُسْلِمٍ فَتَشَبَّثْ بِهِ مَا اسْتَطَعْتَ.

وكيع بن الجرَّاح، كتاب الزهد

اليوم ٣٠٤

قَالَ عَبْدُ اللهِ: النَّجَاةُ فِي اثْنَتَيْنِ وَالْهَلَكَةُ فِي اثْنَتَيْنِ: النَّجَاةُ فِي النِّيَّةِ وَالنُّهَى وَالْهَلَكَةُ فِي الْقُنُوطِ وَالْإِعْجَابِ.

وكيع بن الجرَّاح، كتاب الزهد

DAY 305

Ubayy ibn Abī Ka'b is reported to have said: "No servant leaves something for the sake of Allah except that Allah shall substitute it for him with that which is better from a source he does not expect."

(Wakī' ibn al-Jarrāḥ, *Kitāb al-Zuhd*)

DAY 306

'Umar ibn al-Khaṭṭāb (may Allah be well pleased with him) said: "There is nothing more beloved to Allah, glorious and exalted is He – nor more beneficial [to people] – than a leader's clemency and gentleness, just as there is nothing more loathed by Allah – nor more harmful [to people] – than a leader's foolishness and folly."

(Wakī' ibn al-Jarrāḥ, *Kitāb al-Zuhd*)

اليوم ٣٠٥

عَنْ أَبِي بْنِ كَعْبٍ قَالَ: مَا مِنْ عَبْدٍ تَرَكَ شَيْئًا للهِ إِلَّا أَبْدَلَهُ اللَّهُ بِهِ مَا هُوَ خَيْرٌ مِنْهُ مِنْ حَيْثُ لَا يَحْتَسِبُ.

وكيع بن الجرَّاح ، كتاب الزهد

اليوم ٣٠٦

قَالَ عُمَرُ بْنُ الْخَطَّابِ: لَيْسَ شَيْءٌ أَحَبَّ إِلَىٰ اللَّهِ عَزَّ وَجَلَّ وَلَا أَعَمَّ نَفْعًا مِنْ حِلْمِ إِمَامٍ وَرِفْقِهِ، وَلَيْسَ شَيْءٌ أَبْغَضَ إِلَىٰ اللَّهِ وَلَا أَعَمَّ ضَرَرًا مِنْ جَهْلِ إِمَامٍ وَخُرْقِهِ.

وكيع بن الجرَّاح ، كتاب الزهد

DAY 307

'Umar ibn al-Khaṭṭāb (may Allah bless him and grant him peace) said: "That you are straitened in your livelihoods is more fearful for me than you becoming destitute. And nothing diminishes when there is a restoration of order while nothing remains when there is corruption. And good management of one's livelihood is better than half of what one earns as a living."

(Wakīʿ ibn al-Jarrāḥ, *Kitāb al-Zuhd*)

DAY 308

Ibn ʿUmar (may Allah be well pleased with him) said to a man: "O you there! Make sure to refine your son's deportment for you are responsible for him and he is responsible for being dutiful to you."

(Ibn Abī al-Dunyā, *al-Nafaqah ʿAlā al-ʿIyāl*)

اليوم ٣٠٧

قَالَ عُمَرُ بْنُ الخطَّابِ: الخرَقُ فِي المَعِيشَةِ أَخْوَفُ عِنْدِي عَلَيْكُمْ مِنَ العَوَزِ، وَلَا يَقِلُّ شَيْءٌ مَعَ الإِصْلَاحِ، وَلَا يَبْقَى شَيْءٌ مَعَ الفَسَادِ، وحُسْنُ التَدْبيرِ فِي المَعِيشَةِ أَفْضَلُ مِنْ نِصْفِ الكَسْبِ.

وكيع بن الجرَّاح، كتاب الزهد

اليوم ٣٠٨

قَالَ ابْنُ عُمَرَ لِرَجُلٍ: يَا هَذَا أَحْسِنْ أَدَبَ ابْنِكَ فَإِنَّكَ مَسْئُولٌ عَنْهُ وَهُوَ مَسْئُولٌ عَنْ بِرِّك.

ابن أبي الدنيا، النفقة على العيال

DAY 309

ʿAlī (may Allah be well pleased with him) said: "Good character lies in three traits: avoiding that which is unlawful; seeking that which is lawful; and being generous with one's family."

(al-Ghazālī, *Iḥyā' 'Ulūm al-Dīn*)

DAY 310

ʿUmar ibn al-Khaṭṭāb (may Allah be well pleased with him) said: "Whoever lacks diffidence, he lacks scrupulousness too; and whoever lacks scrupulousness, his heart dies."

(Ibn Abī al-Dunyā, *Makārim al-Akhlāq*)

اليوم ٣٠٩

قَالَ عَلِيٌّ: حُسْنُ الْخُلُقِ فِي ثَلَاثِ خِصَالٍ: اجْتِنَابُ الْمَحَارِمِ وَطَلَبُ الْحَلَالِ وَالتَّوْسِعَةُ عَلَى الْعِيَالِ.

الإمام الغزالي، إحياء علوم الدين

اليوم ٣١٠

قَالَ عُمَرُ: مَنْ قَلَّ حَيَاؤُهُ قَلَّ وَرَعُهُ وَمَنْ قَلَّ وَرَعُهُ مَاتَ قَلْبُهُ.

ابن أبي الدنيا، مكارم الأخلاق

DAY
311

Abū Bakr al-Ṣiddīq, may Allah be well pleased with him, said: "The best form of truthfulness is trustworthiness while the worst form of lying is treachery."

(Al-Bayhaqī, *al-Sunan al-Kubrā*)

DAY
312

Abū Bakr al-Ṣiddīq, may Allah be well pleased with him, said: "Watch out for Muhammad, Allah bless him and grant him peace, regarding the members of his household."

(al-Bukhārī)

اليوم ٣١١

قَالَ أَبُو بَكْرٍ الصِّدِيقُ: أَصْدَقُ الصِّدْقِ الأَمَانَةُ وَأَكْذَبُ الكَذِبِ الخِيَانَةُ.

البيهقي، السنن الكبرى

اليوم ٣١٢

قَالَ أَبُو بَكْرٍ الصِّدِيقُ: ارْقُبُوا مُحَمَّدًا صَلَّى اللهُ عَلَيْهِ وَسَلَّمَ فِي أَهْلِ بَيْتِهِ.

البخاري

DAY 313

'Umar Ibn al-Khaṭṭāb, may Allah be well pleased with him, used to say: "Do not busy yourselves with the mention of others for that is a misfortune, but do busy yourselves with the remembrance of Allah for that is a mercy."

(Ibn Abī al-Dunyā, *Dhamm al-Ghībah wa'l-Namīmah*)

DAY 314

It is reported that 'Umar Ibn al-Khaṭṭāb, may Allah be well pleased with him, said: "Whoever puts himself in a compromising position should not blame others who think ill of him."

(Abū Dāwūd, *Kitāb al-Zuhd*)

اليوم
٣١٣

كَانَ عُمَرُ بْنُ الْخَطَّابِ يَقُولُ: لَا تَشْغَلُوا أَنْفُسَكُمْ بِذِكْرِ النَّاسِ فَإِنَّهُ بَلَاءٌ وَعَلَيْكُمْ بِذِكْرِ اللهِ فَإِنَّهُ رَحْمَةٌ.

ابن أبي الدنيا، ذم الغيبة والنميمة

اليوم
٣١٤

عَنْ عُمَرَ بْنِ الْخَطَّابِ قَالَ: مَنْ عَرَّضَ نَفْسَهُ لِلتُّهَمَةِ فَلَا يَلُومَنَّ مَنْ أَسَاءَ بِهِ الظَّنَّ.

أبو داود، كتاب الزهد

DAY 315

'Umar Ibn al-Khaṭṭāb, may Allah be well pleased with him, said: "Whoever is granted making supplications will not be denied being answered; and whoever is granted gratitude [for any blessings] will not be denied an increase [of those blessings]."
(al-Balādhurī, *Ansāb al-Ashrāf*)

DAY 316

'Umar Ibn al-Khaṭṭāb, may Allah be well pleased with him, said: "If you are religious, then you you are of noble descent; if you have a sound mind, then you are of good stock; and if you have good character traits, then you have a sense of honour. Otherwise, you are worse than a donkey."

(Ibn 'Abd Rabbih, *al-'Iqd al-Farīd*)

اليوم
٣١٥

قَالَ عُمَرُ: مَنْ أُعْطِيَ الدُّعَاءَ لَمْ يُحْرَمِ الإِجَابَةَ، وَمَنْ أُعْطِيَ الشُّكْرَ لَمْ يُحْرَمِ الزِّيَادَةَ، وَمَنْ أُعْطِيَ الاسْتِغْفَارَ لَمْ يُمْنَعَ الْقَبُولَ.

البلاذري ، أنساب الاشراف

اليوم
٣١٦

قَالَ عُمَرُ بْنُ الخَطَّابِ: إِنْ كَانَ لَكَ دِينٌ فَإِنَّ لَكَ حَسَبًا وَإِنْ كَانَ لَكَ عَقْلٌ فَإِنَّ لَكَ أَصْلًا وَإِنْ كَانَ لَكَ خُلُقٌ فَلَكَ مُرُوءَةٌ وَإِلَّا فَأَنْتَ شَرٌّ مِنْ حِمَارٍ.

ابن عبد ربه ، العقد الفريد

DAY 317

ʿUmar Ibn al-Khaṭṭāb, may Allah be well pleased with him, wrote the following to Abū Mūsā al-Ashʿarī, may Allah be well pleased with him: "Wisdom does not come with old age but it is rather a gift that Allah bestows on whomever He wills. So beware of vileness and lowly character traits."

(Ibn Abī al-Dunyā, *al-Ishrāf Fī Manāzil al-Ashrāf*)

DAY 318

ʿUmar Ibn al-Khaṭṭāb, may Allah be well pleased with him, said: "The most openhanded person is the one who gives to those whose reward he does not expect; and the most clement of people is the one who pardons when he is able to retaliate; and the most miserly person is the one who does not give the greeting of peace; and the most incapable of people is the one who fails to supplicate to Allah."

(Ibn Abī Shaybah, *al-Muṣannaf*)

اليوم ٣١٧

كَتَبَ عُمَرُ بْنُ الخطَّابِ لِأَبِي مُوسَىٰ الأَشْعَرِيِّ: إِنَّ الحِكْمَةَ لَيْسَتْ عَنْ كِبَرِ السِّنِّ، وَلَكِنَّهُ عَطَاءُ اللهِ يُعْطِيهِ مَنْ يَشَاءُ، فَإِيَّاكَ وَدَنَاءَةِ الأُمُورِ وَمُرَّا قِ الأَخْلَاقِ.

ابن أبي الدنيا، الإشراف في منازل الأشراف

اليوم ٣١٨

قَالَ عُمَرُ بْنُ الخطَّابِ: إِنَّ أَجْوَدَ النَّاسِ مَنْ جَادَ عَلَىٰ مَنْ لَا يَرْجُو ثَوَابَهُ، وَإِنَّ أَحْلَمَ النَّاسِ مَنْ عَفَا بَعْدَ القُدْرَةِ، وَإِنَّ أَبْخَلَ النَّاسِ الَّذِي يَبْخَلُ بِالسَّلَامِ، وَإِنَّ أَعْجَزَ النَّاسِ الَّذِي يَعْجزُ فِي دُعَاءِ اللهِ.

ابن أبي شيبة، المصنّف

DAY 319

'Uthmān ibn 'Affān, may Allah be well pleased with him, said: "If our hearts were pure, we would not have enough of the speech of our Lord; indeed, I hate that a day passes without me looking at the *Muṣḥaf*."

(al-Bayhaqī, *Shu'ab al-Īmān*)

DAY 320

Abū Bakr al-Ṣiddīq, may Allah be well pleased with him, used to say in his sermon: "Where are those bright ones with pretty faces who are conceited regarding their youth? Where are those kings who built cities and fortified them with solid protecting walls? Where are those who were given victory in wars? They are all perished and are now in dark graves. Hasten to safety! Hasten to safety!"

(Abū Nu'aym al-Aṣfahānī, *Ḥilyat al-Awliyā'*)

اليوم
٣١٩

قال عُثْمَانُ بْنُ عفَّانَ: لَوْ أَنَّ قُلُوبَنَا طَهُرَتْ مَا شَبِعْنَا مِنْ كَلَامِ رَبِّنَا، وَإِنِّي لَأَكْرَهُ أَنْ يَأْتِيَ عَلَيَّ يَوْمٌ لَا أَنْظُرُ فِي الْمُصْحَفِ.

البيهقي ، شعب الإيمان

اليوم
٣٢٠

كَانَ أَبُو بَكْرٍ الصِّدِّيقَ يَقُولُ فِي خُطْبَتِهِ: أَيْنَ الْوِضَاءُ وَالْحَسَنَةُ وُجُوهُهُمْ، الْمُعْجَبُونَ بِشَبَابِهِمْ؟ أَيْنَ الْمُلُوكُ الَّذِينَ بَنَوُا الْمَدَائِنَ وَحَصَّنُوهَا بِالْحِيطَانِ؟ أَيْنَ الَّذِينَ كَانُوا يُعْطَوْنَ الْغَلَبَةَ فِي مَوَاطِنِ الْحَرْبِ؟ قَدْ تَضَعْضَعَ بِهِمُ الدَّهْرُ وَأَصْبَحُوا فِي ظُلُمَاتِ الْقُبُورِ الْوَحَاءَ الْوَحَاءَ، النَّجَاءَ النَّجَاءَ.

أبو نعيم الأصفهاني ، حلية الأولياء

DAY 321

ʿAlī ibn Abī Ṭālib, may Allah be well pleased with him, said: "Blessedness is for those who are not attached to this world and are desirous of the afterlife. Those are the ones who have taken the ground of the earth as their couch, its dust as their cover, its water as their musk, the Book as their emblem and supplication as their blanket. They have lent Allah a loan following the example of the anointed ʿĪsā ibn Maryam, Allah bless him."

(Ibn Abī al-Dunyā, *al-Tawāḍuʿ wa'l-Khumūl*)

DAY 322

ʿUmar Ibn al-Khaṭṭāb, may Allah be well pleased with him, said: "By Allah, compared to the hereafter, this world is like the distance of one rabbit's hop."

(Ibn Abī al-Dunyā, *Kitāb al-Zuhd*)

قَالَ عَلِيُّ بْنُ أَبِي طَالِبٍ: طُوبَى لِلزَّاهِدِينَ فِي الدُّنْيَا وَالرَّاغِبِينَ فِي الْآخِرَةِ أُولَئِكَ قَوْمٌ اتَّخَذُوا الْأَرْضَ بِسَاطًا وَتُرَابَهَا فِرَاشًا وَمَاءَهَا طِيبًا وَالْكِتَابَ شِعَارًا وَالدُّعَاءَ دِثَارًا أَقْرَضُوا اللَّهَ قَرْضًا عَلَى مِنْهَاجِ الْمَسِيحِ عِيسَى ابْنِ مَرْيَمَ صَلَوَاتُ اللَّهِ عَلَيْهِ.

ابن أبي الدنيا، التواضع والخمول

قَالَ عُمَرُ بْنُ الْخَطَّابِ: وَاللَّهِ مَا الدُّنْيَا فِي الْآخِرَةِ إِلَّا كَنَفْجَةِ أَرْنَبٍ.

ابن أبي الدنيا، كتاب الزهد

DAY 323

Muʿādh ibn Jabal, may Allah be well pleased with him said:"O Memorisers of the Qur'ān! How about a world that cuts off your heads? So whomever Allah has placed richness in his heart, such a person will surely succeed; and whoever is not thus, this world of his will not benefit him."

(Ibn Abī al-Dunyā, *Kitāb al-Zuhd*)

DAY 324

ʿAlī ibn Abī Ṭālib, may Allah be well pleased with him, said: "Whoever is unattached to this world deems misfortunes as insignificant; and whoever anticipates death hastens to do good deeds."

(Ibn Abī al-Dunyā, *Kitāb al-Zuhd*)

اليوم ٣٢٣

قَالَ مُعَاذُ بْنُ جَبَلٍ: يَا مَعْشَرَ الْقُرَّاءِ، كَيْفَ بِدُنْيَا تَقْطَعُ رِقَابَكُمْ؟ فَمَنْ جَعَلَ اللهُ عَزَّ وَجَلَّ غِنَاهُ فِي قَلْبِهِ فَقَدْ أَفْلَحَ، وَمَنْ لَا فَلَيْسَ بِنَافِعَتِهِ دُنْيَاهُ.

ابن أبي الدنيا، كتاب الزهد

اليوم ٣٢٤

قَالَ عَلِيُّ بْنُ أَبِي طَالِبٍ: مَنْ زَهِدَ فِي الدُّنْيَا هَانَتْ عَلَيْهِ الْمُصِيبَاتُ، وَمَنِ ارْتَقَبَ الْمَوْتَ سَارَعَ فِي الْخَيْرَاتِ.

ابن أبي الدنيا، كتاب الزهد

DAY 325

Abū'l-Dardā, may Allah be well pleased with him said:"If you were to swear to me that a particular man is the most unattached one to this world amongst you, I would swear to you that he is the best amongst you."

(Ibn Abī al-Dunyā, *Kitāb al-Zuhd*)

DAY 326

'Umar Ibn al-Khaṭṭāb, may Allah be well pleased with him, said: "Do not be saddened that whatever you like of the things of this world is hastened to you as long as you have a desire for the afterlife"

(Ibn Abī al-Dunyā, *Kitāb al-Zuhd*)

اليوم ٣٢٥

قَالَ أَبُو الدَّرْدَاءِ: لَئِنْ حَلَفْتُمْ لِي عَلَى رَجُلٍ مِنْكُمْ أَنَّهُ أَزْهَدُكُمْ، لَأَحْلِفَنَّ لَكُمْ أَنَّهُ خَيْرُكُمْ.

ابن أبي الدنيا، كتاب الزهد

اليوم ٣٢٦

قَالَ عُمَرُ بْنُ الْخَطَّابِ: لَا تَحْزَنْ أَنْ يُعَجَّلَ لَكَ كَثِيرٌ مِمَّا تُحِبُّ مِنْ أَمْرِ دُنْيَاكَ إِذَا كُنْتَ ذَا رَغْبَةٍ فِي أَمْرِ آخِرَتِكَ.

ابن أبي الدنيا، كتاب الزهد

DAY 327

Muʿāwiyah ibn Abī Sufyān, may Allah be well pleased with him, said: "The servant shall not attain to a position of authority and sound opinion until his forbearance has the upper hand over his anger, and his patience has the upper hand over desire and he shall not attain this except through forbearance."

(Ibn Abī al-Dunyā, *al-Ḥilm*)

DAY 328

ʿAlī ibn Abī Ṭālib, may Allah be well pleased with him, said: "The tongue is the prop of the body: if the tongue is upright, then all the other limbs are upright; and if the tongue is perturbed, then no other limb is well."

(Ibn Abī al-Dunyā, *al-Ṣamt wa-Āfāt al-Lisān*)

اليوم ٣٢٧

قَالَ مُعَاوِيَةُ بْنِ أَبِي سُفْيَانَ: لَا يَبْلُغُ العَبْدُ مَبْلَغَ الرَّأْيِ حَتَّىٰ يَغْلِبَ حِلْمُهُ جَهْلَهُ، وَصَبْرُهُ شَهْوَتَهُ، وَلَا يَبْلُغُ ذَلِكَ إِلَّا بِقُوَّةِ الحِلْمِ.

ابن أبي الدنيا ، الحلم

اليوم ٣٢٨

قَالَ عَلِيٌّ بْنُ أَبِي طَالِبٍ: اللِّسَانُ قِوَامُ الْبَدَنِ، فَإِذَا اسْتَقَامَ اللِّسَانُ اسْتَقَامَتِ الْجَوَارِحُ، وَإِذَا اضْطَرَبَ اللِّسَانُ لَمْ يَقُمْ لَهُ جَارِحَةٌ.

ابن أبي الدنيا ، الصمت وآفات اللسان

DAY 329

The Mother of the Believers, ʿĀ'ishah, may Allah be well pleased with her, said: "Indeed, good character traits lie in ten things: being truthful in speech, being genuine in Allah's obedience, giving to the Begger, rewarding for what is being done for one, keeping one's tie of kinship, giving back what is entrusted to one, taking care of the neighbour, taking care of one's companion, giving hospitality to the guest, and at the peak of all these is bashfulness."

(Ibn Abī al-Dunyā, *Makārim al-Akhlāq*)

DAY 330

ʿAlī ibn Abī Ṭālib, may Allah be well pleased with him, said: "Knowledge is an aspect of religion that one is measured by; through it, one obtains others' obedience in one's life and good mention after one's death."

(al-Sharīf al-Raḍī, *Nahj al-Balāghah*)

اليوم
٣٢٩

قَالَتْ أُمُّ المُؤْمِنِينَ عَائِشَةَ: إِنَّ مَكَارِمَ الْأَخْلَاقِ عَشَرَةٌ: صِدْقُ الْحَدِيثِ، وَصِدْقُ الْبَأْسِ فِي طَاعَةِ اللهِ، وَإِعْطَاءُ السَّائِلِ، وَمُكَافَأَةُ الصَّنِيعِ، وَصِلَةُ الرَّحِمِ، وَأَدَاءُ الْأَمَانَةِ، وَالتَّذَمُّمُ لِلْجَارِ، وَالتَّذَمُّمُ لِلصَّاحِبِ، وَقِرَىٰ الضَّيْفِ، وَرَأْسُهُنَّ الْحَيَاءُ.

ابن أبي الدنيا، مكارم الأخلاق

اليوم
٣٣٠

قَالَ عَلِيُّ بْنُ أَبِي طَالِبٍ: العِلْمُ دِينٌ يُدَانُ بِهِ، بِهِ يَكْسِبُ الْإِنْسَانُ الطَّاعَةَ فِي حَيَاتِهِ، وَجَمِيلَ الْأُحْدُوثَةِ بَعْدَ وَفَاتِهِ.

الشّريف الرَّضي، نهج البلاغة

DAY
331

ʿAlī ibn Abī Ṭālib, may Allah be well pleased with him, said: "The most deserving of people to pardon others is the one who is most capable of punishing them."

(al-Sharīf al-Rāḍī, *Nahj al-Balāghah*)

DAY
332

ʿAlī ibn Abī Ṭālib, may Allah be well pleased with him, said: "There is no wealth like a sound reasoning faculty, and there is no utter need like ignorance, just as there is no inheritance like propriety and no assistant like consultation."

(al-Sharīf al-Raḍī, *Nahj al-Balāghah*)

اليوم ٣٣١

قَالَ عَلِيُّ بْنُ أَبِي طَالِبٍ: أَوْلَى النَّاسِ بِالْعَفْوِ أَقْدَرُهُمْ عَلَى الْعُقُوبَةِ.

الشّريف الرَّضي، نهج البلاغة

اليوم ٣٣٢

قَالَ عَلِيُّ بْنُ أَبِي طَالِبٍ: لَا غِنَى كَالْعَقْلِ وَلَا فَقْرَ كَالْجَهْلِ وَلَا مِيرَاثَ كَالْأَدَبِ وَلَا ظَهِيرَ كَالْمُشَاوَرَةِ.

الشّريف الرَّضي، نهج البلاغة

DAY 333

ʿAlī ibn Abī Ṭālib, may Allah be well pleased with him, said: "Generosity is when one gives without being asked. As for giving when one is asked, it is nothing but diffidence and taking care of someone's need."

(al-Sharīf al-Raḍī, *Nahj al-Balāghah*)

DAY 334

ʿAlī ibn Abī Ṭālib, may Allah be well pleased with him, said: "Contentedness is wealth that is never depleted."

(al-Sharīf al-Raḍī, *Nahj al-Balāghah*)

اليوم
٣٣٣

قَالَ عَلِيُّ بْنُ أَبِي طَالِبٍ: السَّخَاءُ مَا كَانَ ابْتِدَاءً فَأَمَّا مَا كَانَ عَنْ مَسْأَلَةٍ فَحَيَاءٌ وَتَذَمُّمٌ.

الشّريف الرَّضي ، نهج البلاغة

اليوم
٣٣٤

قَالَ عَلِيُّ بْنُ أَبِي طَالِبٍ: الْقَنَاعَةُ مَالٌ لَا يَنْفَدُ.

الشّريف الرَّضي ، نهج البلاغة

DAY 335

ʿAlī ibn Abī Ṭālib, may Allah be well pleased with him, said: "Do not be shy to give what is little, for being debarred is even less than that little."

(al-Sharīf al-Raḍī, *Nahj al-Balāghah*)

DAY 336

ʿAlī ibn Abī Ṭālib, may Allah be well pleased with him, said: "Restraint is the adornment of poverty while gratitude is the adornment of wealth."

(al-Sharīf al-Raḍī, *Nahj al-Balāghah*)

اليوم ٣٣٥

قَالَ عَلِيُّ بْنُ أَبِي طَالِبٍ: لَا تَسْتَحِ مِنْ إِعْطَاءِ الْقَلِيلِ فَإِنَّ الْحِرْمَانَ أَقَلُّ مِنْهُ.

الشّريف الرَّضي، نهج البلاغة

اليوم ٣٣٦

قَالَ عَلِيُّ بْنُ أَبِي طَالِبٍ: الْعَفَافُ زِينَةُ الْفَقْرِ وَالشُّكْرُ زِينَةُ الْغِنَى.

الشّريف الرَّضي، نهج البلاغة

DAY 337

ʿAlī ibn Abī Ṭālib, may Allah be well pleased with him, said: "Whoever fixes what is between him and Allah, Allah will fix what is between him and other people; and whoever fixes the matter of his afterlife, Allah will fix for him the matter of this world; and whoever has an admonisher from within himself, he will find from Allah that which shall protect him."

(al-Sharīf al-Raḍī, *Nahj al-Balāghah*)

DAY 338

ʿAlī ibn Abī Ṭālib, may Allah be well pleased with him, said: "No deed is paltry when it is accompanied with Godfearingness, for how could what is accepted [by Allah] be ever paltry?"

(al-Sharīf al-Raḍī, *Nahj al-Balāghah*)

اليوم
٣٣٧

قَالَ عَلِيُّ بْنُ أَبِي طَالِبٍ: مَنْ أَصْلَحَ مَا بَيْنَهُ وَبَيْنَ اللهِ أَصْلَحَ اللهُ مَا بَيْنَهُ وَبَيْنَ النَّاسِ وَمَنْ أَصْلَحَ أَمْرَ آخِرَتِهِ أَصْلَحَ اللهُ لَهُ أَمْرَ دُنْيَاهُ وَمَنْ كَانَ لَهُ مِنْ نَفْسِهِ وَاعِظٌ كَانَ عَلَيْهِ مِنَ اللهِ حَافِظٌ.

الشّريف الرَّضي، نهج البلاغة

اليوم
٣٣٨

قَالَ عَلِيُّ بْنُ أَبِي طَالِبٍ: لَا يَقِلُّ عَمَلٌ مَعَ التَّقْوَى[١] وَكَيْفَ يَقِلُّ مَا يُتَقَبَّلُ.

الشّريف الرَّضي، نهج البلاغة

DAY 339

Abū'l-Dardā', may Allah be well pleased with him said: "When a man wakes up in the morning, his whimsical tendency and work come together. Then, if his work is carried out according to his whimsical tendency, his day shall be an evil day. But if his whimsical tendency is made to follow his work, then his day shall be a good day."

(Ibn Abī al-Dunyā, *Muḥāsabat al-Nafs*)

DAY 340

Salmān al-Fārisī, may Allah be well pleased with him, said: "Three things amazed me to the point they made me laugh: a person who has great hopes in this world while death is chasing him; a person who is completely oblivious of everything while everything he does is taken into account; a person who keeps laughing when he does not know whether the Lord of the worlds is angry with him

اليوم ٣٣٩

قَالَ أَبُو الدَّرْدَاءِ: إِذَا أَصْبَحَ الرَّجُلُ اِجْتَمَعَ هَوَاهُ وَعَمَلُهُ، فَإِنْ كَانَ عَمَلُهُ تَبَعًا لِهَوَاهُ فَيَوْمُهُ يَوْمُ سُوءٍ، وَإِنْ كَانَ هَوَاهُ تَبَعًا لِعَمَلِهِ فَيَوْمُهُ يَوْمٌ صَالِحٌ.

ابن أبي الدنيا، محاسبة النفس

اليوم ٣٤٠

قَالَ سَلْمَانُ الفَارِسِيُّ: ثَلَاثٌ أَعْجَبَتْنِي حَتَّى أَضْحَكَتْنِي: مُؤَمِّلُ الدُّنْيَا، وَالْمَوْتُ يَطْلُبُهُ، وَغَافِلٌ وَلَيْسَ بِمَغْفُولٍ عَنْهُ، وَضَاحِكٌ لَا يَدْرِي أَسَاخِطٌ عَلَيْهِ رَبُّ الْعَالَمِينَ أَمْ رَاضٍ، وَثَلَاثٌ

or pleased. And there are three things that saddened me to the point they made me cry: the departure of Muhammad, Allah bless him and grant him peace and his party – or he said: Muhammad, Allah bless him and grant him peace, and the beloved ones; the horrors of the Day of Judgement; and standing before Allah, exalted and glorified is He, and not knowing whether I shall be led to Paradise or Hell."

(Ibn Abī al-Dunyā, *Qiṣar al-Amal*)

DAY 341

Abū Bakr al-Ṣiddīq, may Allah be well pleased with him, said: "Whoever detests himself for the Countenance of Allah, Allah shall keep him safe from His detestation."

(Ibn Abī al-Dunyā, *Muḥāsabat al-Nafs*)

أَحْزَنَتْنِي حَتَّىٰ أَبْكَتْنِي: فِرَاقُ مُحَمَّدٍ صَلىٰ اللهُ عَلَيْهِ وَعَلىٰ آلِهِ وَصَحْبِهِ وَسَلَّمَ وَحِزْبِهِ - أَوْ قَالَ: فِرَاقُ مُحَمَّدٍ وَالْأَحِبَّةَ - وَهَوْلُ الْمَطْلَعِ، وَالْوُقُوفُ بَيْنَ يَدَيِ اللهِ عَزَّ وَجَلَّ، لَا أَدْرِي إِلَىٰ جَنَّةٍ يُؤْمَرُ بِي أَوْ إِلَىٰ نَارٍ.

ابن أبي الدنيا، قصر الأمل

اليوم ٣٤١

قَالَ أَبُو بَكْرٍ الصِّدِّيقُ: مَنْ مَقَتَ نَفْسَهُ فِي ذَاتِ اللهِ آمَنَهُ اللهُ مِنْ مَقْتِهِ.

ابن أبي الدنيا، محاسبة النفس

DAY
342

Abū'l-Dardā', may Allah be well pleased with him, used to supplicate: "O Allah! I ask You for perpetual faith, beneficial knowledge and precious guidance."

(Ibn Abī Shaybah, *al-Muṣannaf*)

DAY
343

Salmān al-Fārisī, may Allah be well pleased with him, said: "The example of the five daily prayers is that of the shares of the spoils of war. The one who gets five shares is better than the one who gets four, and the one who gets four is better than the one who gets three, and the one who gets three is better than the one who gets two, and the one who gets two is better than the one who gets one. And Allah does not equate someone with one share in Islam with someone who does not have any share whatsoever."

(Ibn Abī Shaybah, *al-Muṣannaf*)

اليوم ٣٤٢

كَانَ أَبُو الدَّرْدَاءِ يَقُولُ: اللَّهُمَّ إِنِّي أَسْأَلُكَ إِيمَانًا دَائِمًا وَعِلْمًا نَافِعًا وَهَدْيًا قَيِّمًا.

ابن أبي شيبة، المصنّف

اليوم ٣٤٣

قَالَ سَلْمَانُ الفَارِسِيُّ: إِنَّ مَثَلَ الصَّلَوَاتِ الْخَمْسِ كَمَثَلِ سِهَامِ الْغَنِيمَةِ، فَمَنْ يَضْرِبُ فِيهَا بِخَمْسَةٍ خَيْرٌ مِمَّنْ يَضْرِبُ فِيهَا بِأَرْبَعَةٍ، وَمَنْ يَضْرِبُ فِيهَا بِأَرْبَعَةٍ خَيْرٌ مِمَّنْ يَضْرِبُ فِيهَا بِثَلَاثَةٍ، وَمَنْ يَضْرِبُ فِيهَا بِثَلَاثَةٍ خَيْرٌ مِمَّنْ يَضْرِبُ فِيهَا بِسَهْمَيْنِ، وَمَنْ يَضْرِبُ فِيهَا بِسَهْمَيْنِ خَيْرٌ مِمَّنْ يَضْرِبُ فِيهَا بِسَهْمٍ، وَمَا جَعَلَ اللَّهُ مَنْ لَهُ سَهْمٌ فِي الْإِسْلَامِ كَمَنْ لَا سَهْمَ لَهُ.

ابن أبي شيبة، المصنّف

DAY 344

Muʿāwiyah ibn Abī Sufyān, may Allah be well pleased with him, said: "No nation has ever split into factions except that Allah gives the upper hand to the proponents of falsehood over the proponents of the truth, and the only exception is this [Muslim] nation."

(Ibn Abī Shaybah, *al-Muṣannaf*)

DAY 345

ʿUmar ibn al-Khaṭṭāb, may Allah be well pleased with him, said: "O Quraysh kinsfolk! I do not fear that people overpower you but I fear that you may overpower people. And, indeed, I have left for you two things which, were you to hold fast to them, you would always be in a good state: justice in governance and justice in distributing the spoils of war."

(Ibn Abī Shaybah, *al-Muṣannaf*)

اليوم ٣٤٤

قَالَ مُعَاوِيَةُ بْنُ أَبِي سُفْيَانَ: مَا تَفَرَّقَتْ أُمَّةٌ قَطُّ إِلَّا أَظْهَرَ اللَّهُ أَهْلَ الْبَاطِلِ عَلَىٰ أَهْلِ الْحَقِّ إِلَّا هَذِهِ الْأُمَّةَ.

ابن أبي شيبة، المصنّف

اليوم ٣٤٥

قَالَ عُمَرُ بْنُ الْخَطَّابِ: يَا مَعْشَرَ قُرَيْشٍ! إِنِّي لَا أَخَافُ النَّاسَ عَلَيْكُمْ، إِنَّمَا أَخَافُكُمْ عَلَىٰ النَّاسِ، وَإِنِّي قَدْ تَرَكْتُ فِيكُمُ اثْنَتَيْنِ لَمْ تَبْرَحُوا بِخَيْرٍ مَا لَزِمْتُمُوهَا: الْعَدْلَ فِي الْحُكْمِ وَالْعَدْلَ فِي الْقَسْمِ.

ابن أبي شيبة، المصنّف

DAY
346

Abū Dharr al-Ghifārī, may Allah be well pleased with him, is reported to have said: "The right measure of supplication compared to one's virtuous deeds should be like the right quantity of salt that is put in one's food."

(Abū Nu'aym al-Aṣfahānī, *Ḥilyat al-Awliyā'*)

DAY
347

Abū Dharr al-Ghifārī, may Allah be well pleased with him, is reported to have said: "Do you see the sheer number of people? There is no good in them unless one of them is a Godfearing person or a repentant one."

(Aḥmad ibn Ḥanbal, *Kitāb al-Zuhd*)

اليوم ٣٤٦

عَنْ أَبِي ذَرٍّ الغِفَارِيِّ أَنَّهُ قَالَ: يَكْفِي مِنَ الدُّعَاءِ مَعَ الْبِرِّ مَا يَكْفِي الْمِلْحُ مِنَ الطَّعَامِ.

أبو نعيم الأصفهاني، حلية الأولياء

اليوم ٣٤٧

قَالَ أَبُو ذَرٍّ الغِفَارِيِّ: هَلْ تَرَىٰ النَّاسَ مَا أَكْثَرَهُمْ؟ مَا فِيهِمْ خَيْرٌ إِلَّا تَقِيٌّ أَوْ تَائِبٌ.

أحمد بن حنبل، كتاب الزهد

DAY 348

Al-Zubayr ibn al-ʿAwwām, may Allah be well pleased with him, said: "Whoever is able to keep some good works secret [between him and Allah], then let him do so."

(Aḥmad ibn Ḥanbal, *Kitāb al-Zuhd*)

DAY 349

Umm al-Dardā', may Allah be well pleased with her, said: "This world is more bewitching for the servant's heart than Hārūt and Mārūt; and no servant ever prefers it [over the afterlife] except that it will destroy him."

(Aḥmad ibn Ḥanbal, *Kitāb al-Zuhd*)

اليوم ٣٤٨

قَالَ الزُّبَيْرُ بْنُ العَوَّامِ: مَنِ اسْتَطَاعَ أَنْ تَكُونَ لَهُ خَبِيئَةٌ مِنْ عَمَلٍ صَالِحٍ فَلْيَفْعَلْ.

أحمد بن حنبل، كتاب الزهد

اليوم ٣٤٩

قَالَتْ أُمُّ الدَّرْدَاءِ: الدُّنْيَا أَسْحَرُ لِقَلْبِ الْعَبْدِ مِنْ هَارُوتَ وَمَارُوتَ، وَمَا آثَرَهَا عَبْدٌ قَطُّ إِلَّا أَصْرَعَتْ خَدَّهُ.

أحمد بن حنبل، كتاب الزهد

DAY 350

ʿAmmār ibn Yāsir, may Allah be well pleased with him, said: "Death is sufficient as an admonisher; certainty is enough as a freedom from need; just as worship is enough as a preoccupation."

(Aḥmad ibn Ḥanbal, *Kitāb al-Zuhd*)

DAY 351

Abū Hurayrah, may Allah be well pleased with him, used to circumambulate the Kaʿbah and say: "Woe unto me from my belly: if I give it its fill, it makes me overfull; and if I make it hungry, it makes me exhausted."

(Aḥmad ibn Ḥanbal, *Kitāb al-Zuhd*)

اليوم
٣٥٠

قال عمَّارُ بْنُ ياسِرٍ: كَفَى بِالْمَوْتِ وَاعِظًا، وَكَفَى بِالْيَقِينِ غِنًى، وَكَفَى بِالْعِبَادَةِ شُغُلًا.

أحمد بن حنبل، كتاب الزهد

اليوم
٣٥١

كَانَ أَبُو هُرَيْرَةَ يَطُوفُ بِالْبَيْتِ وَهُوَ يَقُولُ: وَيْلٌ لِي مِنْ بَطْنِي، إِنْ أَشْبَعْتُهُ كَظَّنِي وَإِنْ أَجَعْتُهُ أَنْصَبَنِي.

أحمد بن حنبل، كتاب الزهد

DAY 352

Abū Hurayrah, may Allah be well pleased with him, said: "He shall not enter the Fire whoever weeps from the utter fear of Allah, glorified and exalted is He, unless milk can go back to the udder from which it was milked."

(Aḥmad ibn Ḥanbal, *Kitāb al-Zuhd*)

DAY 353

Abū Mas'ūd, may Allah be well pleased with him, said: "Beware of being changeable regarding religion such that what you consider to be correct today you deem it to be wrong tomorrow and what you consider to be wrong today you deem it to be correct tomorrow."

(Aḥmad ibn Ḥanbal, *Kitāb al-Zuhd*)

اليوم
٣٥٢

قَالَ عَبْدُ اللهِ بْنُ مَسْعُودٍ: خَيْرُ الْعَمَلِ مَا نَفَعَ وَخَيْرُ الْهَدْيِ مَا اتُّبِعَ وَخَيْرُ مَا أُلْقِيَ فِي الْقَلْبِ الْيَقِينُ.

القضاعي، مُسْنَد الشهاب القضاعي

اليوم
٣٥٣

قَالَ أَبُو مَسْعُودٌ الأَنْصَارِيُّ: إِيَّاكُمْ وَالتَّلَوُّنَ فِي الدِّينِ مَا عَرَفْتُمُ الْيَوْمَ فَلَا تُنْكِرُوهُ غَدًا، وَمَا أَنْكَرْتُمُوهُ الْيَوْمَ فَلَا تَعْرِفُوهُ غَدًا.

أحمد بن حنبل، كتاب الزهد

DAY
354

It is reported that Abū Dharr al-Ghifārī said: "My intimate friend [i.e. the Prophet, Allah bless him and grant him peace,] counselled me with the following: he commanded me to love the destitute and to draw closer to them; and he commanded me to consider those who are less fortunate than me and not look at those who are better off than me; and he commanded me not to ask anyone for anything; and he commanded me to keep my ties of kinship even if they do not; and he commanded me to say the truth even if it be bitter; and he commanded me not to fear the censoring of any censor; and he commanded me to say abundantly: 'there is no motion or strength except through Allah' for they are of the treasure that is placed under the Throne."

(Ibn Sa'd, *al-Ṭabaqāt al-Kubrā*)

اليوم
٣٥٤

عَنْ أَبِي ذَرٍّ قَالَ: أَوْصَانِي خَلِيلِي بِسَبْعٍ: أَمَرَنِي بِحُبِّ الْمَسَاكِينِ وَالدُّنُوِّ مِنْهُمْ، وَأَمَرَنِي أَنْ أَنْظُرَ إِلَىٰ مَنْ هُوَ دُونِي وَلَا أَنْظُرَ إِلَىٰ مَنْ هُوَ فَوْقِي، وَأَمَرَنِي أَنْ لَا أَسْأَلَ أَحَدًا شَيْئًا، وَأَمَرَنِي أَنْ أَصِلَ الرَّحِمَ وَإِنْ أَدْبَرَتْ، وَأَمَرَنِي أَنْ أَقُولَ الْحَقَّ وَإِنْ كَانَ مُرًّا، وَأَمَرَنِي أَنْ لَا أَخَافَ فِي اللَّهِ لَوْمَةَ لَائِمٍ، وَأَمَرَنِي أَنْ أُكْثِرَ مِنْ لَا حَوْلَ وَلَا قُوَّةَ إِلَّا بِاللَّهِ، فَإِنَّهُنَّ مِنْ كَنْزٍ تَحْتَ الْعَرْشِ.

ابن سعد، الطبقات الكبرى

DAY 355

Muʿādh ibn Jabal, may Allah be well pleased with him, said: "If a person does one of three things, then he has exposed himself to [Allah's] detestation: laughing without experiencing any sense of wonder; sleeping without staying awake at night; and eating without feeling hungry."

(Aḥmad ibn Ḥanbal, *Kitāb al-Zuhd*)

DAY 356

Abū Bakr al-Ṣiddīq, may Allah be well pleased with him, said: "The highest form of intelligence lies in Godfearingness, and the worse form of stupidity lies in immorality. The strongest amongst you in my sight is the weak person until I restore to him his right, and the weakest amongst you in my sight is the strong person until I take away from him the right he usurped."

(al-Baqillānī, *Iʿjāz al-Qur'ān*)

اليوم ٣٥٥

قَالَ مُعَاذُ بْنُ جَبَلٍ: ثَلَاثٌ مَنْ فَعَلَهُنَّ فَقَدْ تَعَرَّضَ لِلْمَقْتِ: الضَّحِكُ مِنْ غَيْرِ عَجَبٍ، وَالنَّوْمُ مِنْ غَيْرِ سَهَرٍ، وَالْأَكْلُ مِنْ غَيْرِ جُوعٍ.

أحمد بن حنبل، كتاب الزهد

اليوم ٣٥٦

قَالَ أَبُو بَكْرٍ الصِّدِّيقُ: إِنَّ أَكْيَسَ الْكَيْسِ التُّقَى، وَإِنَّ أَحْمَقَ الْحُمْقِ الْفُجُورُ، وإِنَّ أَقْوَاكُمْ عِنْدِي الضَّعِيفُ حَتَّىٰ آخُذَ لَهُ بِحَقِّهِ، وَإِنَّ أَضْعَفَكُمْ عِنْدِي الْقَوِيُّ حَتَّىٰ آخُذَ مِنْهُ الْحَقَّ.

الإمام الباقلاني، إعجاز القرآن

DAY 357

Ibn ʿAbbās, may Allah be well pleased with father and son, said: "The Final Hour will not take place as long as there is one single person saying: Allah! Allah!'"

(Aḥmad ibn Ḥanbal, *Kitāb al-Zuhd*)

DAY 358

Ibn ʿUmar, may Allah be well pleased with him, said: "When one's earning is lawful and wholesome, one's expending of it is also lawful and wholesome."

(Aḥmad ibn Ḥanbal, *Kitāb al-Zuhd*)

اليوم ٣٥٧

قَالَ ابْنُ عَبَّاسٍ: لَا تَقُومُ السَّاعَةُ وَوَاحِدٌ يَقُولُ: اللهُ اللهُ.

أحمد بن حنبل، كتاب الزهد

اليوم ٣٥٨

قَالَ ابْنِ عُمَرَ: إِذَا طَابَ الْمَكْسَبُ زَكَتِ النَّفَقَةُ.

أحمد بن حنبل، كتاب الزهد

DAY 359

Ibn ʿUmar, may Allah be well pleased with him, said: "I would not be worried if I had the like of Uḥud in gold, provided I knew its exact measure and I pay its poor-due."

(Aḥmad ibn Ḥanbal, *Kitāb al-Zuhd*)

DAY 360

Abū'l-Dardā', may Allah be well pleased with him, said: "Shall I not inform you of the day of my utter poverty? It is the day I am put in my grave."

(al-Ghazālī, *Iḥyā' ʿUlūm al-Dīn*)

اليوم
٣٥٩

قَالَ ابْنُ عُمَرَ: مَا أُبَالِي لَوْ أَنَّ لِي مِثْلَ أُحُدٍ ذَهَبًا أَعْرِفُ عَدَدَهُ وَأُؤَدِّي زَكَاتَهُ.

أحمد بن حنبل، كتاب الزهد

اليوم
٣٦٠

قَالَ أَبُو الدَّرْدَاءِ: أَلَا أُخْبِرُكُمْ بِيَوْمِ فَقْرِي؟ يَوْمَ أُنْزِلُ قَبْرِي.

الإمام الغزالي، إحياء علوم الدين

DAY 361

It is related that ʿAbdullāh ibn Masʿūd, may Allah be well pleased with him, said: "A man enters on the ruler while he has his religion intact but departs without anything of it left."

(Jamāl al-Dīn ibn Manẓūr, *Mukhtaṣar Tārīkh Dimashq*)

DAY 362

It is related from ʿAbdullāh ibn Masʿūd, may Allah be well pleased with him, that he said: "Had the folk of knowledge protected this knowledge and placed it with those who deserve it, they would have become the masters of the people of their era. However, they placed it with those who are after this world to obtain a share of their world, and so they became insignificant."

(al-Bukhārī, *al-Tārīkh al-Kabīr*)

اليوم ٣٦١

عَنْ اِبْنِ مَسْعُودٍ أَنَّهُ قَالَ: يَدْخُلُ الرَّجُلُ عَلَى السُّلْطَانِ ومَعَهُ دِينُهُ، فَيَخْرُجُ ومَا مَعَهُ شَيْءٌ.

جمال الدين بن منظور ، مختصر تاريخ دمشق من ابن عساكر

اليوم ٣٦٢

رُوِيَ عَنْ اِبْنِ مَسْعُودٍ أَنَّهُ قَالَ: لَوْ أَنَّ أَهْلَ العِلْمِ صَانُوا العِلْمَ ووضَعُوهُ عِنْدَ أَهْلِهِ لَسَادُوا به أَهْلَ زَمَانِهِمْ، ولَكِنَّهُمْ بَذَلُوهُ لِأَهْلِ الدُّنْيَا لِيَنَالُوا به مِنْ دُنْيَاهُمْ فهَانُوا عَلَيْهِ.

البخاري ، التاريخ الكبير

DAY 363

ʿAlī ibn Abī Ṭālib, may Allah be well pleased with him, said: "Knowledge keeps watch over you while you keep watch over wealth. However, a watchman cannot turn his eyes away from what he is watching over otherwise it would be lost or wasted."

(Abū Nuʿaym al-Aṣfahānī, *Ḥilyat al-Awliyā'*)

DAY 364

Abū'l-Dardā', may Allah be well pleased with him, said: "I have known people who were leaves without thorns and now they have become thorns without leaves; if you disapprove of them, they disapprove of you, but if you leave them alone, they do not leave you alone." He was asked: "What shall we do then?" he said: "You let them tear up at your honour, the reward of which you will find when you need it most [i.e. on the Day of Judgement]."

(Ibn Abī al-Dunyā, *Mudārāt al-Nufūs*)

اليوم ٣٦٣

قَالَ عَلِيُّ بْنُ أَبِي طَالِبٍ: الْعِلْمُ يَحْرُسُكَ وَأَنْتَ تحْرُسُ الْمَالَ والحارسُ لا يَتسَنَّىٰ لَهُ أَنْ يَلْتَفِتَ عَنِ الشَّيْءِ الذي يَحْرُسُهُ وإلّا تعَرَّضَ للضَّيَاعِ والبَدَدِ.

أبو نعيم الأصفهاني، حلية الأولياء

اليوم ٣٦٤

قَالَ أَبُو الدَّرْدَاءِ: أَدْرَكْتُ النَّاسَ وَرَقًا لَا شَوْكَ فِيهِ فَأَصْبَحُوا شَوْكًا لَا وَرَقَ فِيهِ، إِنْ نَقَدْتَهُمْ نَقَدُوكَ وَإِنْ تَرَكْتَهُمْ لَا يَتْرُكُوكَ. قَالُوا: فَكَيْفَ نَصْنَعُ؟ قَالَ: تُقْرِضُهُمْ مِنْ عِرْضِكَ لِيَوْمِ فَقْرِكَ.

ابن أبي الدنيا، مداراة النفوس

DAY
365

ʿAlī ibn Abī Ṭālib, may Allah be well pleased with him, said: "Knowledge is better than wealth."

(al-Sharīf al-Raḍī, *Nahj al-Balāghah*)

اليوم
٣٦٥

قَالَ عَلِيٌّ بْنُ أَبِي طَالِبٍ: الْعِلْمُ خَيْرٌ مِنَ الْمَالِ.

الشّريف الرّضي، نهج البلاغة

SUBJECT INDEX

INDEX

Note: Reference is made in this index to where the English terms appear according to the page numbers; Arabic translations are on the facing pages.